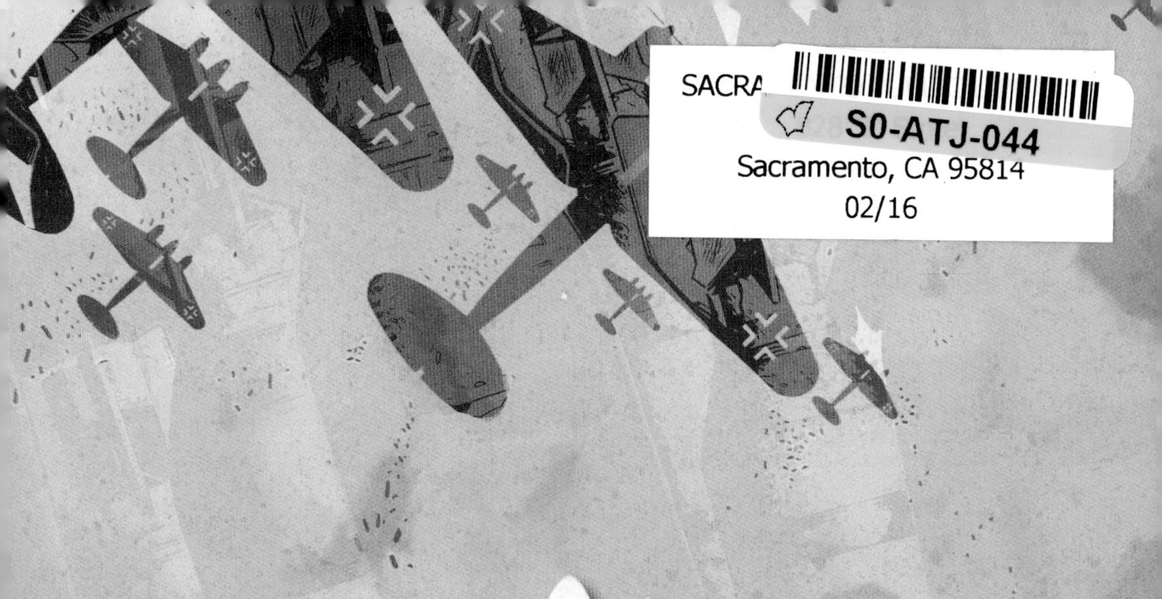

THE ROYALS
MASTERS OF WAR

written by
ROB WILLIAMS

pencils by
SIMON COLEBY

inks by
SIMON COLEBY (chapters 1-3)
GARY ERSKINE (chapters 4-6)

colors by
J.D. METTLER

letters by
WES ABBOTT

cover art and original series covers by
SIMON COLEBY & J.D. METTLER

THE ROYALS created by
ROB WILLIAMS & SIMON COLEBY

Ben Abernathy Will Dennis Editors – Original Series
Greg Lockard Associate Editor – Original Series
Kristy Quinn Assistant Editor – Original Series
Scott Nybakken Editor
Robbin Brosterman Design Director – Books
Sarabeth Kett Publication Design

Shelly Bond Executive Editor – Vertigo
Hank Kanalz Senior VP – Vertigo & Integrated Publishing

Diane Nelson President
Dan DiDio and Jim Lee Co-Publishers
Geoff Johns Chief Creative Officer
Amit Desai Senior VP – Marketing & Franchise Management
Amy Genkins Senior VP – Business & Legal Affairs
Nairi Gardiner Senior VP – Finance
Jeff Boison VP – Publishing Planning
Mark Chiarello VP – Art Direction & Design
John Cunningham VP – Marketing
Terri Cunningham VP – Editorial Administration
Larry Ganem VP – Talent Relations & Services
Alison Gill Senior VP – Manufacturing & Operations
Jay Kogan VP – Business & Legal Affairs, Publishing
Jack Mahan VP – Business Affairs, Talent
Nick Napolitano VP – Manufacturing Administration
Sue Pohja VP – Book Sales
Fred Ruiz VP – Manufacturing Operations
Courtney Simmons Senior VP – Publicity
Bob Wayne Senior VP – Sales

THE ROYALS: MASTERS OF WAR

Published by DC Comics. Compilation Copyright © 2014
Rob Williams and Simon Coleby. All Rights Reserved.

Originally published in single magazine form as
THE ROYALS 1-6. Copyright © 2014 Rob Williams and Simon
Coleby. All Rights Reserved. All characters, their distinctive
likenesses and related elements featured in this publication are
trademarks of DC Comics. VERTIGO is a trademark of DC Comics.
The stories, characters and incidents featured in this publication
are entirely fictional. DC Comics does not read or accept
unsolicited submissions of ideas, stories or artwork.

DC Comics, 1700 Broadway, New York, NY 10019
A Warner Bros. Entertainment Company
Printed in the USA. First Printing.
ISBN: 978-1-4012-5054-6

Library of Congress Cataloging-in-Publication Data

Williams, Rob (Robert Glyndwr) author.
  The Royals : masters of war / Rob Williams, writer ; Simon
Coleby, artist.
    pages cm
  ISBN 978-1-4012-5054-6 (paperback)
  1. World War, 1939-1945—Comic books, strips, etc. 2. Royal
households—Great Britain—Comic books, strips, etc. 3.
England—Comic books, strips, etc. 4. Graphic novels. I. Coleby,
Simon, illustrator. II. Title.

PN6737.W45R69 2014
741.5'942—dc23

                                        2014027374

SUSTAINABLE
FORESTRY
INITIATIVE

Certified Chain of Custody
20% Certified Forest Content,
80% Certified Sourcing
www.sfiprogram.org
SFI-01042
APPLIES TO TEXT STOCK ONLY

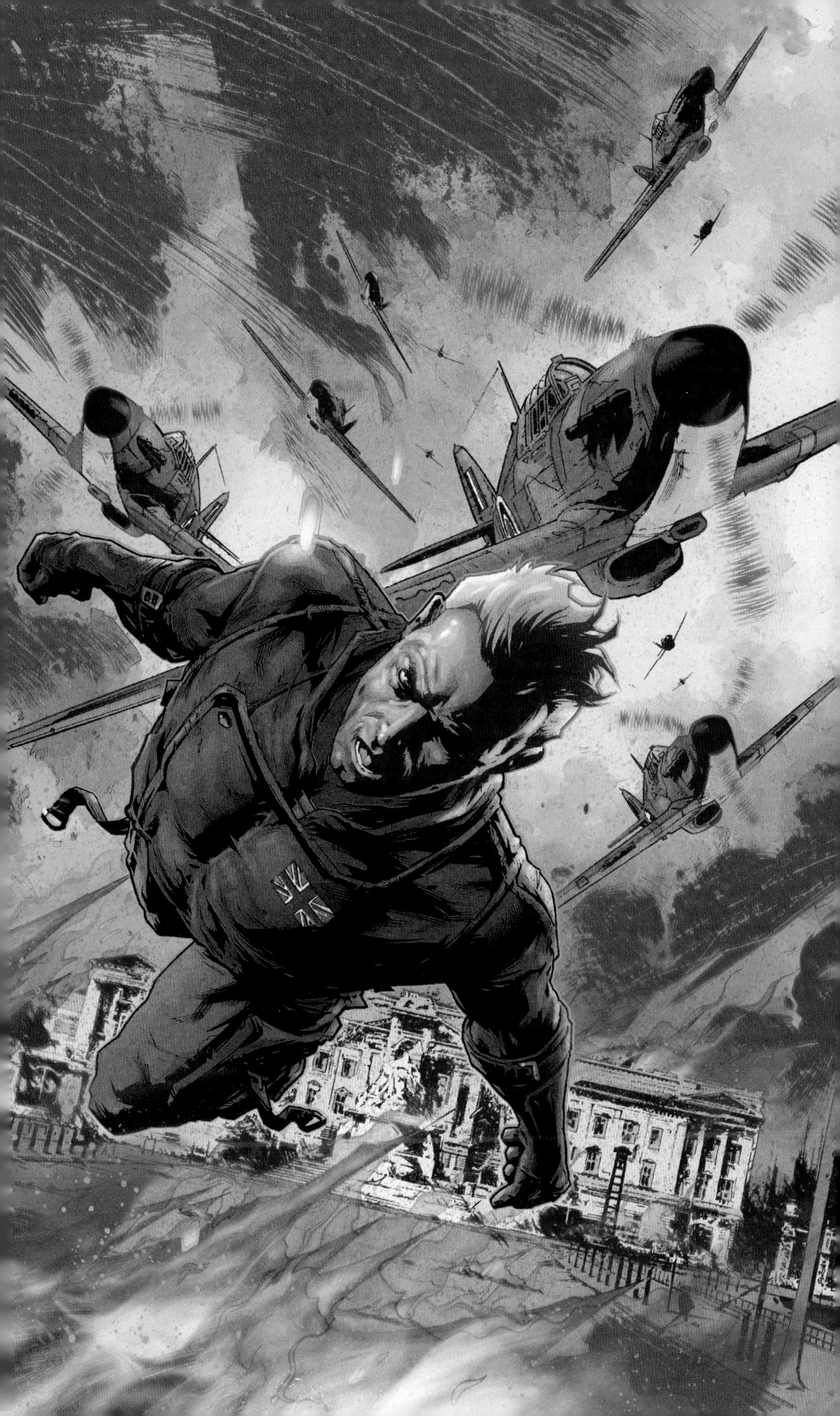

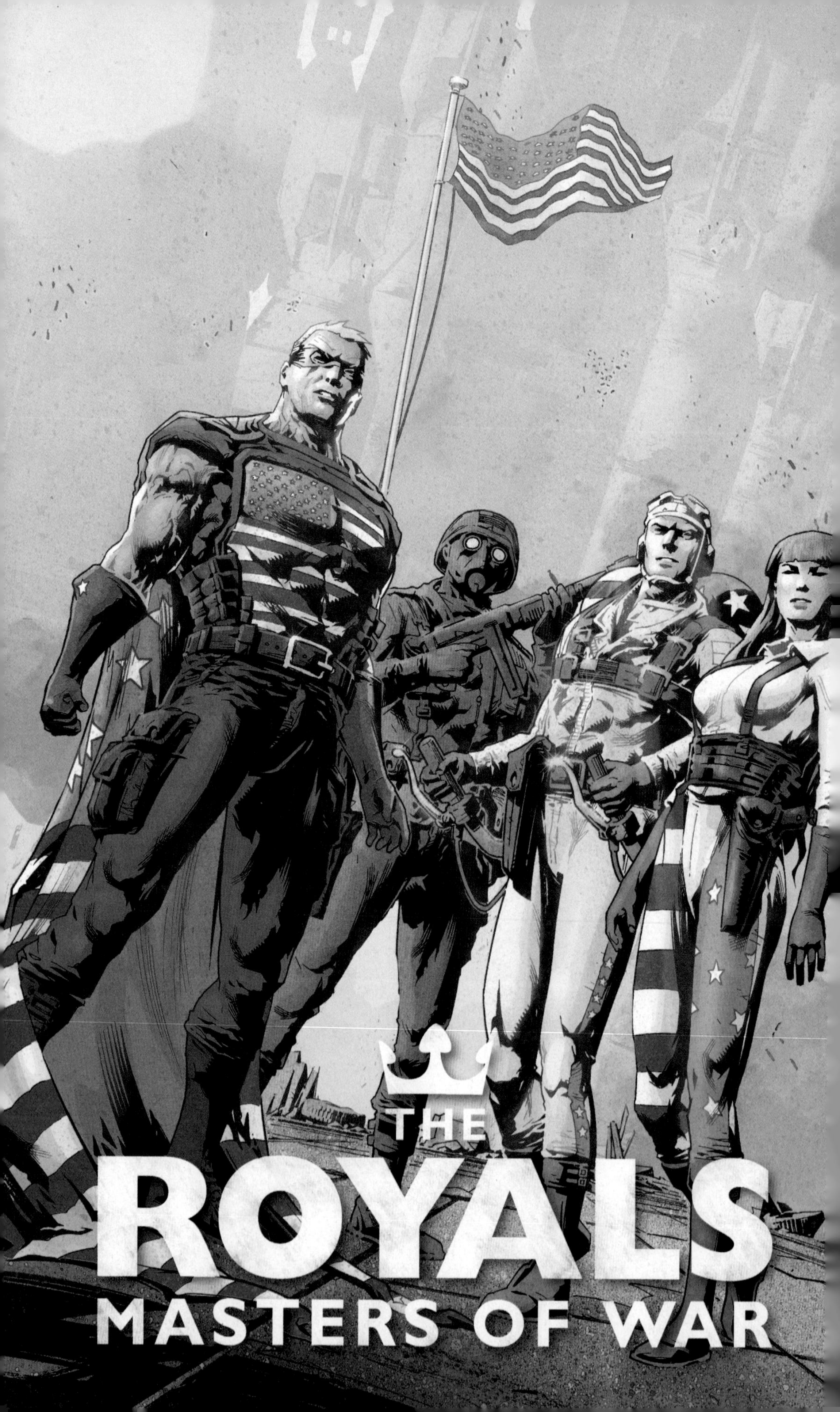
THE
ROYALS
MASTERS OF WAR

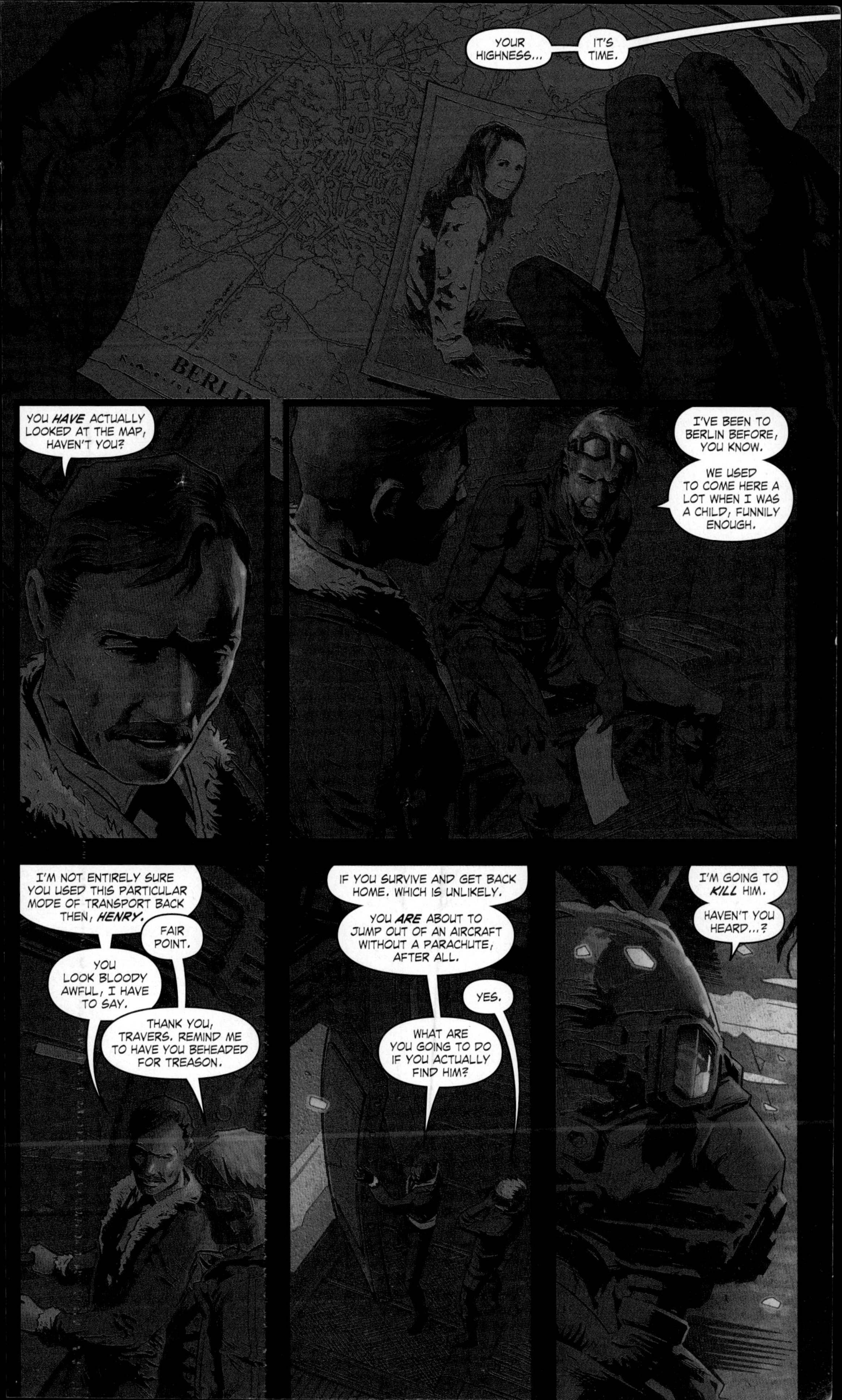
YOUR HIGHNESS...
IT'S TIME.
BERLI
YOU HAVE ACTUALLY LOOKED AT THE MAP, HAVEN'T YOU?
I'VE BEEN TO BERLIN BEFORE, YOU KNOW.
WE USED TO COME HERE A LOT WHEN I WAS A CHILD, FUNNILY ENOUGH.
I'M NOT ENTIRELY SURE YOU USED THIS PARTICULAR MODE OF TRANSPORT BACK THEN, HENRY.
FAIR POINT.
YOU LOOK BLOODY AWFUL, I HAVE TO SAY.
THANK YOU, TRAVERS. REMIND ME TO HAVE YOU BEHEADED FOR TREASON.
IF YOU SURVIVE AND GET BACK HOME. WHICH IS UNLIKELY.
YOU ARE ABOUT TO JUMP OUT OF AN AIRCRAFT WITHOUT A PARACHUTE, AFTER ALL.
YES.
WHAT ARE YOU GOING TO DO IF YOU ACTUALLY FIND HIM?
I'M GOING TO KILL HIM.
HAVEN'T YOU HEARD...?

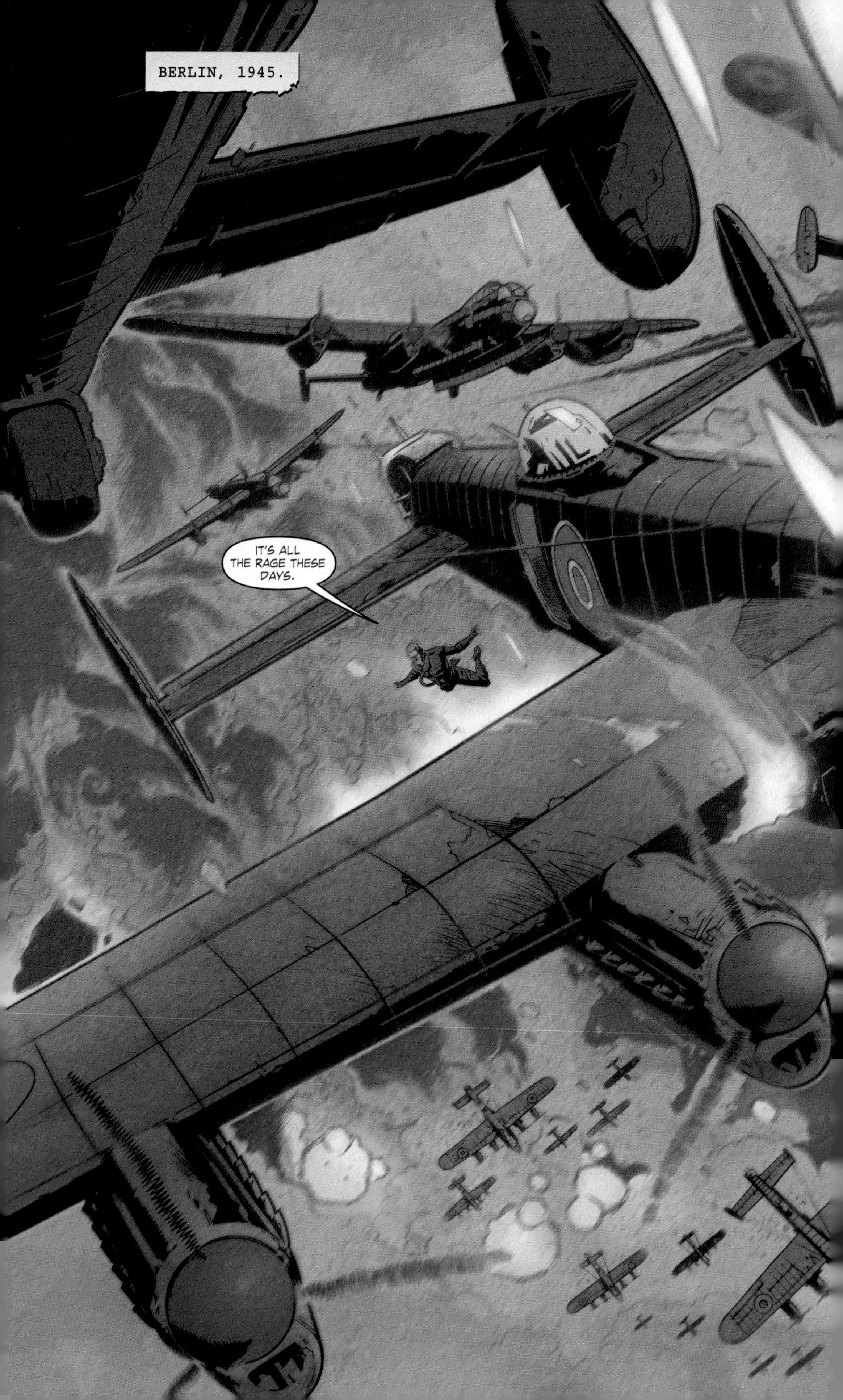
BERLIN, 1945.
IT'S ALL THE RAGE THESE DAYS.

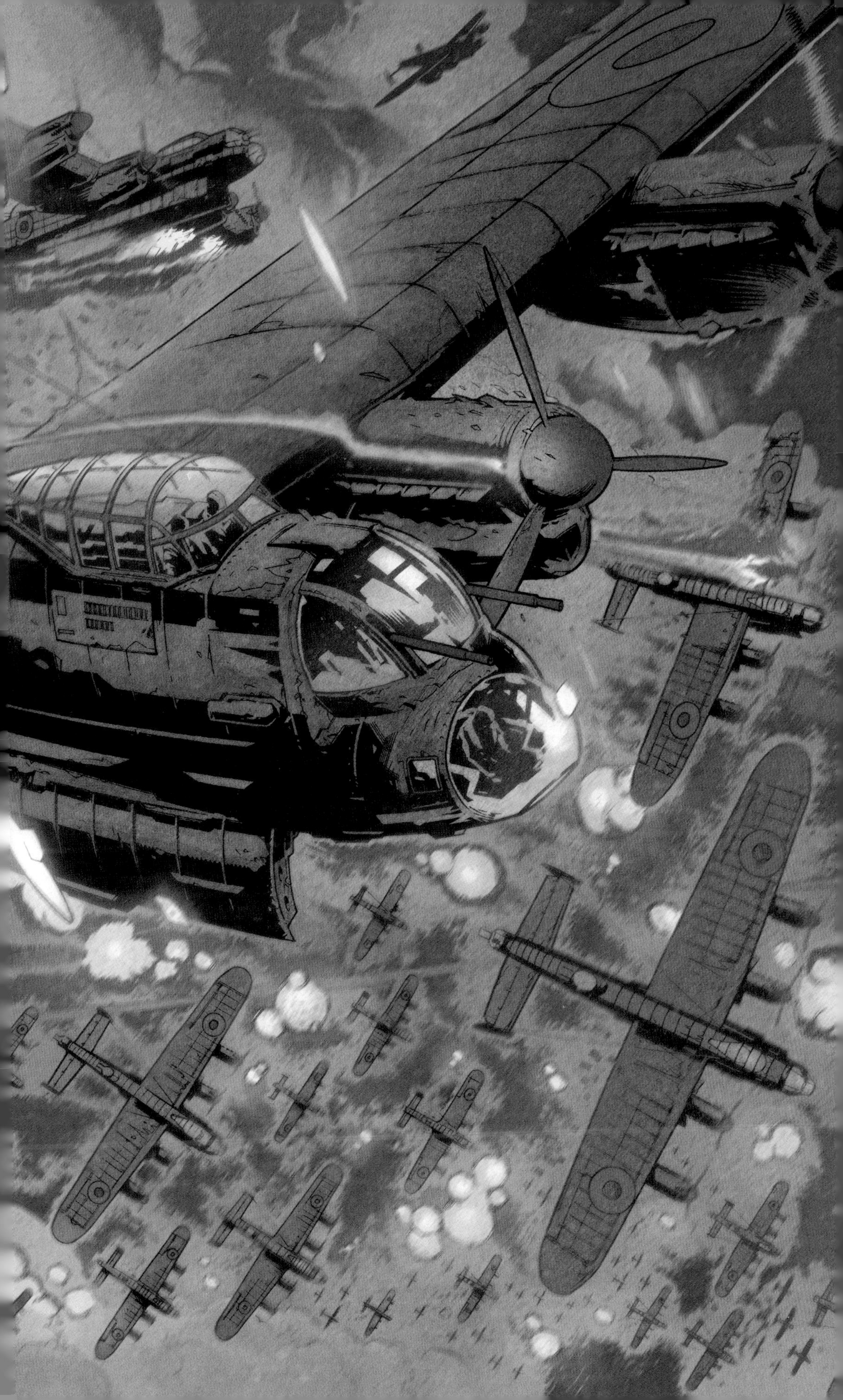

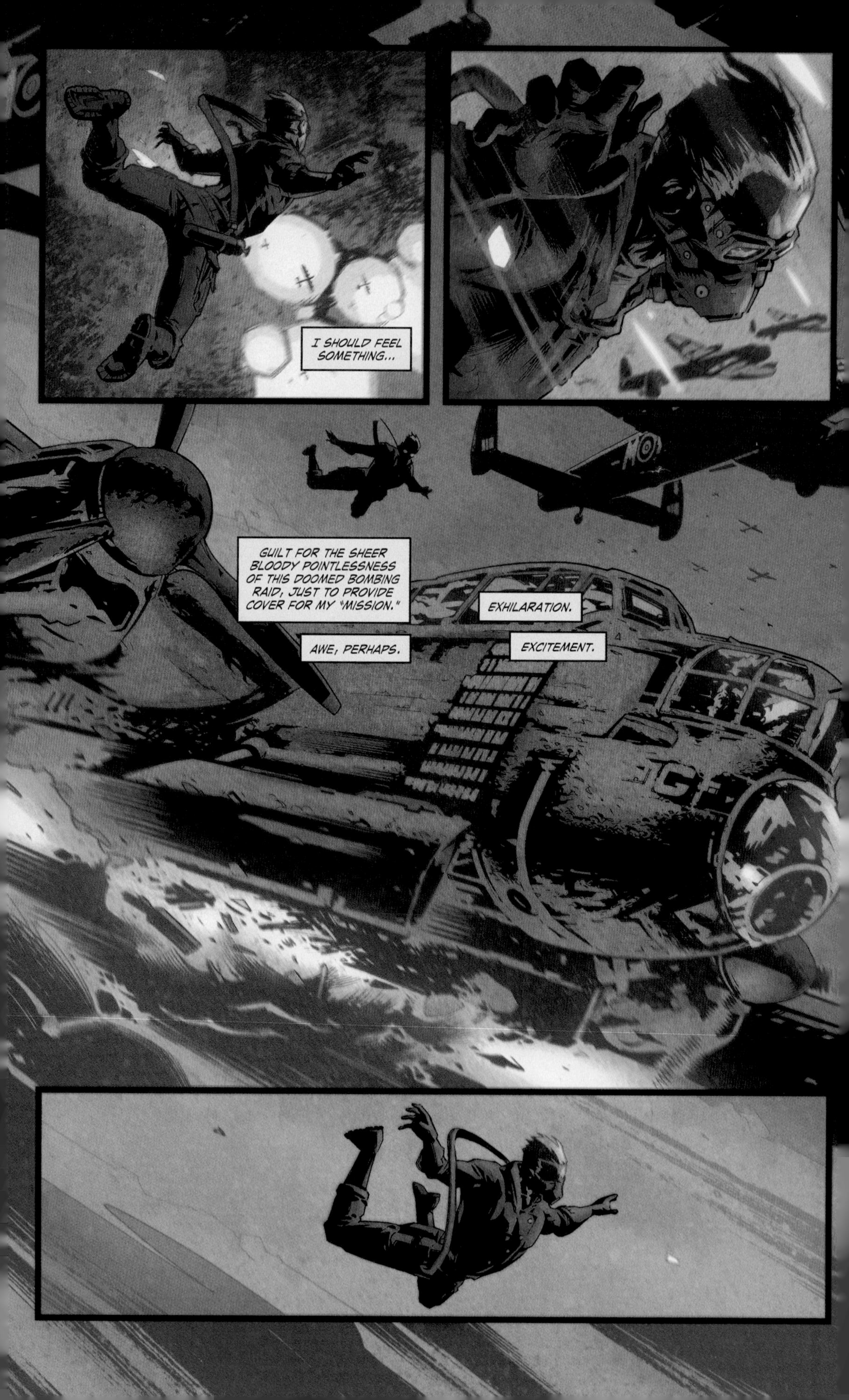
I SHOULD FEEL SOMETHING...
GUILT FOR THE SHEER BLOODY POINTLESSNESS OF THIS DOOMED BOMBING RAID, JUST TO PROVIDE COVER FOR MY "MISSION."
AWE, PERHAPS.
EXHILARATION.
EXCITEMENT.

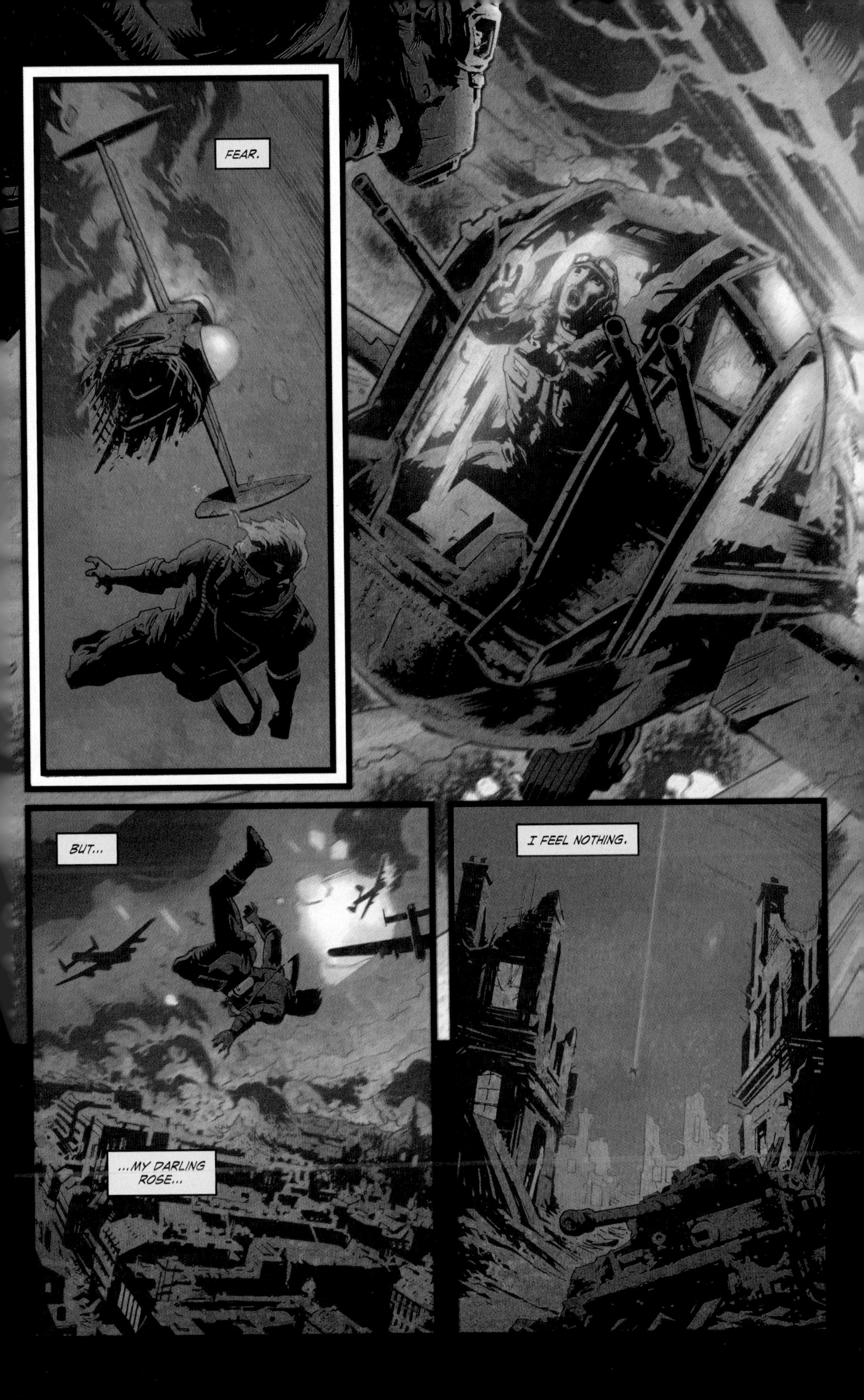
FEAR.
BUT...
...MY DARLING ROSE...
I FEEL NOTHING.

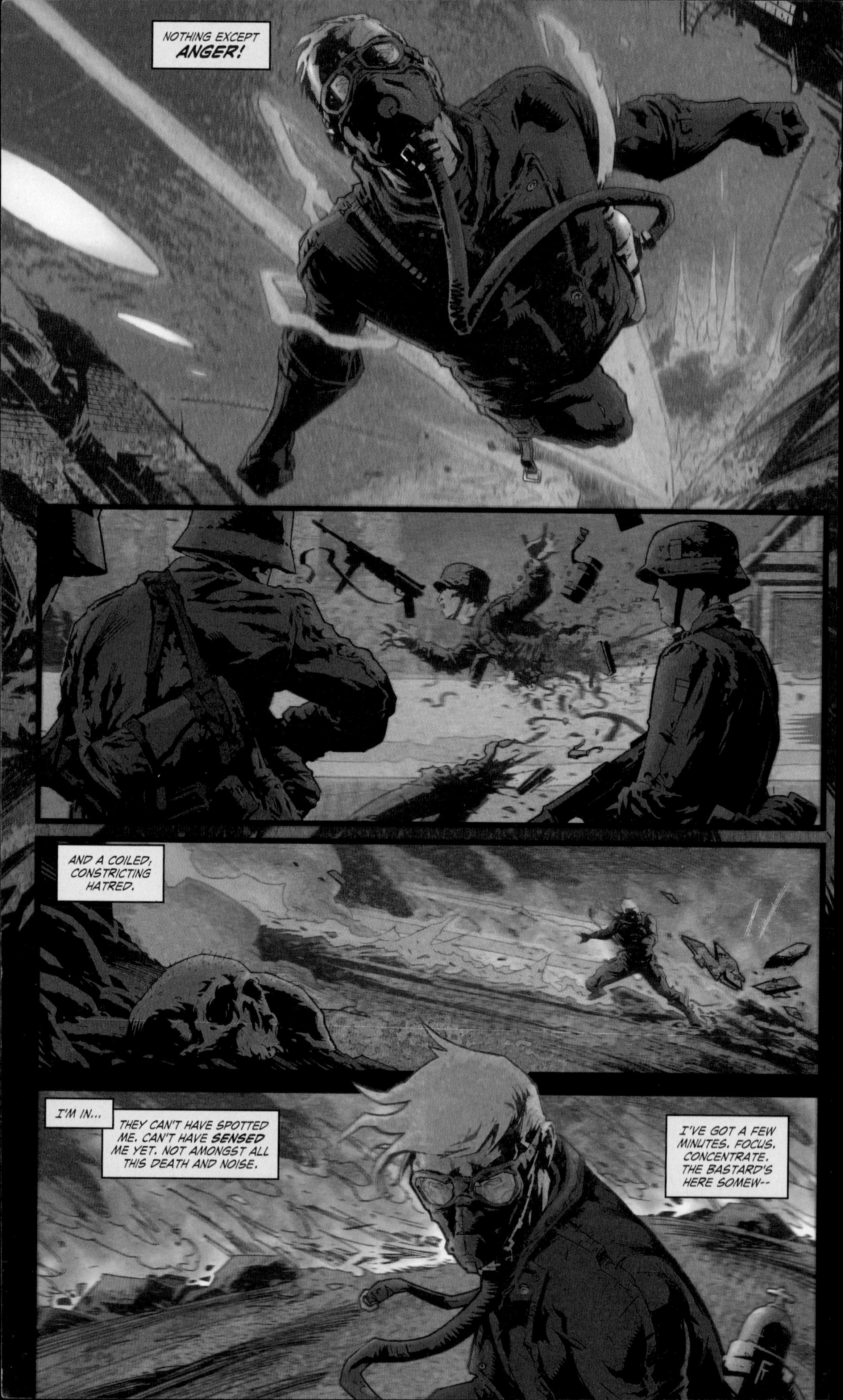
NOTHING EXCEPT ANGER!
AND A COILED, CONSTRICTING HATRED.
I'M IN...
THEY CAN'T HAVE SPOTTED ME. CAN'T HAVE SENSED ME YET. NOT AMONGST ALL THIS DEATH AND NOISE.
I'VE GOT A FEW MINUTES. FOCUS. CONCENTRATE. THE BASTARD'S HERE SOMEW--

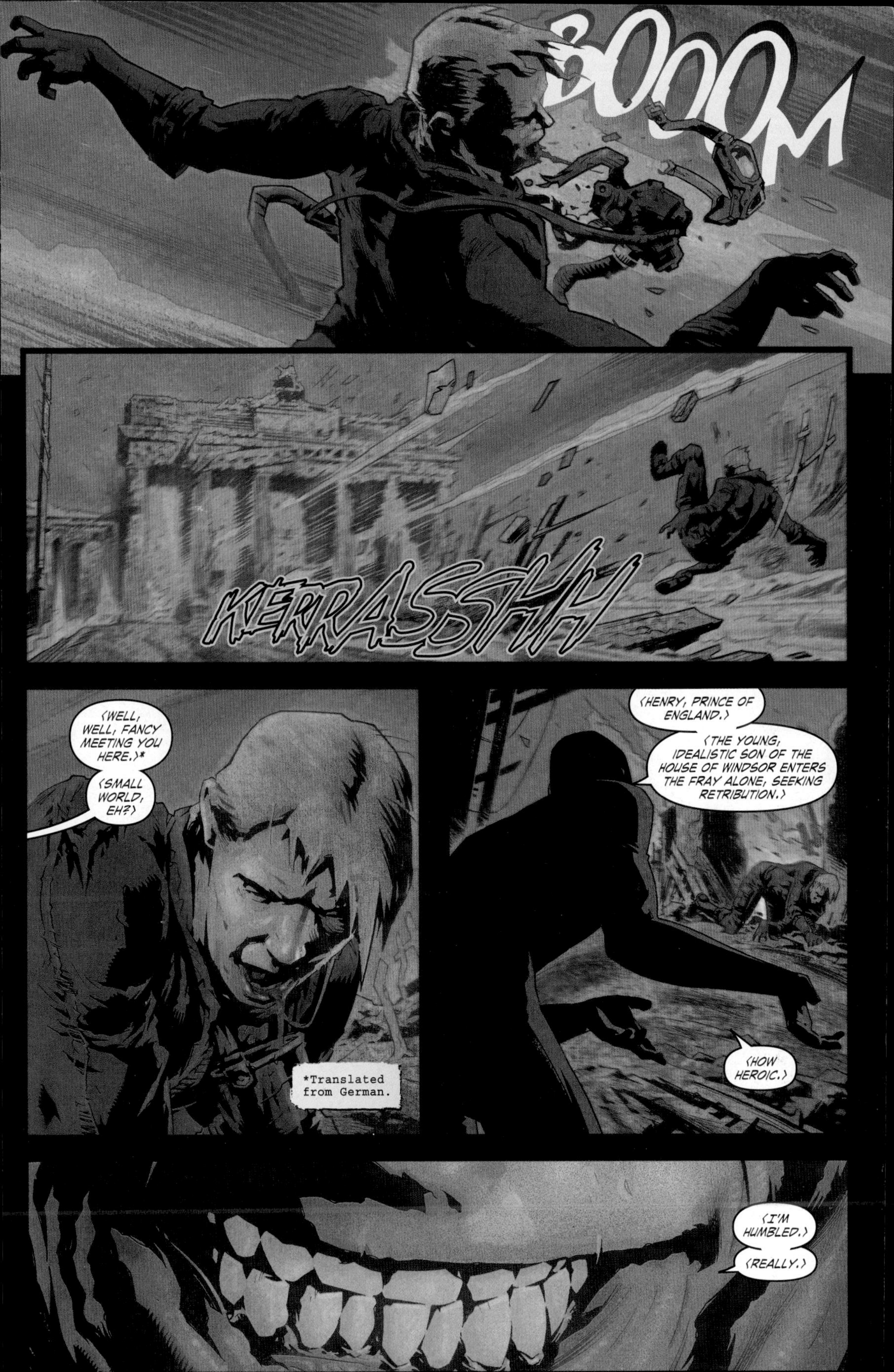
BOOOM
KERRASSHH
‹WELL, WELL, FANCY MEETING YOU HERE.›*
‹SMALL WORLD, EH?›
*Translated from German.
‹HENRY, PRINCE OF ENGLAND.›
‹THE YOUNG, IDEALISTIC SON OF THE HOUSE OF WINDSOR ENTERS THE FRAY ALONE, SEEKING RETRIBUTION.›
‹HOW HEROIC.›
‹I'M HUMBLED.›
‹REALLY.›

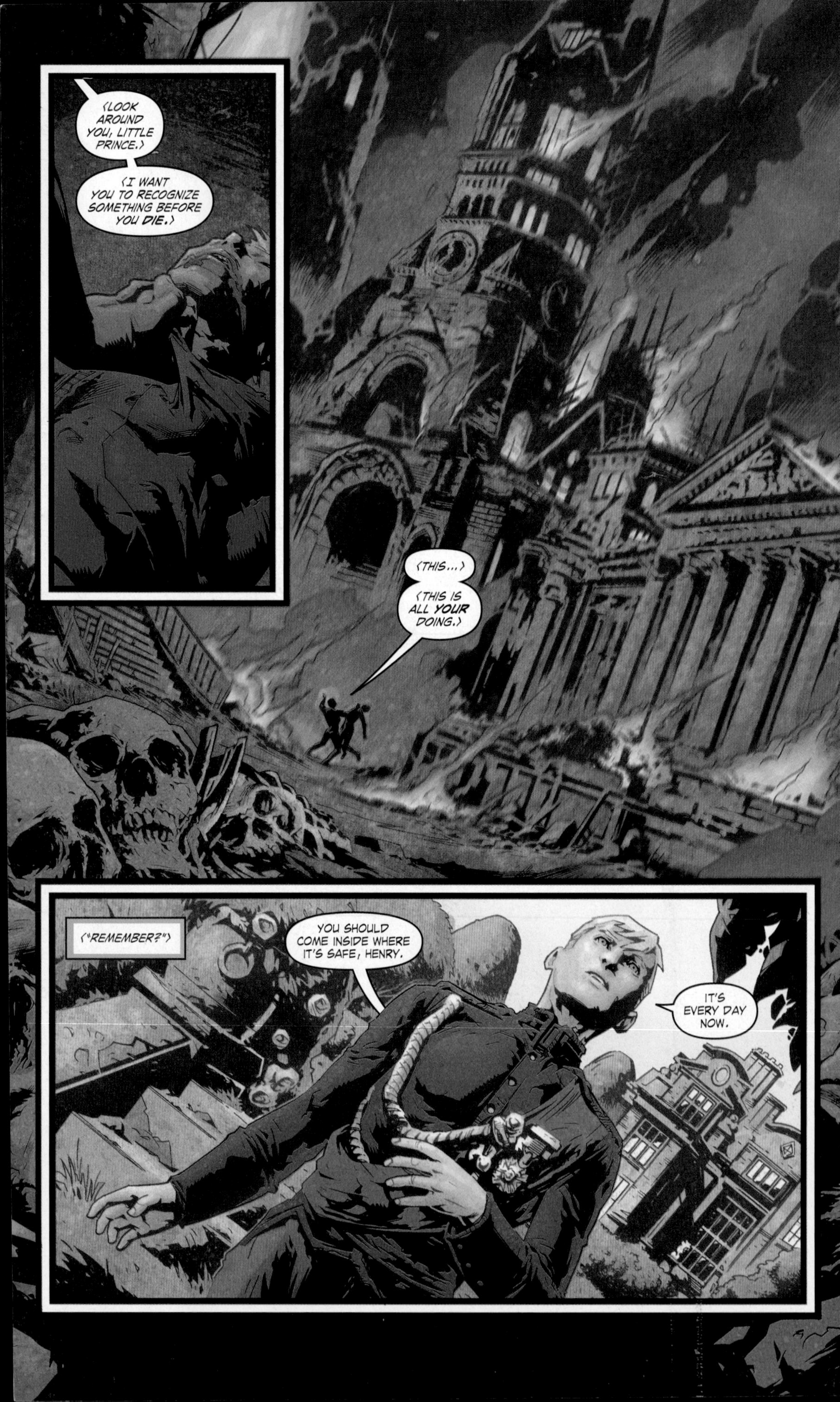
⟨LOOK AROUND YOU, LITTLE PRINCE.⟩
⟨I WANT YOU TO RECOGNIZE SOMETHING BEFORE YOU DIE.⟩
⟨THIS...⟩
⟨THIS IS ALL YOUR DOING.⟩
⟨"REMEMBER?"⟩
YOU SHOULD COME INSIDE WHERE IT'S SAFE, HENRY.
IT'S EVERY DAY NOW.

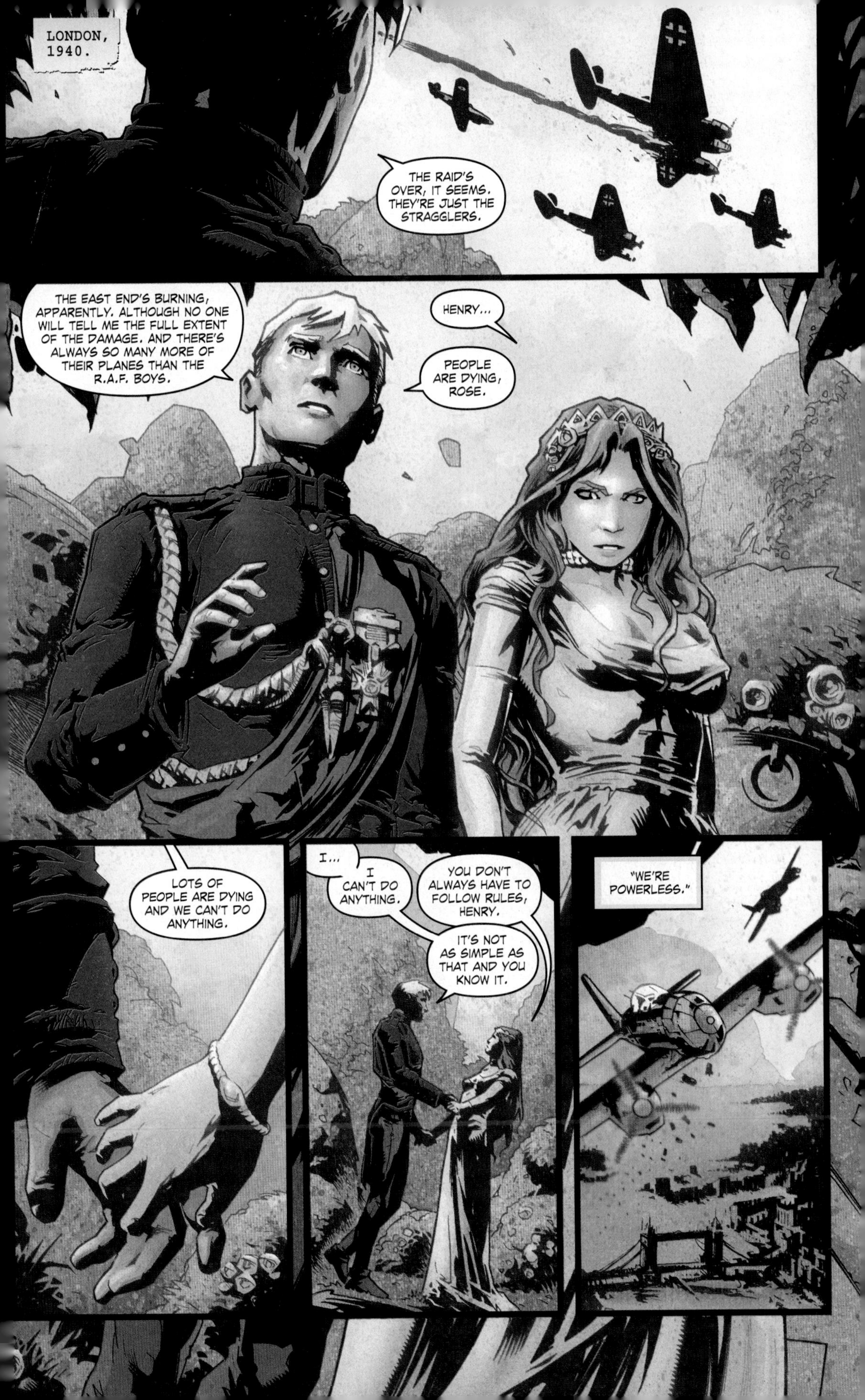
LONDON, 1940.
THE RAID'S OVER, IT SEEMS. THEY'RE JUST THE STRAGGLERS.
THE EAST END'S BURNING, APPARENTLY. ALTHOUGH NO ONE WILL TELL ME THE FULL EXTENT OF THE DAMAGE. AND THERE'S ALWAYS SO MANY MORE OF THEIR PLANES THAN THE R.A.F. BOYS.
HENRY...
PEOPLE ARE DYING, ROSE.
LOTS OF PEOPLE ARE DYING AND WE CAN'T DO ANYTHING.
I...
I CAN'T DO ANYTHING.
YOU DON'T ALWAYS HAVE TO FOLLOW RULES, HENRY.
IT'S NOT AS SIMPLE AS THAT AND YOU KNOW IT.
"WE'RE POWERLESS."

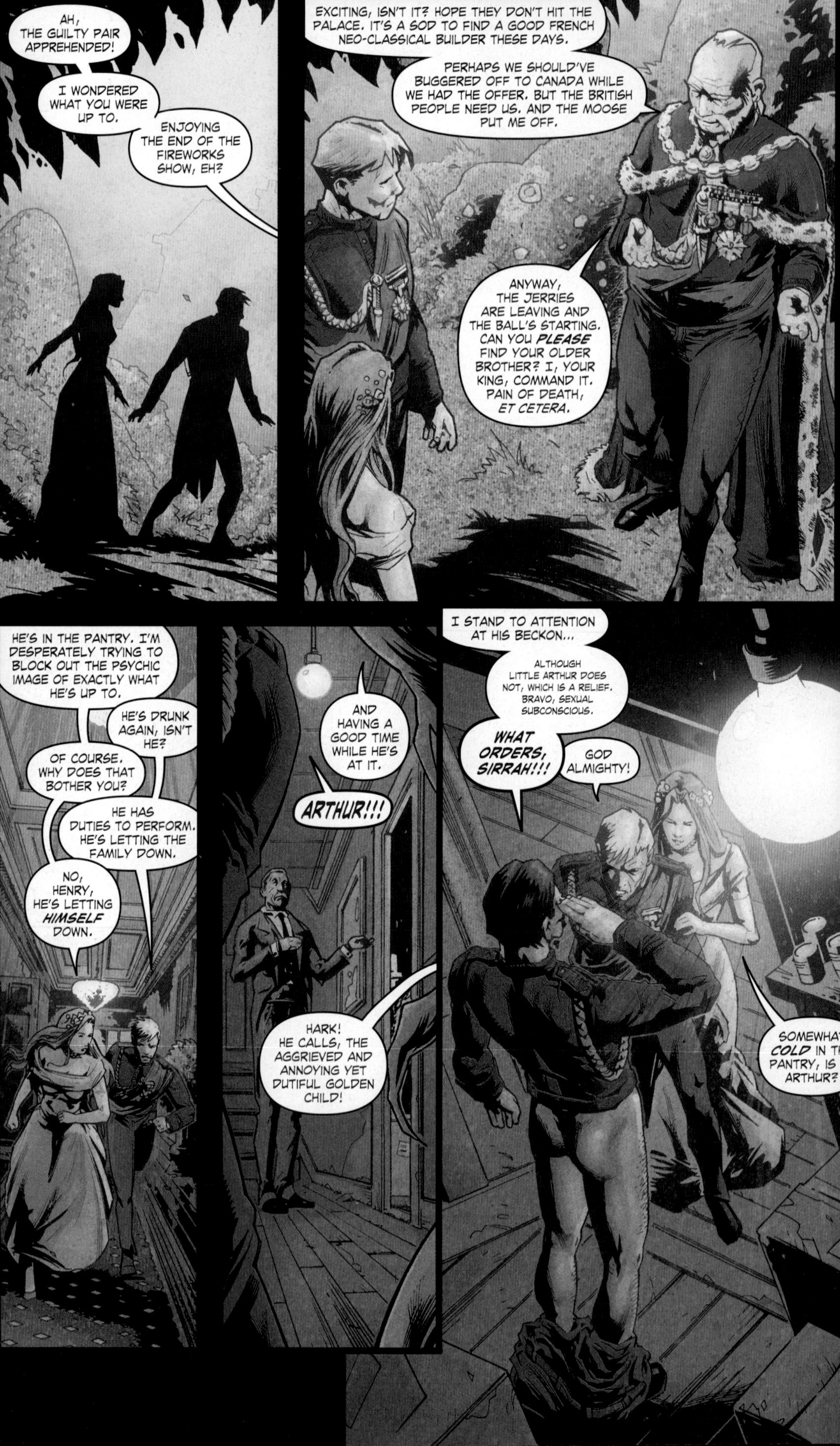

AH, THE GUILTY PAIR APPREHENDED!
I WONDERED WHAT YOU WERE UP TO.
ENJOYING THE END OF THE FIREWORKS SHOW, EH?
EXCITING, ISN'T IT? HOPE THEY DON'T HIT THE PALACE. IT'S A SOD TO FIND A GOOD FRENCH NEO-CLASSICAL BUILDER THESE DAYS.
PERHAPS WE SHOULD'VE BUGGERED OFF TO CANADA WHILE WE HAD THE OFFER. BUT THE BRITISH PEOPLE NEED US. AND THE MOOSE PUT ME OFF.
ANYWAY, THE JERRIES ARE LEAVING AND THE BALL'S STARTING. CAN YOU PLEASE FIND YOUR OLDER BROTHER? I, YOUR KING, COMMAND IT. PAIN OF DEATH, ET CETERA.
HE'S IN THE PANTRY. I'M DESPERATELY TRYING TO BLOCK OUT THE PSYCHIC IMAGE OF EXACTLY WHAT HE'S UP TO.
HE'S DRUNK AGAIN, ISN'T HE?
OF COURSE. WHY DOES THAT BOTHER YOU?
HE HAS DUTIES TO PERFORM. HE'S LETTING THE FAMILY DOWN.
NO, HENRY, HE'S LETTING HIMSELF DOWN.
AND HAVING A GOOD TIME WHILE HE'S AT IT.
ARTHUR!!!
HARK! HE CALLS, THE AGGRIEVED AND ANNOYING YET DUTIFUL GOLDEN CHILD!
I STAND TO ATTENTION AT HIS BECKON...
ALTHOUGH LITTLE ARTHUR DOES NOT, WHICH IS A RELIEF. BRAVO, SEXUAL SUBCONSCIOUS.
WHAT ORDERS, SIRRAH!!!
GOD ALMIGHTY!
SOMEWHAT COLD IN TH PANTRY, IS ARTHUR?

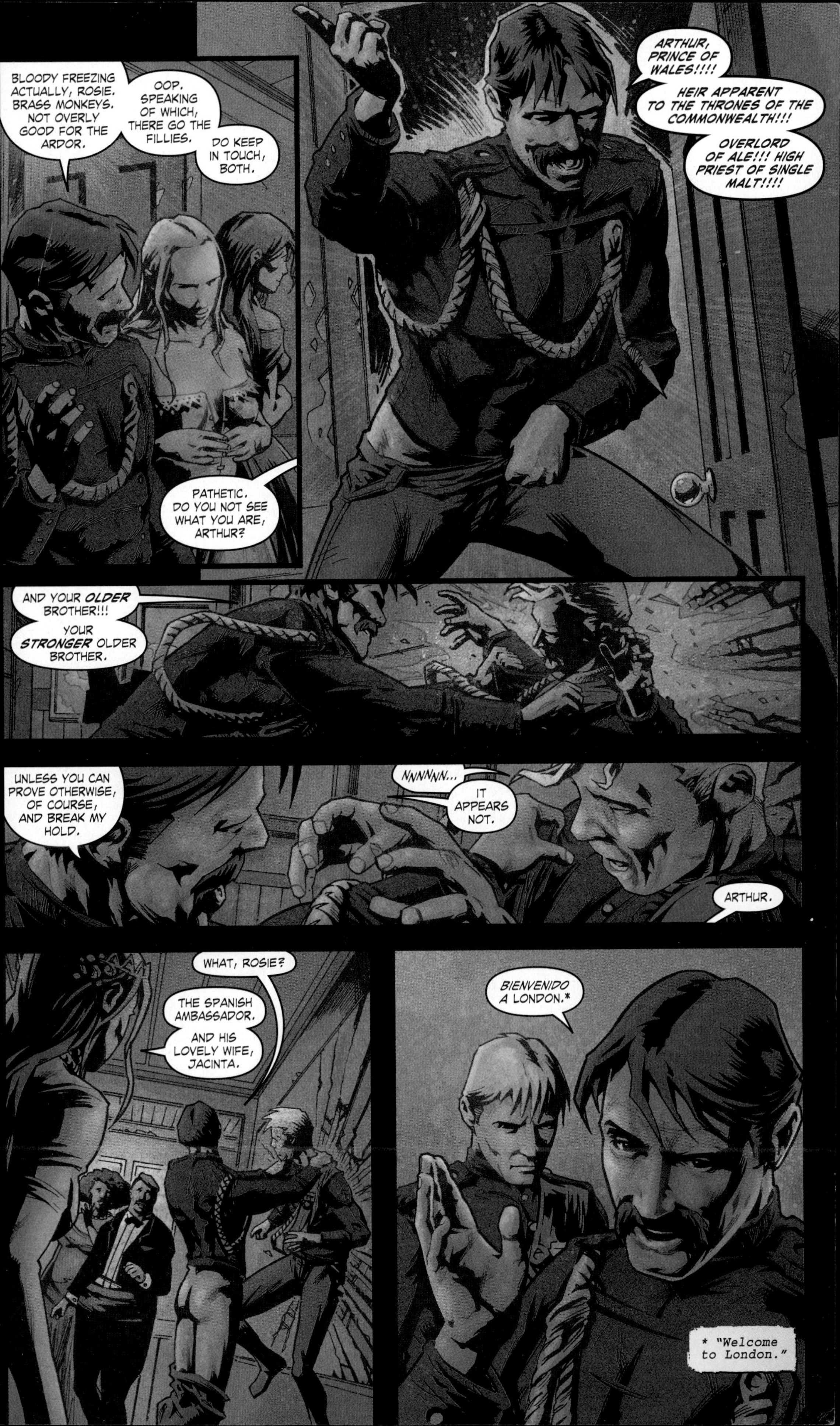

BLOODY FREEZING ACTUALLY, ROSIE. BRASS MONKEYS. NOT OVERLY GOOD FOR THE ARDOR.
OOP. SPEAKING OF WHICH, THERE GO THE FILLIES.
DO KEEP IN TOUCH, BOTH.
PATHETIC. DO YOU NOT SEE WHAT YOU ARE, ARTHUR?
ARTHUR, PRINCE OF WALES!!!!
HEIR APPARENT TO THE THRONES OF THE COMMONWEALTH!!!
OVERLORD OF ALE!!! HIGH PRIEST OF SINGLE MALT!!!!
AND YOUR OLDER BROTHER!!!
YOUR STRONGER OLDER BROTHER.
UNLESS YOU CAN PROVE OTHERWISE, OF COURSE, AND BREAK MY HOLD.
NNNNNN...
IT APPEARS NOT.
ARTHUR.
WHAT, ROSIE?
THE SPANISH AMBASSADOR.
AND HIS LOVELY WIFE, JACINTA.
BIENVENIDO A LONDON.*
* "Welcome to London."

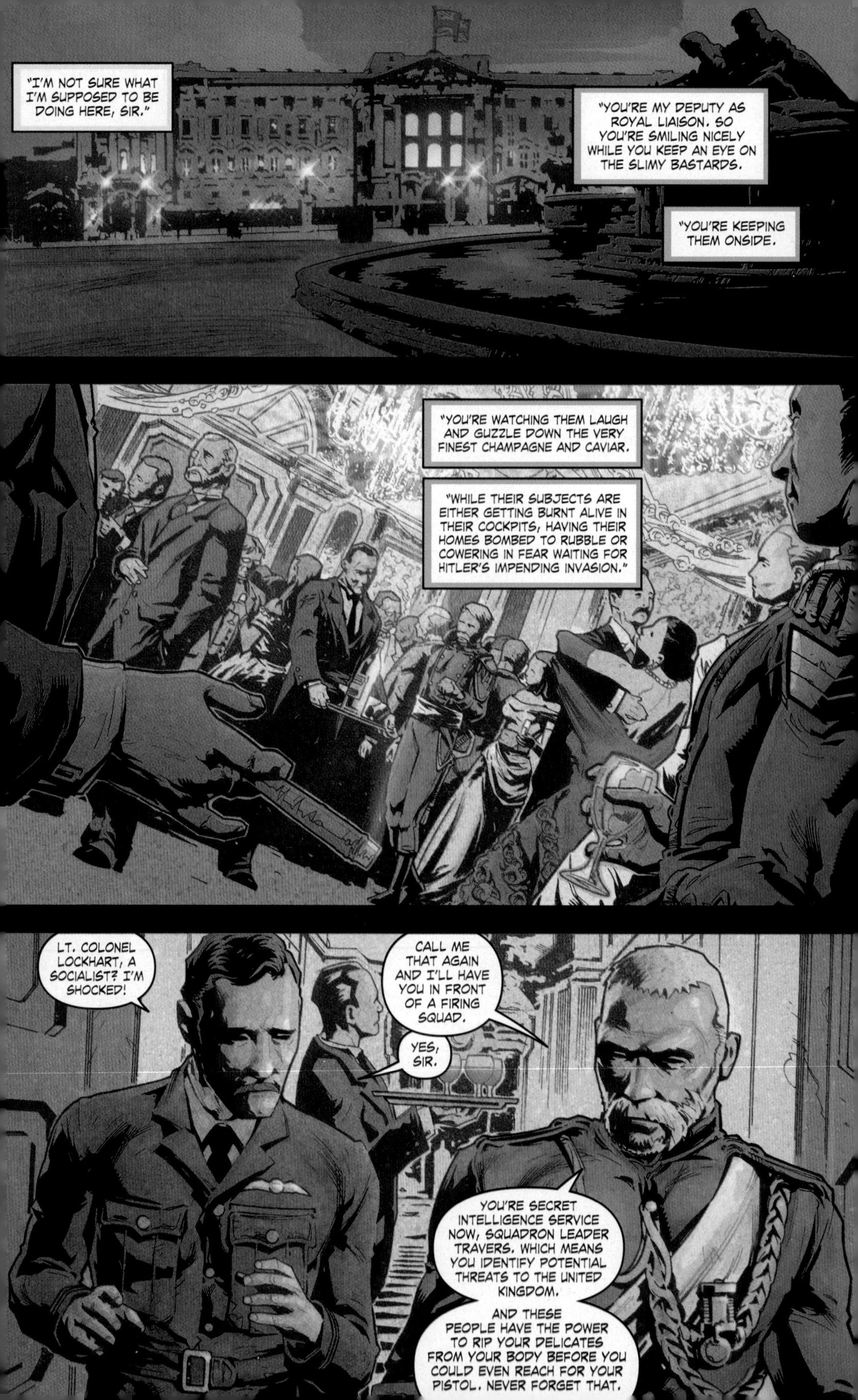
"I'M NOT SURE WHAT I'M SUPPOSED TO BE DOING HERE, SIR."
"YOU'RE MY DEPUTY AS ROYAL LIAISON. SO YOU'RE SMILING NICELY WHILE YOU KEEP AN EYE ON THE SLIMY BASTARDS.
"YOU'RE KEEPING THEM ONSIDE.
"YOU'RE WATCHING THEM LAUGH AND GUZZLE DOWN THE VERY FINEST CHAMPAGNE AND CAVIAR.
"WHILE THEIR SUBJECTS ARE EITHER GETTING BURNT ALIVE IN THEIR COCKPITS, HAVING THEIR HOMES BOMBED TO RUBBLE OR COWERING IN FEAR WAITING FOR HITLER'S IMPENDING INVASION."
LT. COLONEL LOCKHART, A SOCIALIST? I'M SHOCKED!
CALL ME THAT AGAIN AND I'LL HAVE YOU IN FRONT OF A FIRING SQUAD.
YES, SIR.
YOU'RE SECRET INTELLIGENCE SERVICE NOW, SQUADRON LEADER TRAVERS. WHICH MEANS YOU IDENTIFY POTENTIAL THREATS TO THE UNITED KINGDOM.
AND THESE PEOPLE HAVE THE POWER TO RIP YOUR DELICATES FROM YOUR BODY BEFORE YOU COULD EVEN REACH FOR YOUR PISTOL. NEVER FORGET THAT.

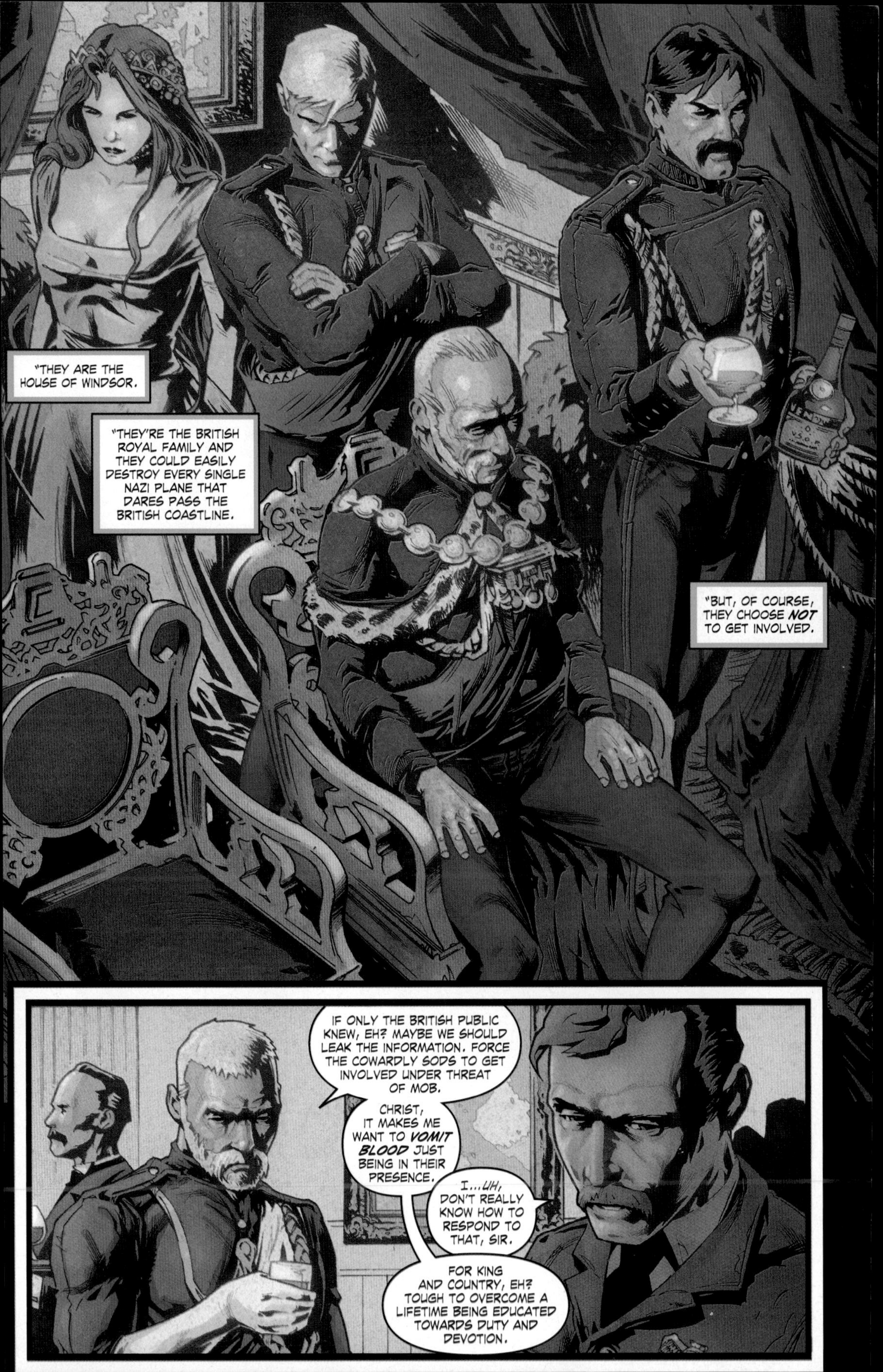
"THEY ARE THE HOUSE OF WINDSOR.
"THEY'RE THE BRITISH ROYAL FAMILY AND THEY COULD EASILY DESTROY EVERY SINGLE NAZI PLANE THAT DARES PASS THE BRITISH COASTLINE.
"BUT, OF COURSE, THEY CHOOSE NOT TO GET INVOLVED.
IF ONLY THE BRITISH PUBLIC KNEW, EH? MAYBE WE SHOULD LEAK THE INFORMATION. FORCE THE COWARDLY SODS TO GET INVOLVED UNDER THREAT OF MOB.
CHRIST, IT MAKES ME WANT TO VOMIT BLOOD JUST BEING IN THEIR PRESENCE.
I...UH, DON'T REALLY KNOW HOW TO RESPOND TO THAT, SIR.
FOR KING AND COUNTRY, EH? TOUGH TO OVERCOME A LIFETIME BEING EDUCATED TOWARDS DUTY AND DEVOTION.

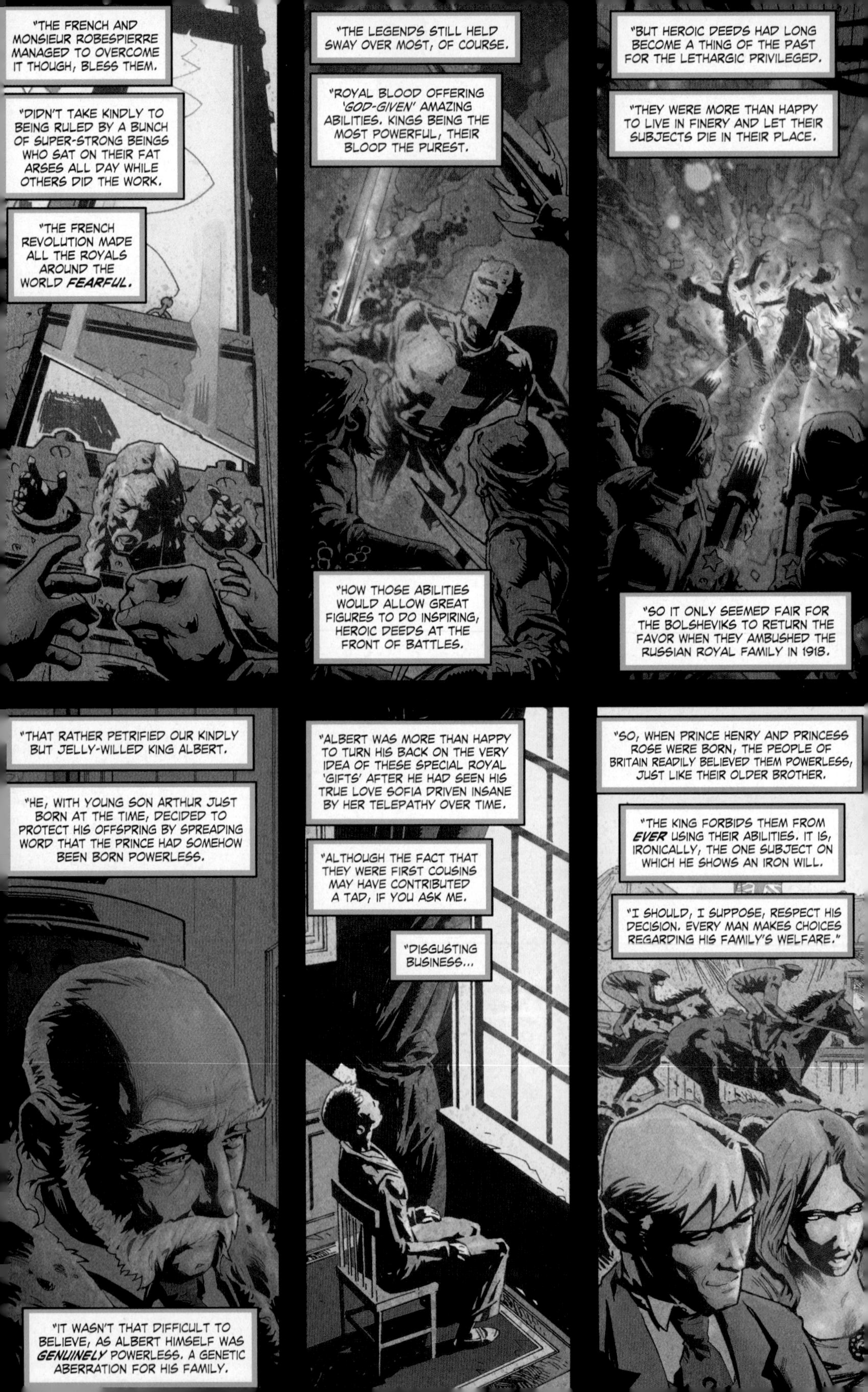
"THE FRENCH AND MONSIEUR ROBESPIERRE MANAGED TO OVERCOME IT THOUGH, BLESS THEM.
"DIDN'T TAKE KINDLY TO BEING RULED BY A BUNCH OF SUPER-STRONG BEINGS WHO SAT ON THEIR FAT ARSES ALL DAY WHILE OTHERS DID THE WORK.
"THE FRENCH REVOLUTION MADE ALL THE ROYALS AROUND THE WORLD FEARFUL.
"THE LEGENDS STILL HELD SWAY OVER MOST, OF COURSE.
"ROYAL BLOOD OFFERING 'GOD-GIVEN' AMAZING ABILITIES. KINGS BEING THE MOST POWERFUL, THEIR BLOOD THE PUREST.
"HOW THOSE ABILITIES WOULD ALLOW GREAT FIGURES TO DO INSPIRING, HEROIC DEEDS AT THE FRONT OF BATTLES.
"BUT HEROIC DEEDS HAD LONG BECOME A THING OF THE PAST FOR THE LETHARGIC PRIVILEGED.
"THEY WERE MORE THAN HAPPY TO LIVE IN FINERY AND LET THEIR SUBJECTS DIE IN THEIR PLACE.
"SO IT ONLY SEEMED FAIR FOR THE BOLSHEVIKS TO RETURN THE FAVOR WHEN THEY AMBUSHED THE RUSSIAN ROYAL FAMILY IN 1918.
"THAT RATHER PETRIFIED OUR KINDLY BUT JELLY-WILLED KING ALBERT.
"HE, WITH YOUNG SON ARTHUR JUST BORN AT THE TIME, DECIDED TO PROTECT HIS OFFSPRING BY SPREADING WORD THAT THE PRINCE HAD SOMEHOW BEEN BORN POWERLESS.
"IT WASN'T THAT DIFFICULT TO BELIEVE, AS ALBERT HIMSELF WAS GENUINELY POWERLESS. A GENETIC ABERRATION FOR HIS FAMILY.
"ALBERT WAS MORE THAN HAPPY TO TURN HIS BACK ON THE VERY IDEA OF THESE SPECIAL ROYAL 'GIFTS' AFTER HE HAD SEEN HIS TRUE LOVE SOFIA DRIVEN INSANE BY HER TELEPATHY OVER TIME.
"ALTHOUGH THE FACT THAT THEY WERE FIRST COUSINS MAY HAVE CONTRIBUTED A TAD, IF YOU ASK ME.
"DISGUSTING BUSINESS...
"SO, WHEN PRINCE HENRY AND PRINCESS ROSE WERE BORN, THE PEOPLE OF BRITAIN READILY BELIEVED THEM POWERLESS, JUST LIKE THEIR OLDER BROTHER.
"THE KING FORBIDS THEM FROM EVER USING THEIR ABILITIES. IT IS, IRONICALLY, THE ONE SUBJECT ON WHICH HE SHOWS AN IRON WILL.
"I SHOULD, I SUPPOSE, RESPECT HIS DECISION. EVERY MAN MAKES CHOICES REGARDING HIS FAMILY'S WELFARE."

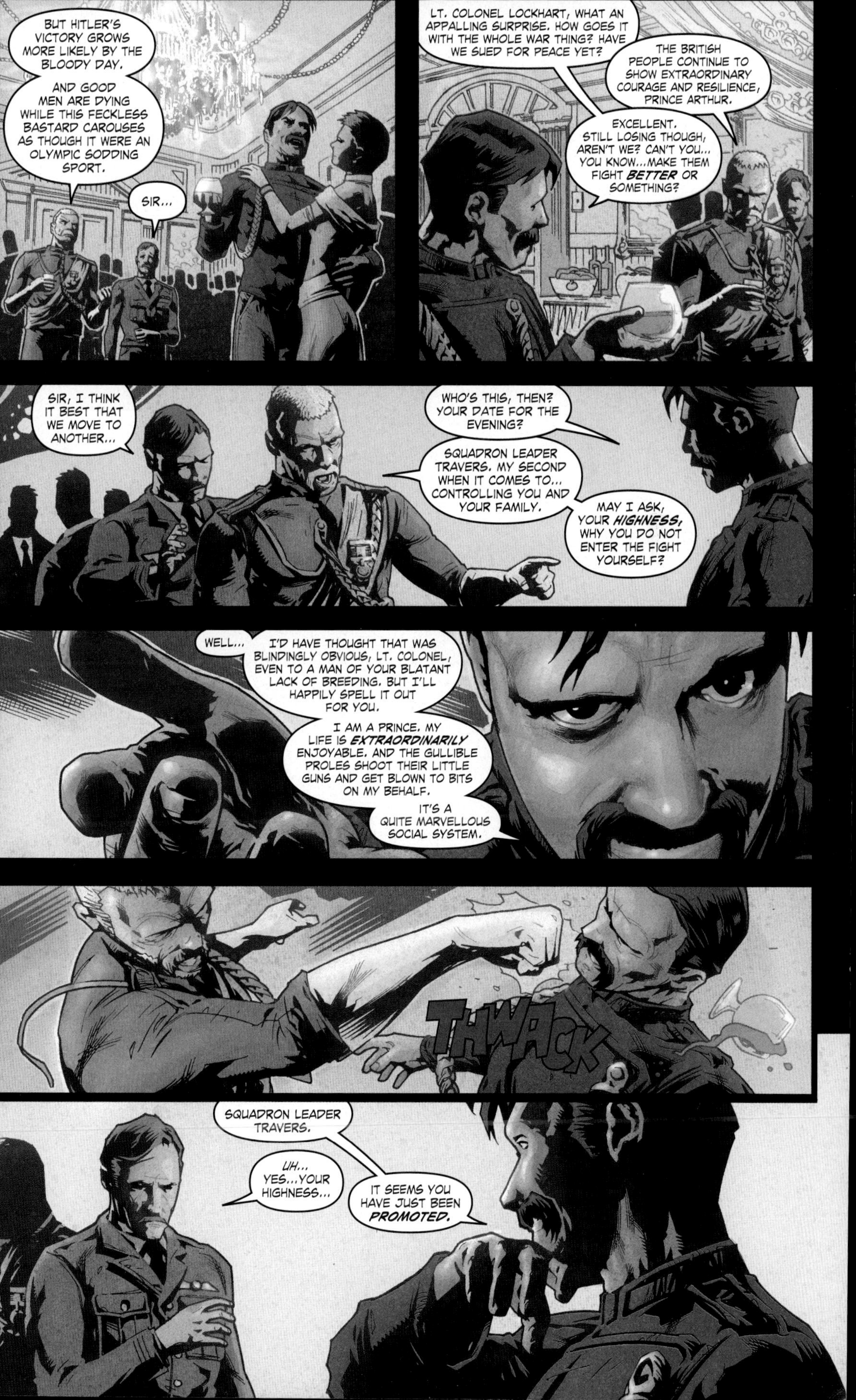

BUT HITLER'S VICTORY GROWS MORE LIKELY BY THE BLOODY DAY.
AND GOOD MEN ARE DYING WHILE THIS FECKLESS BASTARD CAROUSES AS THOUGH IT WERE AN OLYMPIC SODDING SPORT.
SIR...
LT. COLONEL LOCKHART, WHAT AN APPALLING SURPRISE. HOW GOES IT WITH THE WHOLE WAR THING? HAVE WE SUED FOR PEACE YET?
THE BRITISH PEOPLE CONTINUE TO SHOW EXTRAORDINARY COURAGE AND RESILIENCE, PRINCE ARTHUR.
EXCELLENT. STILL LOSING THOUGH, AREN'T WE? CAN'T YOU... YOU KNOW...MAKE THEM FIGHT **BETTER** OR SOMETHING?
SIR, I THINK IT BEST THAT WE MOVE TO ANOTHER...
WHO'S THIS, THEN? YOUR DATE FOR THE EVENING?
SQUADRON LEADER TRAVERS. MY SECOND WHEN IT COMES TO... CONTROLLING YOU AND YOUR FAMILY.
MAY I ASK, YOUR **HIGHNESS**, WHY YOU DO NOT ENTER THE FIGHT YOURSELF?
WELL...
I'D HAVE THOUGHT THAT WAS BLINDINGLY OBVIOUS, LT. COLONEL, EVEN TO A MAN OF YOUR BLATANT LACK OF BREEDING. BUT I'LL HAPPILY SPELL IT OUT FOR YOU.
I AM A PRINCE. MY LIFE IS **EXTRAORDINARILY** ENJOYABLE. AND THE GULLIBLE PROLES SHOOT THEIR LITTLE GUNS AND GET BLOWN TO BITS ON MY BEHALF.
IT'S A QUITE MARVELLOUS SOCIAL SYSTEM.
THWACK
SQUADRON LEADER TRAVERS.
UH... YES...YOUR HIGHNESS...
IT SEEMS YOU HAVE JUST BEEN **PROMOTED.**

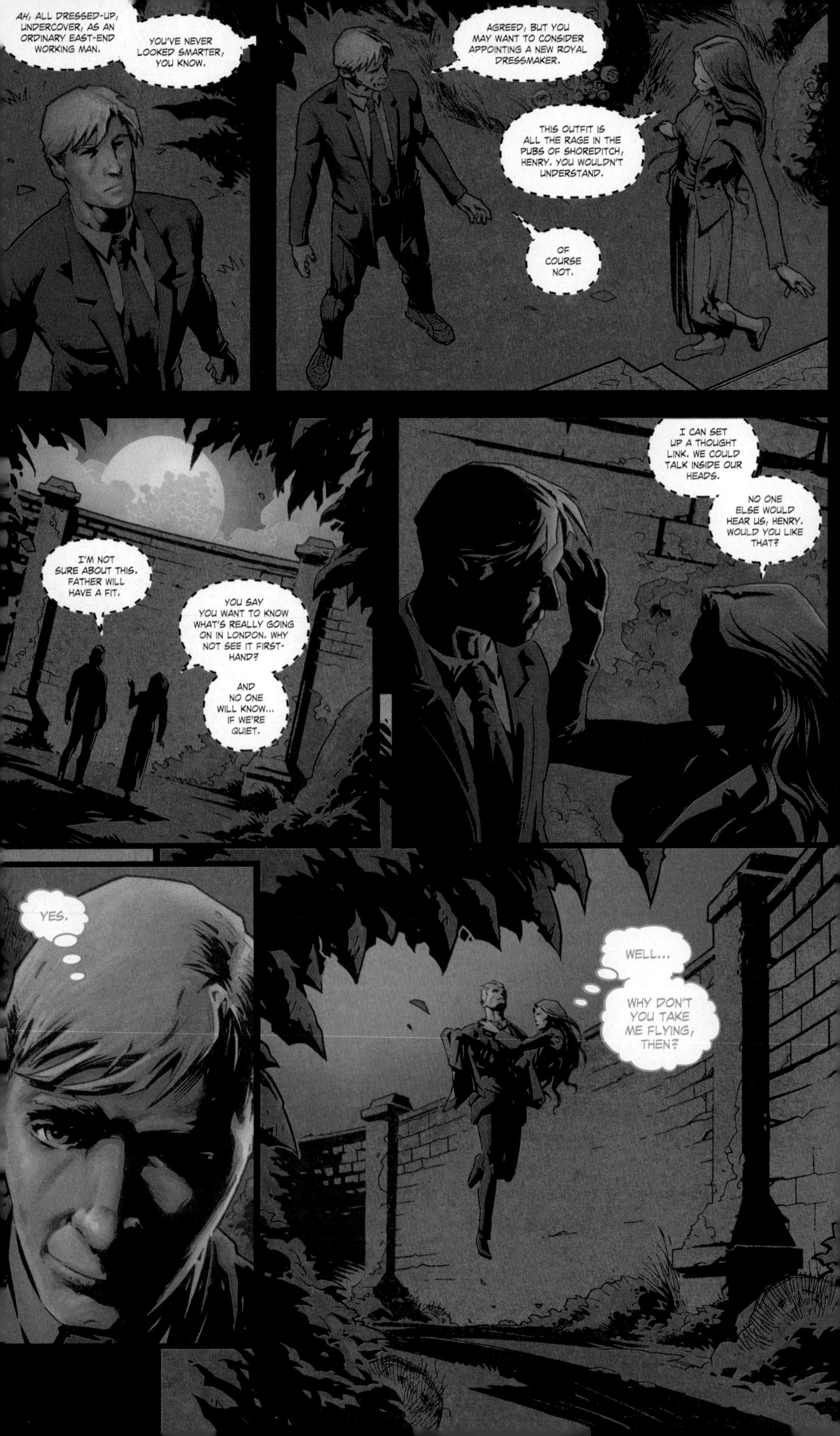
AH, ALL DRESSED-UP, UNDERCOVER, AS AN ORDINARY EAST-END WORKING MAN.
YOU'VE NEVER LOOKED SMARTER, YOU KNOW.
AGREED, BUT YOU MAY WANT TO CONSIDER APPOINTING A NEW ROYAL DRESSMAKER.
THIS OUTFIT IS ALL THE RAGE IN THE PUBS OF SHOREDITCH, HENRY. YOU WOULDN'T UNDERSTAND.
OF COURSE NOT.
I'M NOT SURE ABOUT THIS. FATHER WILL HAVE A FIT.
YOU SAY YOU WANT TO KNOW WHAT'S REALLY GOING ON IN LONDON. WHY NOT SEE IT FIRST-HAND?
AND NO ONE WILL KNOW... IF WE'RE QUIET.
I CAN SET UP A THOUGHT LINK. WE COULD TALK INSIDE OUR HEADS.
NO ONE ELSE WOULD HEAR US, HENRY. WOULD YOU LIKE THAT?
YES.
WELL...
WHY DON'T YOU TAKE ME FLYING, THEN?

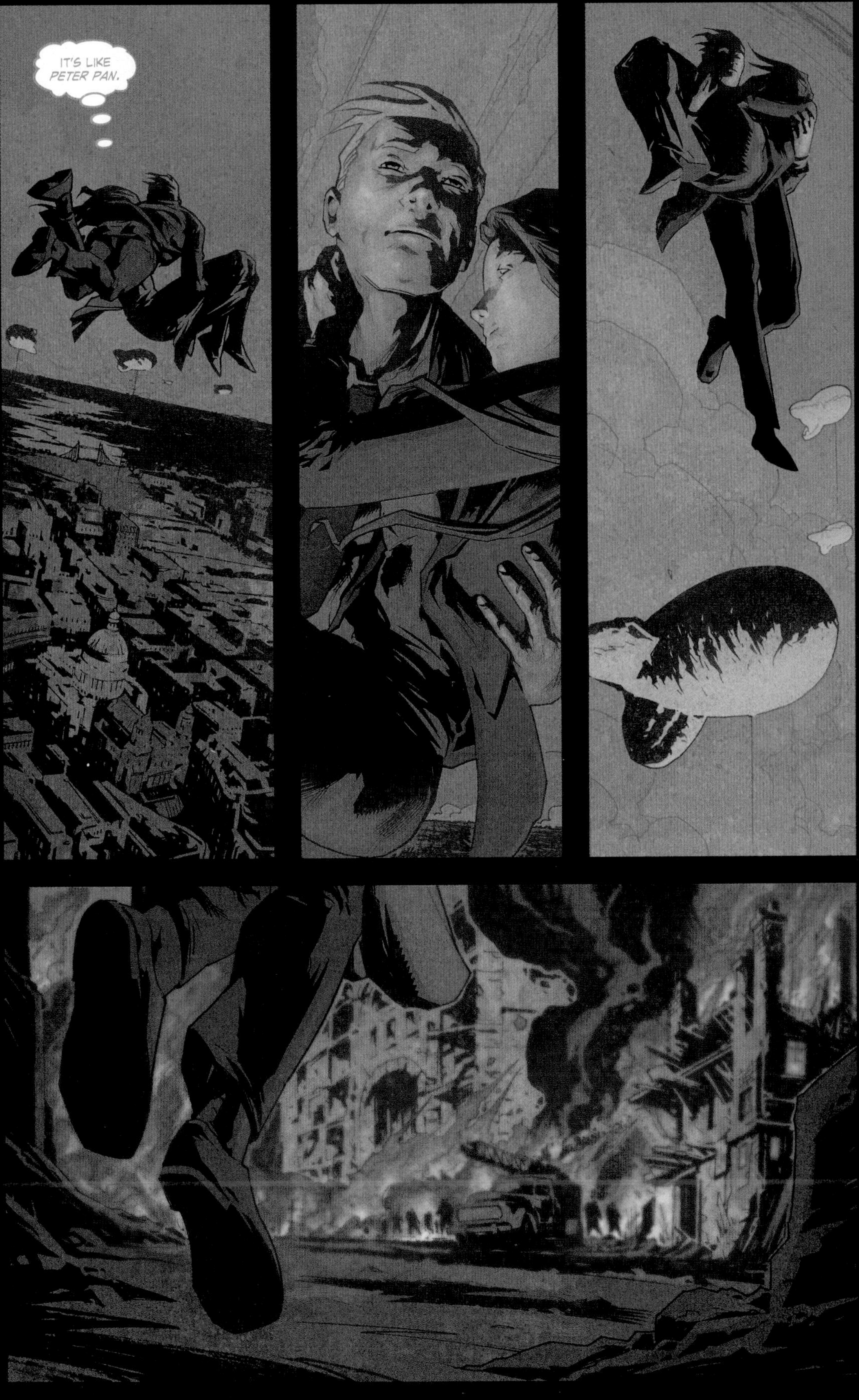
IT'S LIKE PETER PAN.

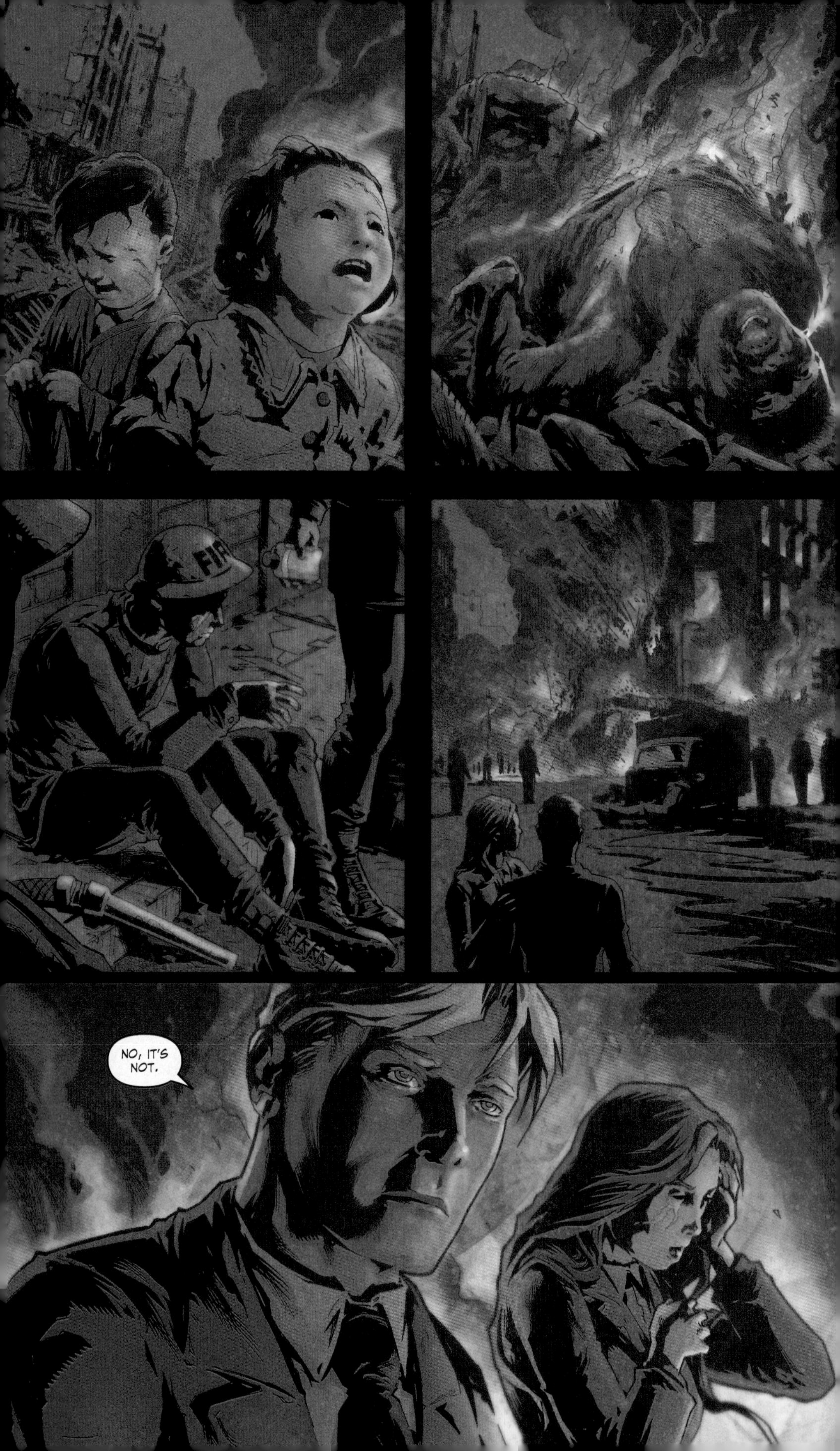
NO, IT'S NOT.

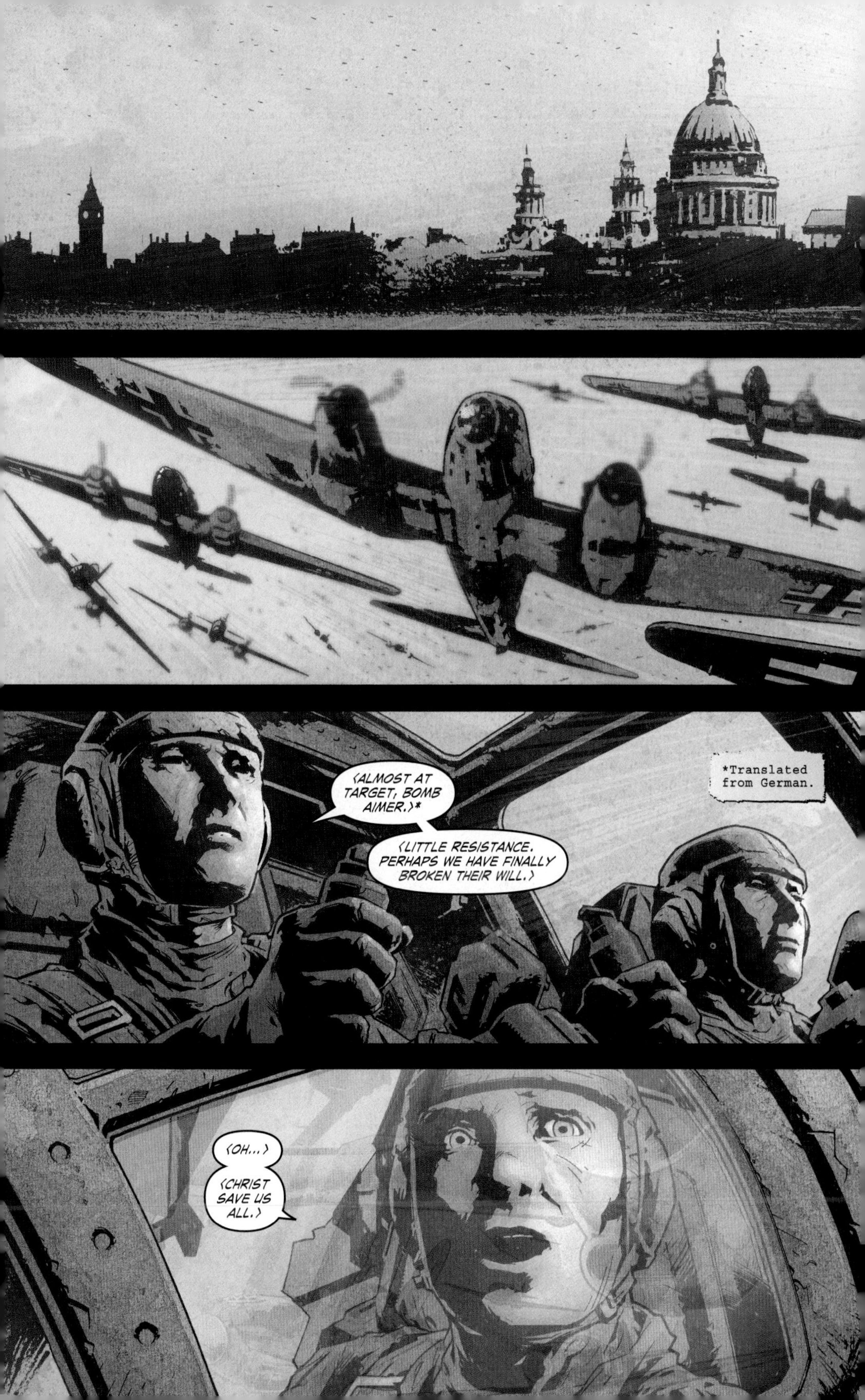

<ALMOST AT TARGET, BOMB AIMER.>*
<LITTLE RESISTANCE. PERHAPS WE HAVE FINALLY BROKEN THEIR WILL.>
*Translated from German.
<OH...>
<CHRIST SAVE US ALL.>

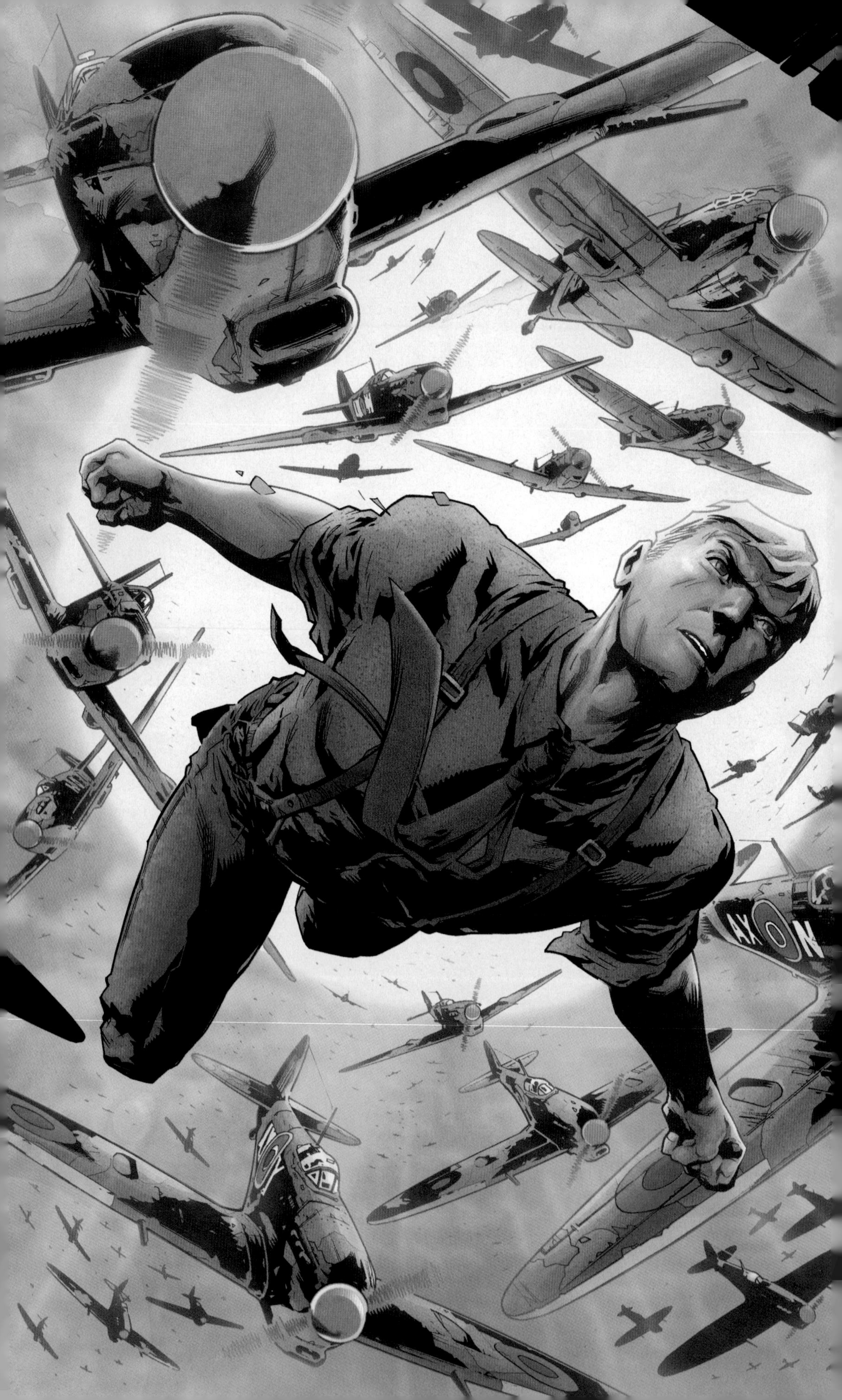

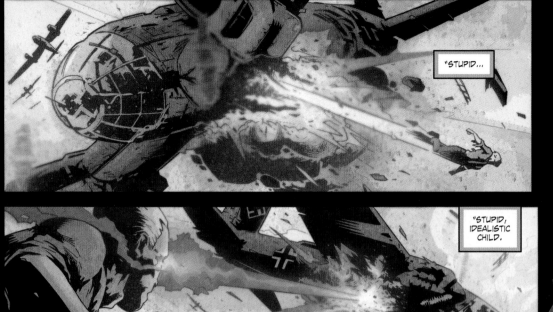

"STUPID...

"STUPID, IDEALISTIC CHILD.

"WHAT HAVE YOU GONE AND DONE?

"WE HAD AN INTERNATIONAL PACT.

"WE WEREN'T GOING TO GET INVOLVED.

"NONE OF US."

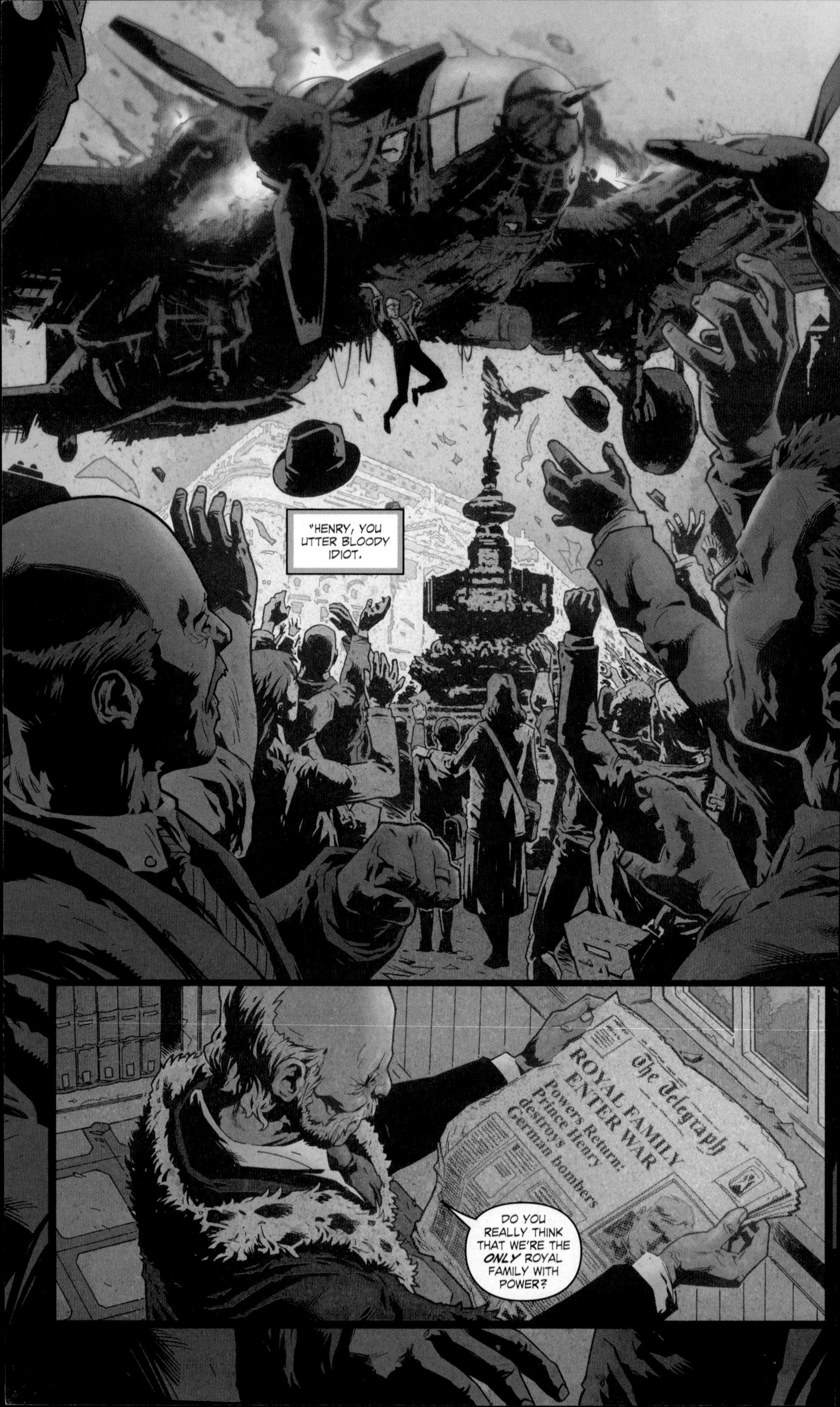
"HENRY, YOU UTTER BLOODY IDIOT.
The Telegraph
ROYAL FAMILY ENTER WAR
Powers Return: Prince Henry destroys German bombers
DO YOU REALLY THINK THAT WE'RE THE *ONLY* ROYAL FAMILY WITH POWER?

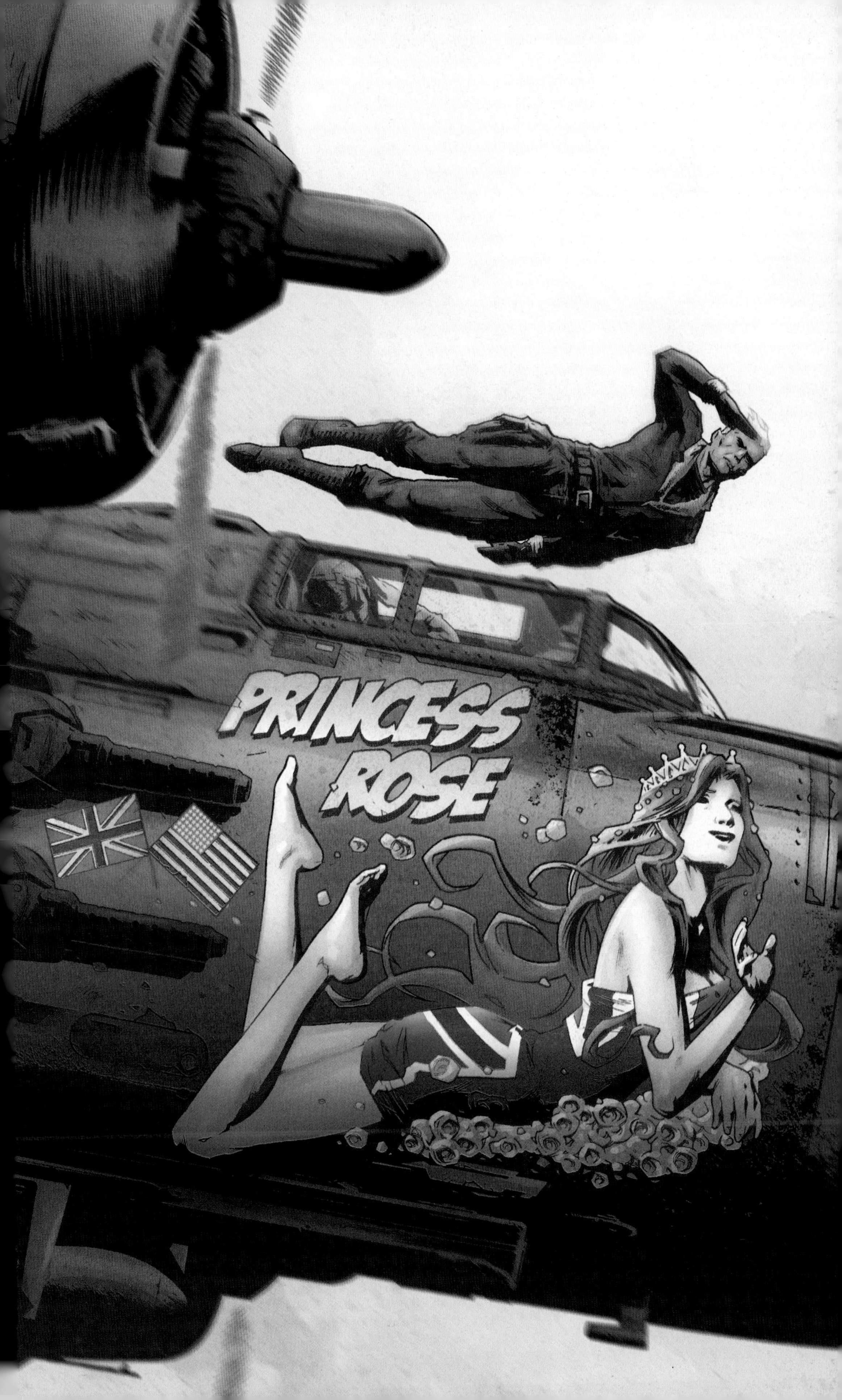
PRINCESS ROSE

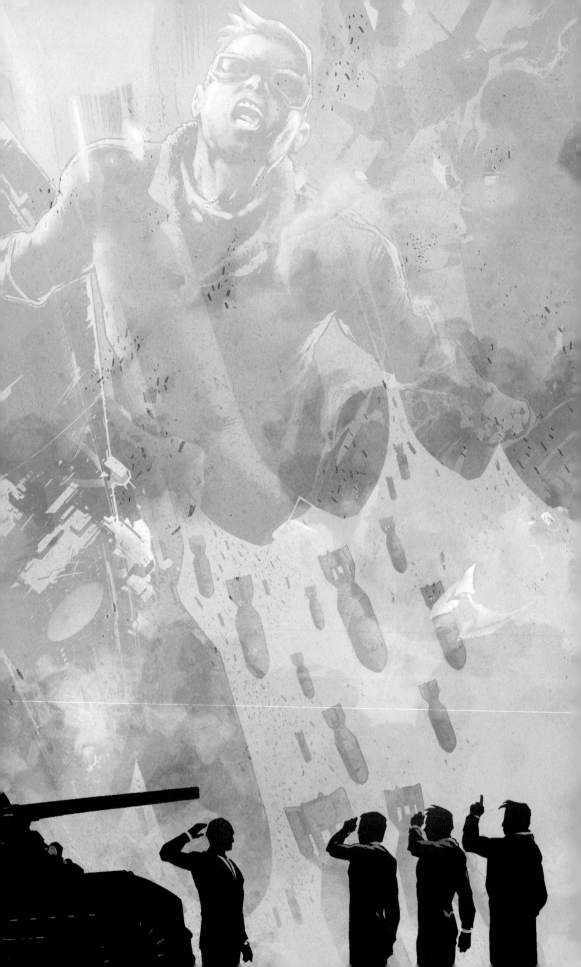

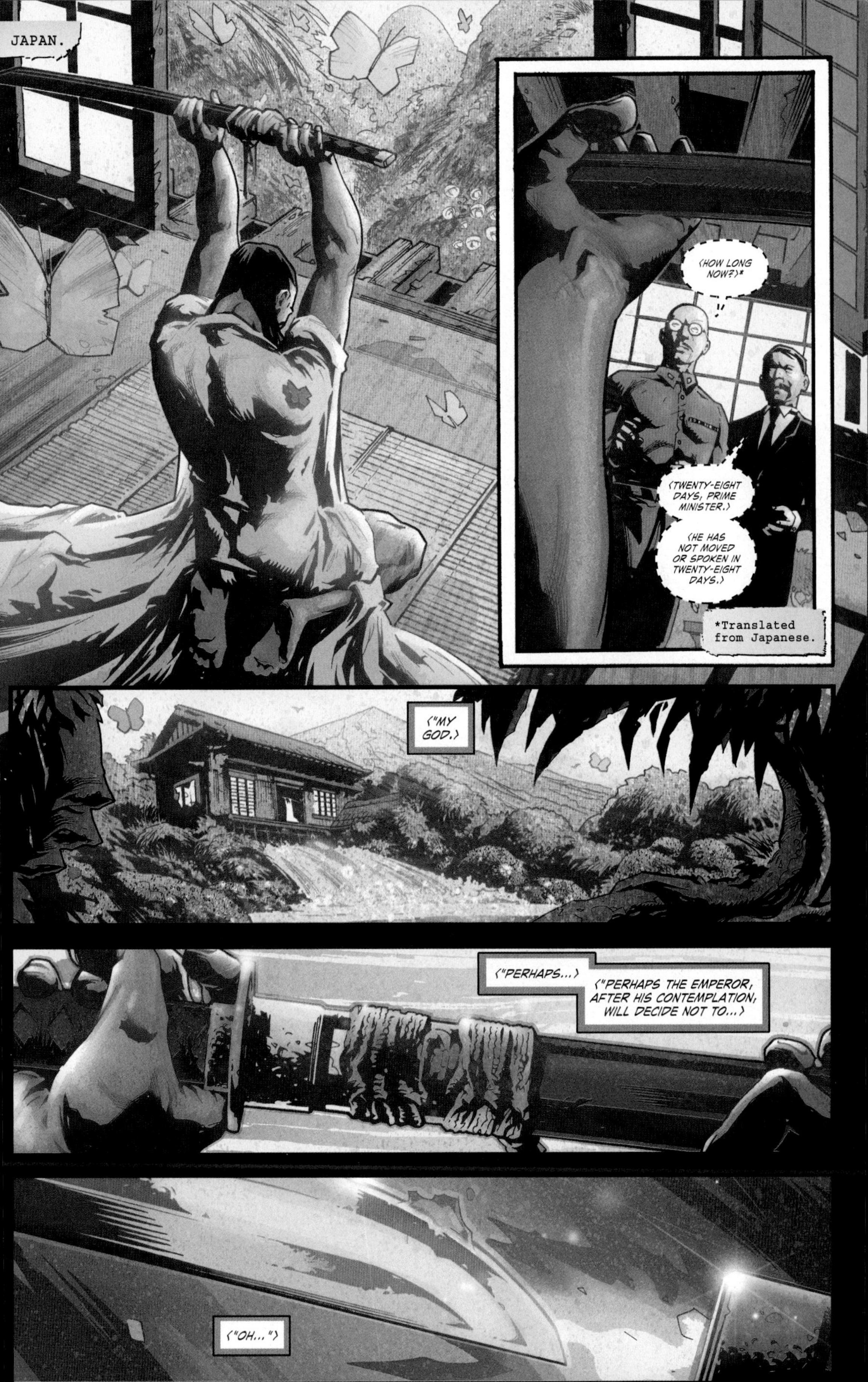
JAPAN.
‹HOW LONG NOW?›*
‹TWENTY-EIGHT DAYS, PRIME MINISTER.›
‹HE HAS NOT MOVED OR SPOKEN IN TWENTY-EIGHT DAYS.›
*Translated from Japanese.
‹"MY GOD.›
‹"PERHAPS...›
‹"PERHAPS THE EMPEROR, AFTER HIS CONTEMPLATION, WILL DECIDE NOT TO...›
‹"OH..."›

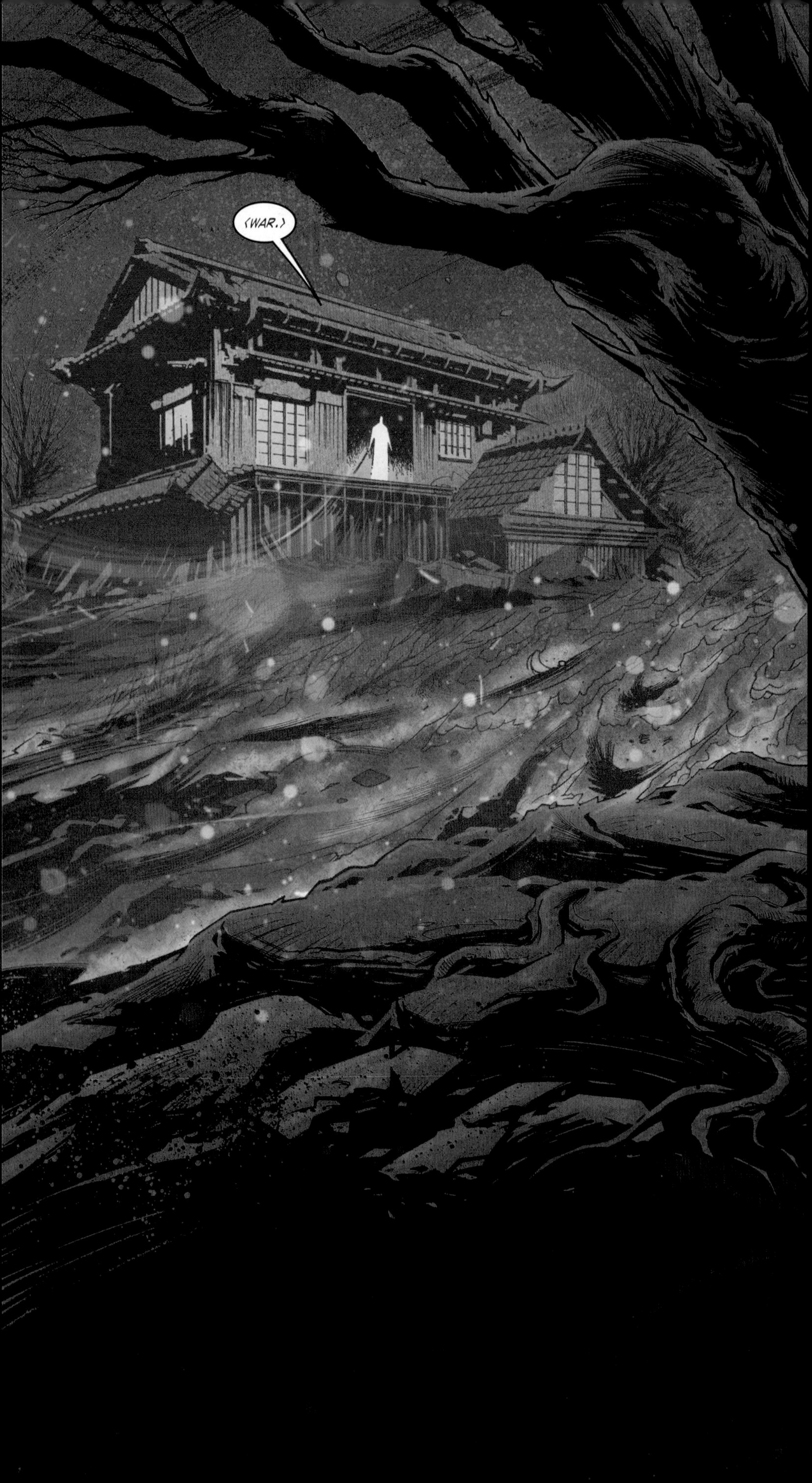

‹WAR.›

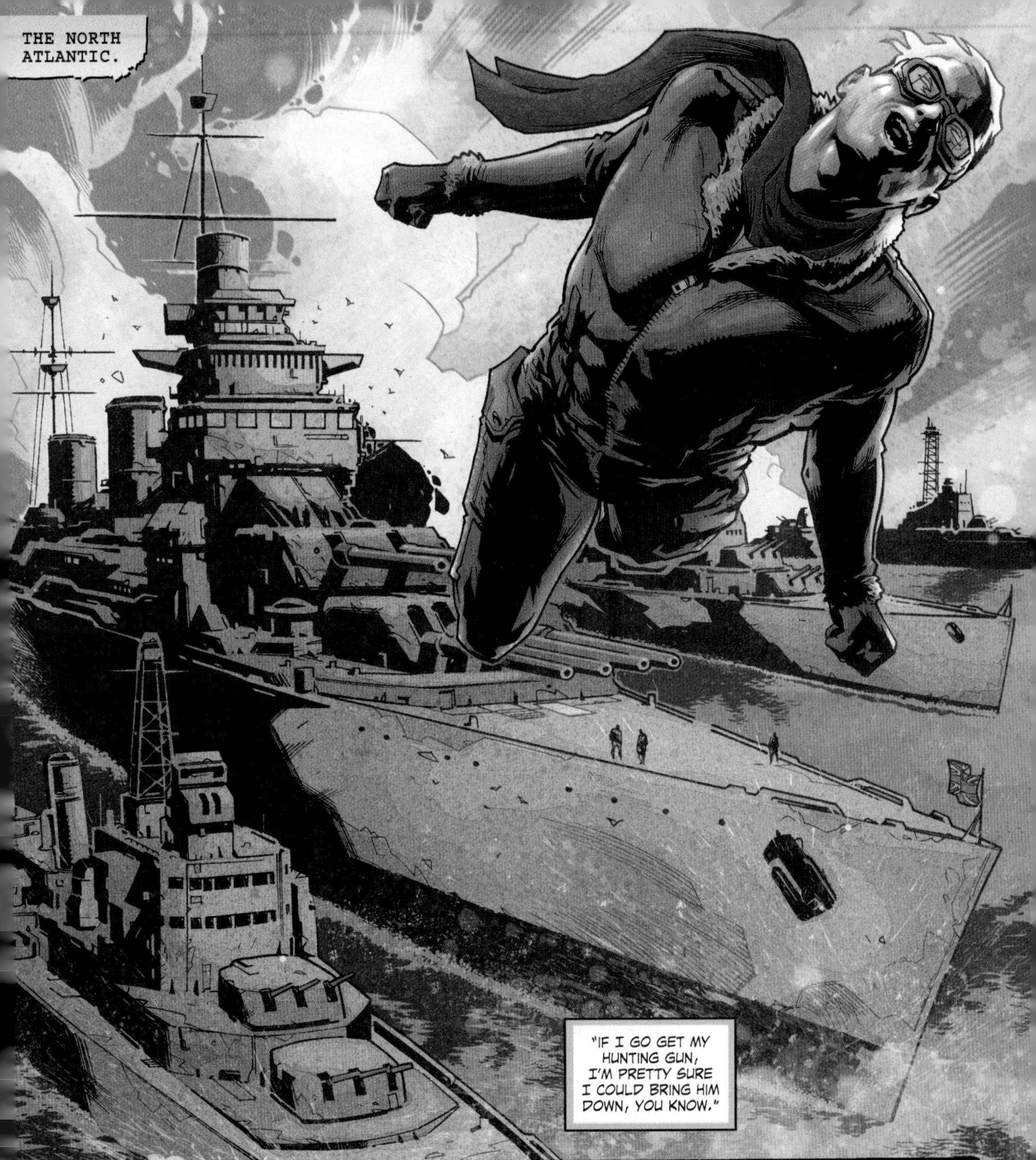
THE NORTH ATLANTIC.
"IF I GO GET MY HUNTING GUN, I'M PRETTY SURE I COULD BRING HIM DOWN, YOU KNOW."

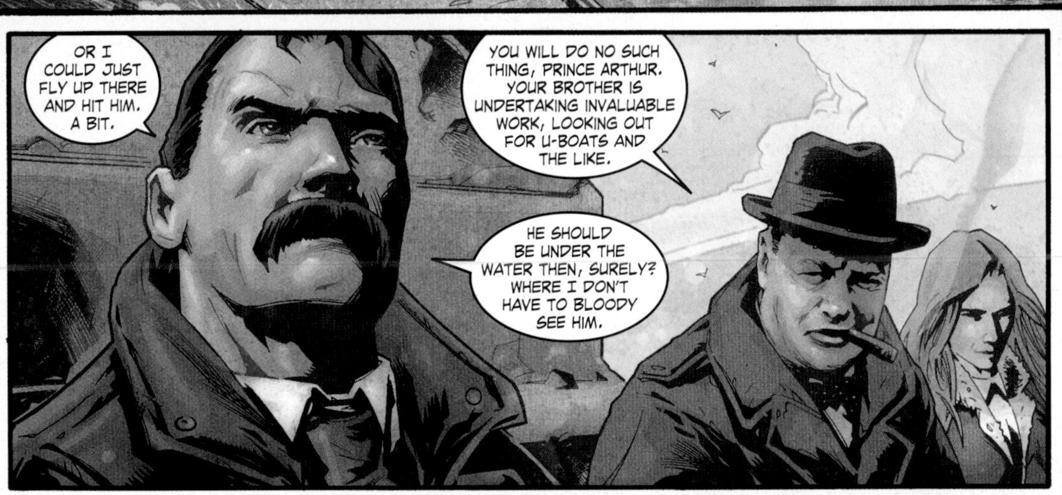
OR I COULD JUST FLY UP THERE AND HIT HIM. A BIT.
YOU WILL DO NO SUCH THING, PRINCE ARTHUR. YOUR BROTHER IS UNDERTAKING INVALUABLE WORK, LOOKING OUT FOR U-BOATS AND THE LIKE.
HE SHOULD BE UNDER THE WATER THEN, SURELY? WHERE I DON'T HAVE TO BLOODY SEE HIM.

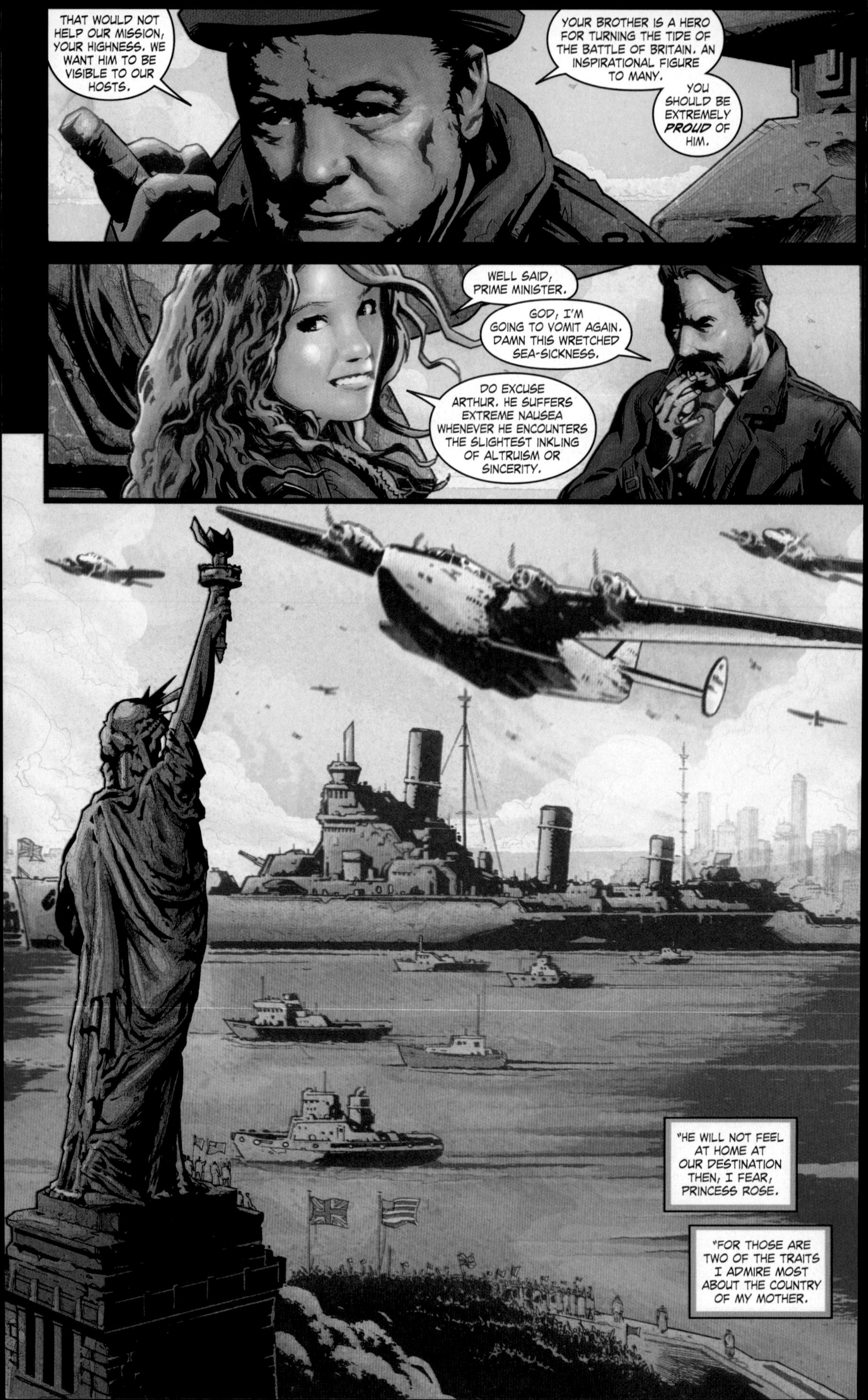
THAT WOULD NOT HELP OUR MISSION, YOUR HIGHNESS. WE WANT HIM TO BE VISIBLE TO OUR HOSTS.
YOUR BROTHER IS A HERO FOR TURNING THE TIDE OF THE BATTLE OF BRITAIN. AN INSPIRATIONAL FIGURE TO MANY.
YOU SHOULD BE EXTREMELY *PROUD* OF HIM.
WELL SAID, PRIME MINISTER.
GOD, I'M GOING TO VOMIT AGAIN. DAMN THIS WRETCHED SEA-SICKNESS.
DO EXCUSE ARTHUR. HE SUFFERS EXTREME NAUSEA WHENEVER HE ENCOUNTERS THE SLIGHTEST INKLING OF ALTRUISM OR SINCERITY.
"HE WILL NOT FEEL AT HOME AT OUR DESTINATION THEN, I FEAR, PRINCESS ROSE.
"FOR THOSE ARE TWO OF THE TRAITS I ADMIRE MOST ABOUT THE COUNTRY OF MY MOTHER.

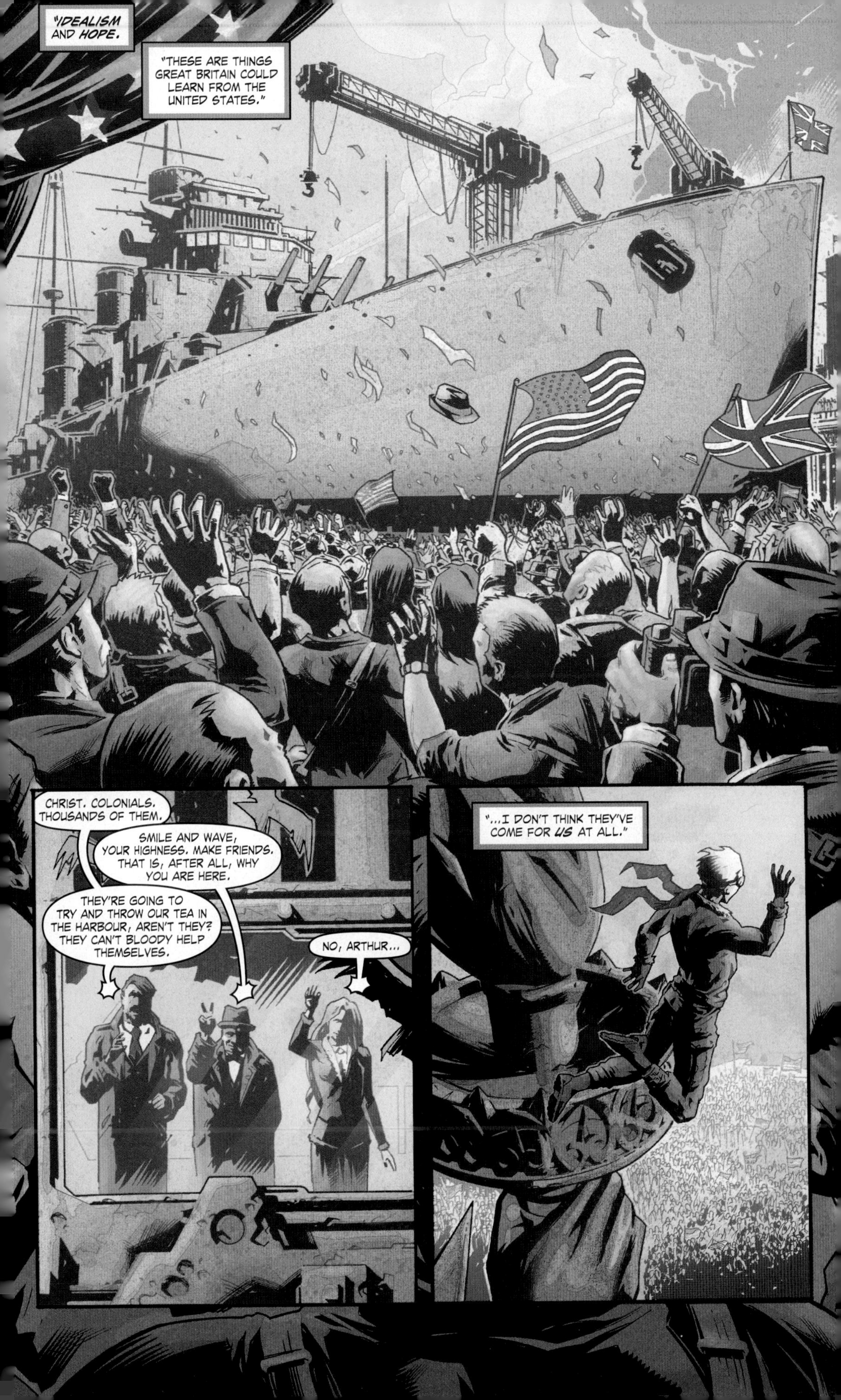
"IDEALISM AND HOPE.
"THESE ARE THINGS GREAT BRITAIN COULD LEARN FROM THE UNITED STATES."
CHRIST. COLONIALS. THOUSANDS OF THEM.
SMILE AND WAVE, YOUR HIGHNESS. MAKE FRIENDS. THAT IS, AFTER ALL, WHY YOU ARE HERE.
THEY'RE GOING TO TRY AND THROW OUR TEA IN THE HARBOUR, AREN'T THEY? THEY CAN'T BLOODY HELP THEMSELVES.
NO, ARTHUR...
"...I DON'T THINK THEY'VE COME FOR US AT ALL."

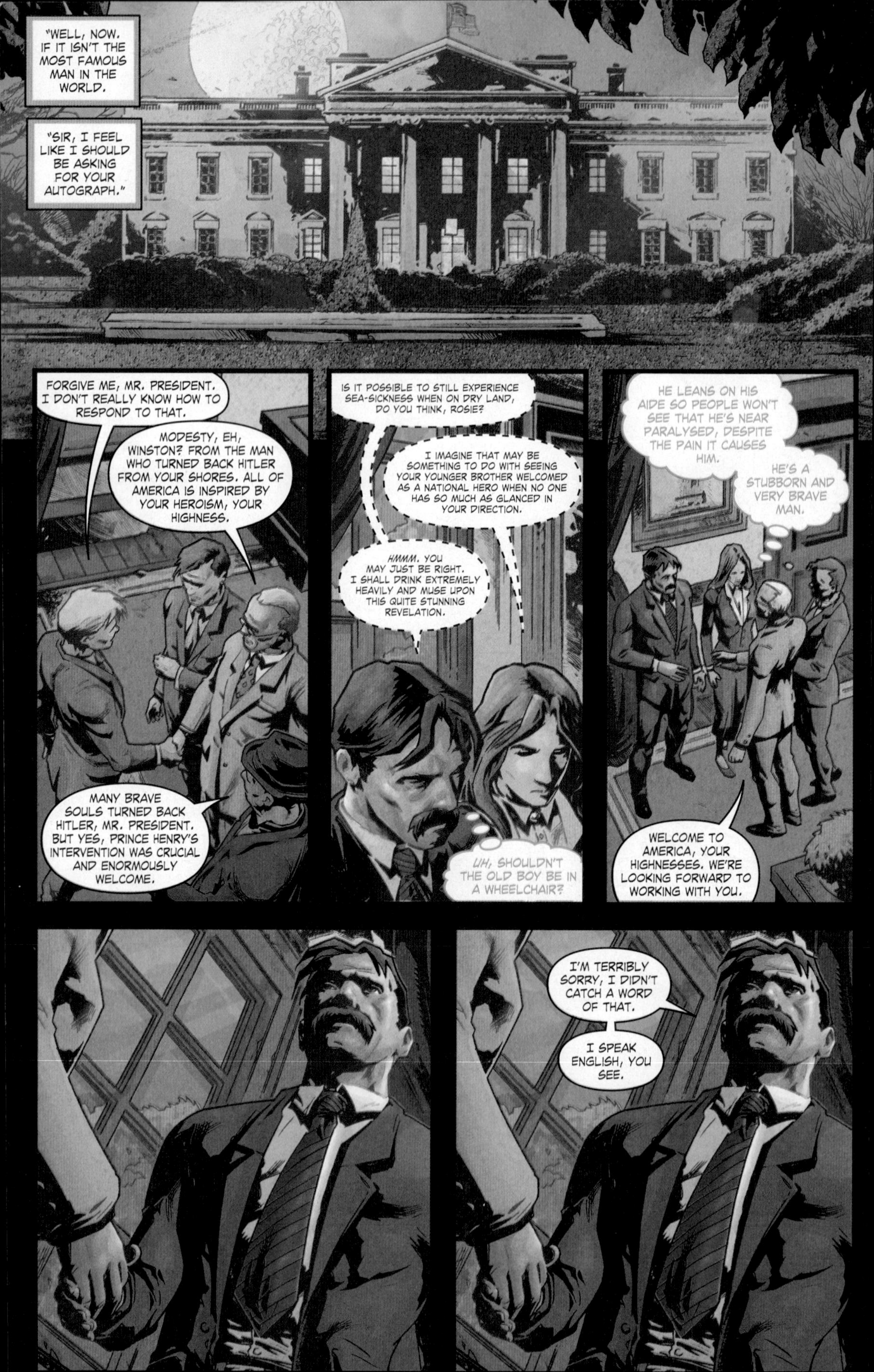
"WELL, NOW. IF IT ISN'T THE MOST FAMOUS MAN IN THE WORLD.
"SIR, I FEEL LIKE I SHOULD BE ASKING FOR YOUR AUTOGRAPH."
FORGIVE ME, MR. PRESIDENT. I DON'T REALLY KNOW HOW TO RESPOND TO THAT.
MODESTY, EH, WINSTON? FROM THE MAN WHO TURNED BACK HITLER FROM YOUR SHORES. ALL OF AMERICA IS INSPIRED BY YOUR HEROISM, YOUR HIGHNESS.
MANY BRAVE SOULS TURNED BACK HITLER, MR. PRESIDENT. BUT YES, PRINCE HENRY'S INTERVENTION WAS CRUCIAL AND ENORMOUSLY WELCOME.
IS IT POSSIBLE TO STILL EXPERIENCE SEA-SICKNESS WHEN ON DRY LAND, DO YOU THINK, ROSIE?
I IMAGINE THAT MAY BE SOMETHING TO DO WITH SEEING YOUR YOUNGER BROTHER WELCOMED AS A NATIONAL HERO WHEN NO ONE HAS SO MUCH AS GLANCED IN YOUR DIRECTION.
HMMM. YOU MAY JUST BE RIGHT. I SHALL DRINK EXTREMELY HEAVILY AND MUSE UPON THIS QUITE STUNNING REVELATION.
UH, SHOULDN'T THE OLD BOY BE IN A WHEELCHAIR?
HE LEANS ON HIS AIDE SO PEOPLE WON'T SEE THAT HE'S NEAR PARALYSED, DESPITE THE PAIN IT CAUSES HIM.
HE'S A STUBBORN AND VERY BRAVE MAN.
WELCOME TO AMERICA, YOUR HIGHNESSES. WE'RE LOOKING FORWARD TO WORKING WITH YOU.
I'M TERRIBLY SORRY, I DIDN'T CATCH A WORD OF THAT.
I SPEAK ENGLISH, YOU SEE.

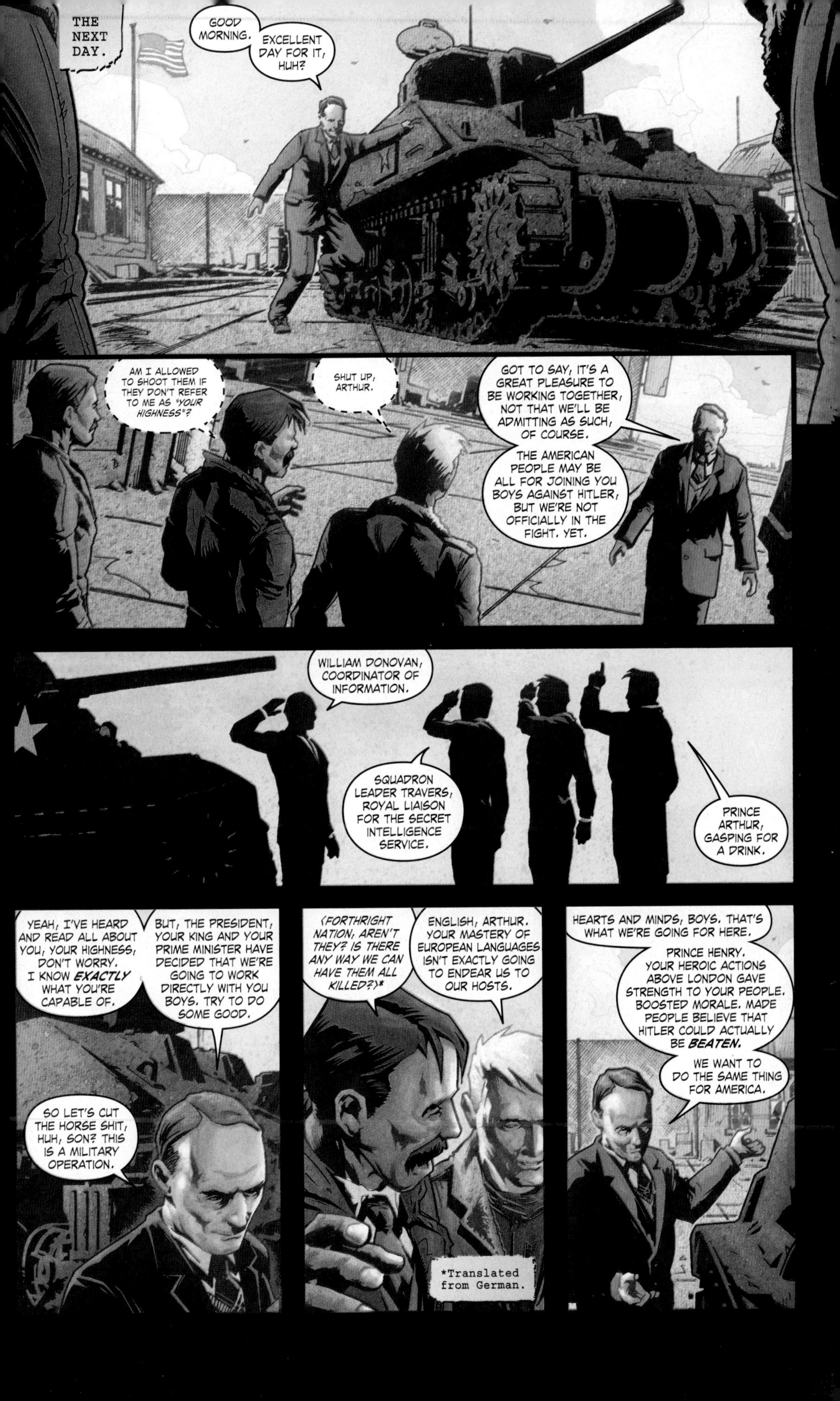
THE NEXT DAY.
GOOD MORNING.
EXCELLENT DAY FOR IT, HUH?
AM I ALLOWED TO SHOOT THEM IF THEY DON'T REFER TO ME AS "YOUR HIGHNESS"?
SHUT UP, ARTHUR.
GOT TO SAY, IT'S A GREAT PLEASURE TO BE WORKING TOGETHER, NOT THAT WE'LL BE ADMITTING AS SUCH, OF COURSE.
THE AMERICAN PEOPLE MAY BE ALL FOR JOINING YOU BOYS AGAINST HITLER, BUT WE'RE NOT OFFICIALLY IN THE FIGHT. YET.
WILLIAM DONOVAN, COORDINATOR OF INFORMATION.
SQUADRON LEADER TRAVERS, ROYAL LIAISON FOR THE SECRET INTELLIGENCE SERVICE.
PRINCE ARTHUR, GASPING FOR A DRINK.
YEAH, I'VE HEARD AND READ ALL ABOUT YOU, YOUR HIGHNESS, DON'T WORRY. I KNOW EXACTLY WHAT YOU'RE CAPABLE OF.
BUT, THE PRESIDENT, YOUR KING AND YOUR PRIME MINISTER HAVE DECIDED THAT WE'RE GOING TO WORK DIRECTLY WITH YOU BOYS. TRY TO DO SOME GOOD.
SO LET'S CUT THE HORSE SHIT, HUH, SON? THIS IS A MILITARY OPERATION.
‹FORTHRIGHT NATION, AREN'T THEY? IS THERE ANY WAY WE CAN HAVE THEM ALL KILLED?›*
ENGLISH, ARTHUR. YOUR MASTERY OF EUROPEAN LANGUAGES ISN'T EXACTLY GOING TO ENDEAR US TO OUR HOSTS.
*Translated from German.
HEARTS AND MINDS, BOYS. THAT'S WHAT WE'RE GOING FOR HERE.
PRINCE HENRY. YOUR HEROIC ACTIONS ABOVE LONDON GAVE STRENGTH TO YOUR PEOPLE. BOOSTED MORALE. MADE PEOPLE BELIEVE THAT HITLER COULD ACTUALLY BE BEATEN.
WE WANT TO DO THE SAME THING FOR AMERICA.

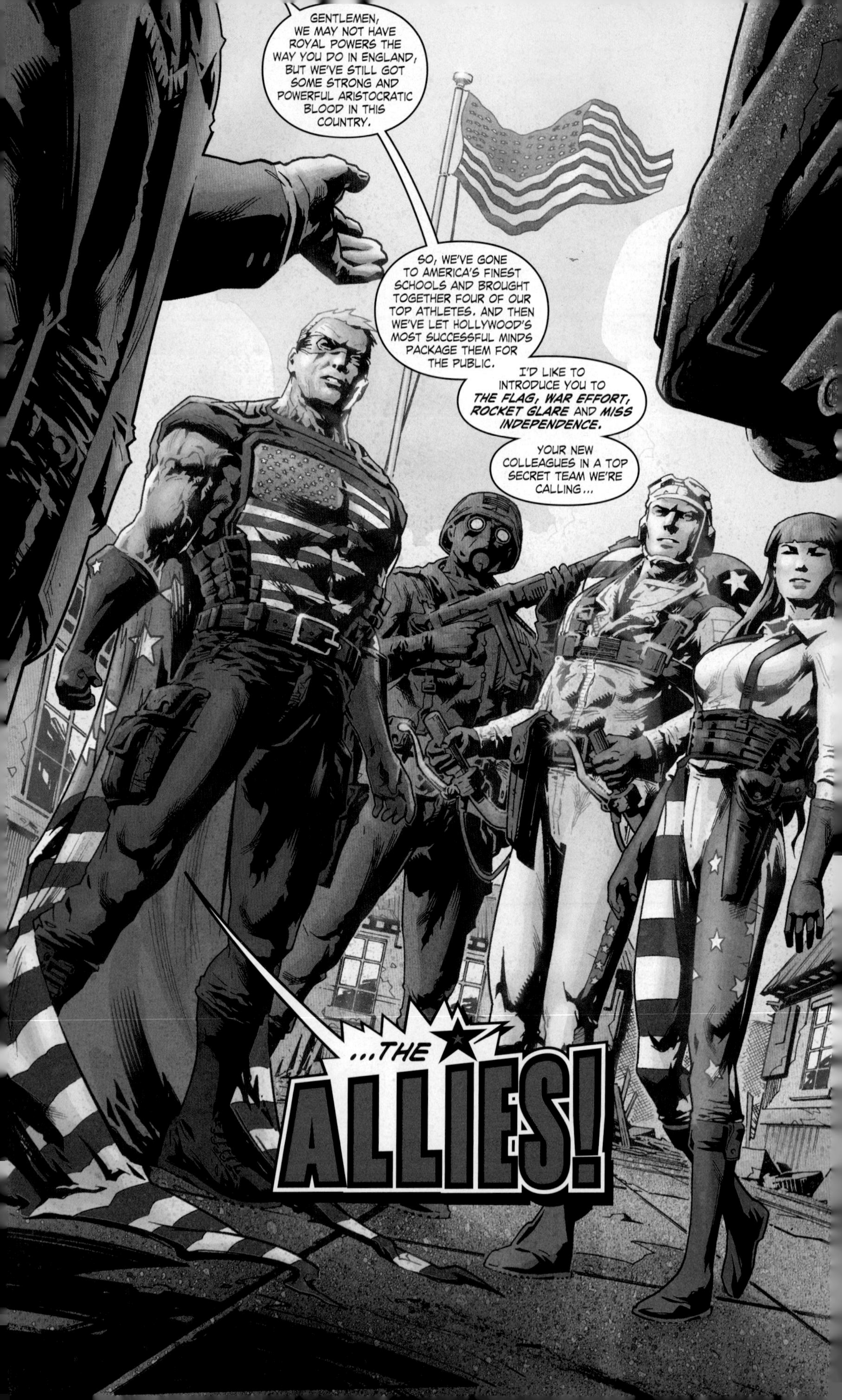

GENTLEMEN, WE MAY NOT HAVE ROYAL POWERS THE WAY YOU DO IN ENGLAND, BUT WE'VE STILL GOT SOME STRONG AND POWERFUL ARISTOCRATIC BLOOD IN THIS COUNTRY.
SO, WE'VE GONE TO AMERICA'S FINEST SCHOOLS AND BROUGHT TOGETHER FOUR OF OUR TOP ATHLETES. AND THEN WE'VE LET HOLLYWOOD'S MOST SUCCESSFUL MINDS PACKAGE THEM FOR THE PUBLIC.
I'D LIKE TO INTRODUCE YOU TO *THE FLAG, WAR EFFORT, ROCKET GLARE* AND *MISS INDEPENDENCE*.
YOUR NEW COLLEAGUES IN A TOP SECRET TEAM WE'RE CALLING...
...THE ALLIES!

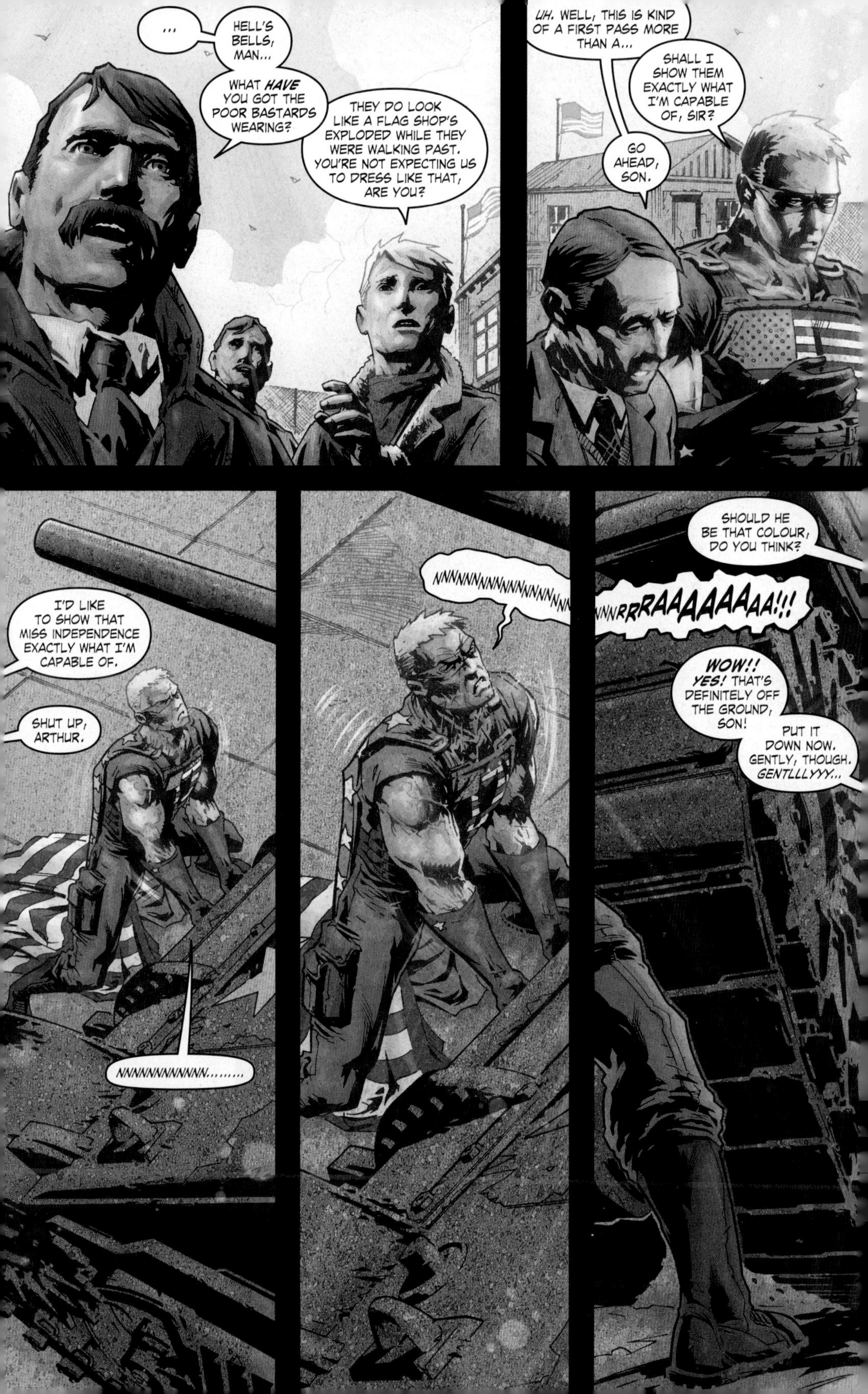
...
HELL'S BELLS, MAN...
WHAT *HAVE* YOU GOT THE POOR BASTARDS WEARING?
THEY DO LOOK LIKE A FLAG SHOP'S EXPLODED WHILE THEY WERE WALKING PAST. YOU'RE NOT EXPECTING US TO DRESS LIKE THAT, ARE YOU?
UH. WELL, THIS IS KIND OF A FIRST PASS MORE THAN A...
SHALL I SHOW THEM EXACTLY WHAT I'M CAPABLE OF, SIR?
GO AHEAD, SON.
I'D LIKE TO SHOW THAT MISS INDEPENDENCE EXACTLY WHAT I'M CAPABLE OF.
SHUT UP, ARTHUR.
NNNNNNNNNNN.........
NNNNNNNNNNNNNNNNNNNNNNNNRRRAAAAAAAAA!!!
SHOULD HE BE THAT COLOUR, DO YOU THINK?
WOW!! YES! THAT'S DEFINITELY OFF THE GROUND, SON!
PUT IT DOWN NOW. GENTLY, THOUGH. *GENTLLLYYY...*

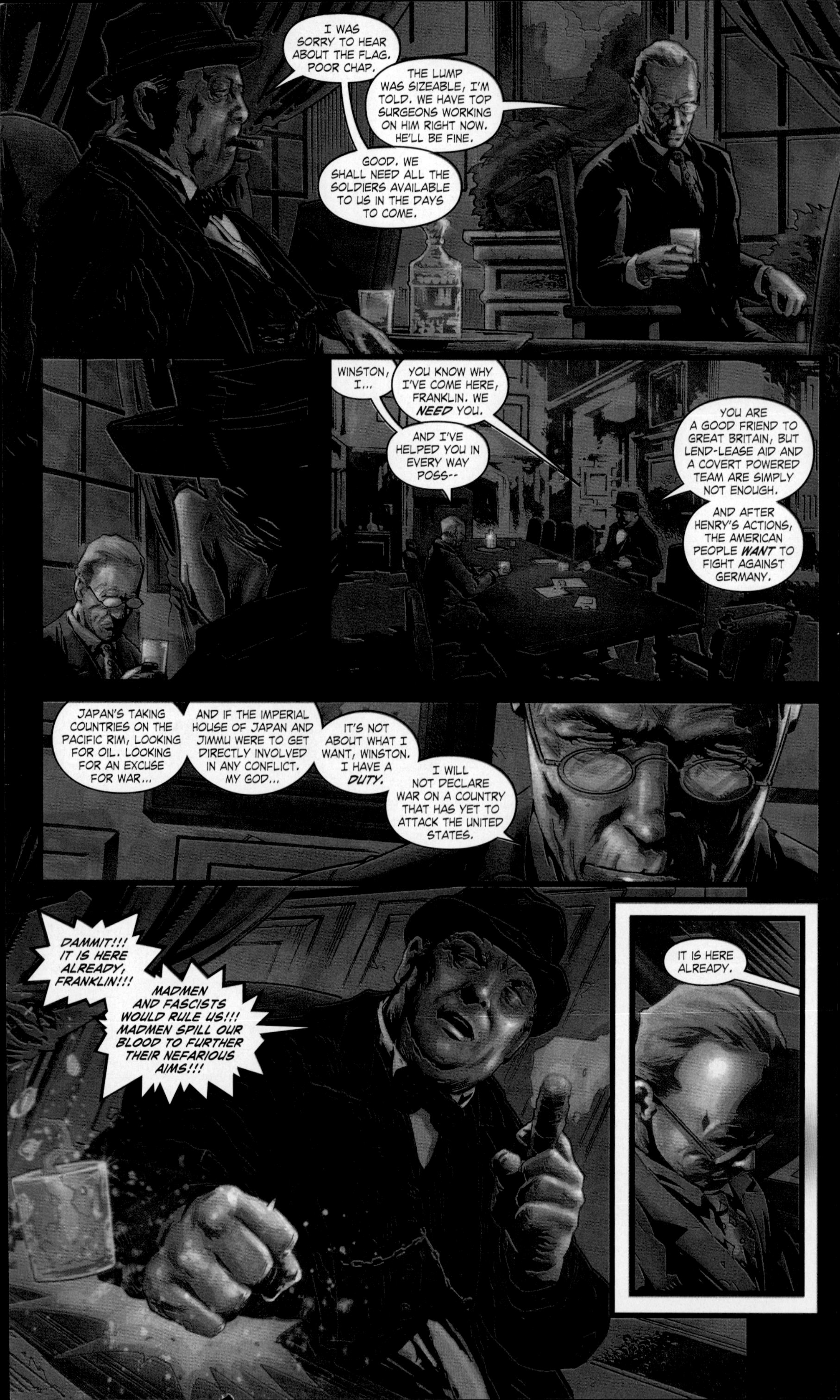
I WAS SORRY TO HEAR ABOUT THE FLAG. POOR CHAP.
THE LUMP WAS SIZEABLE, I'M TOLD. WE HAVE TOP SURGEONS WORKING ON HIM RIGHT NOW. HE'LL BE FINE.
GOOD. WE SHALL NEED ALL THE SOLDIERS AVAILABLE TO US IN THE DAYS TO COME.
WINSTON, I...
YOU KNOW WHY I'VE COME HERE, FRANKLIN. WE *NEED* YOU.
AND I'VE HELPED YOU IN EVERY WAY POSS--
YOU ARE A GOOD FRIEND TO GREAT BRITAIN, BUT LEND-LEASE AID AND A COVERT POWERED TEAM ARE SIMPLY NOT ENOUGH.
AND AFTER HENRY'S ACTIONS, THE AMERICAN PEOPLE *WANT* TO FIGHT AGAINST GERMANY.
JAPAN'S TAKING COUNTRIES ON THE PACIFIC RIM, LOOKING FOR OIL. LOOKING FOR AN EXCUSE FOR WAR...
AND IF THE IMPERIAL HOUSE OF JAPAN AND JIMMU WERE TO GET DIRECTLY INVOLVED IN ANY CONFLICT. MY GOD...
IT'S NOT ABOUT WHAT I WANT, WINSTON. I HAVE A *DUTY.*
I WILL NOT DECLARE WAR ON A COUNTRY THAT HAS YET TO ATTACK THE UNITED STATES.
DAMMIT!!! IT IS HERE ALREADY, FRANKLIN!!!
MADMEN AND FASCISTS WOULD RULE US!!! MADMEN SPILL OUR BLOOD TO FURTHER THEIR NEFARIOUS AIMS!!!
IT IS HERE ALREADY.

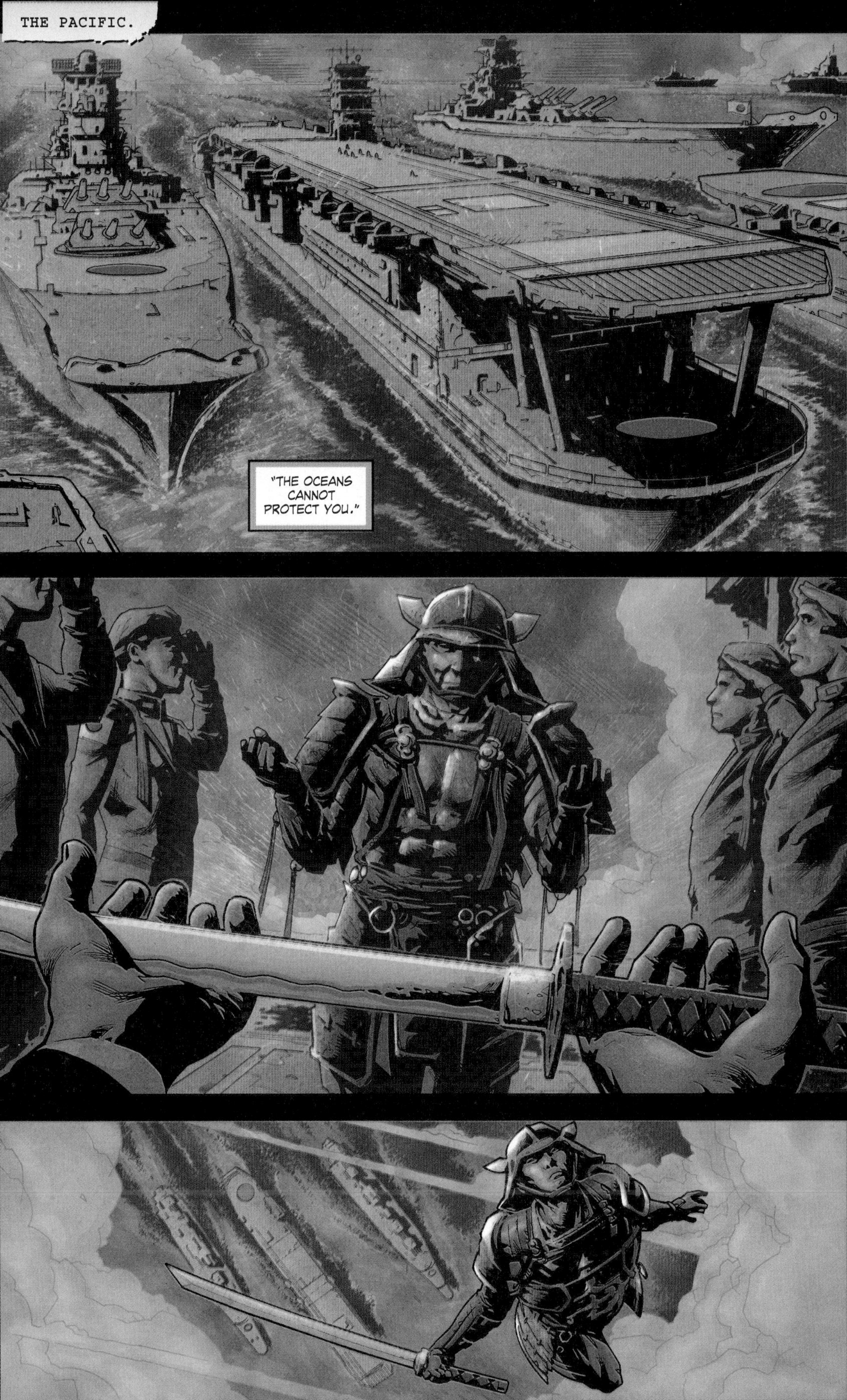
THE PACIFIC.
"THE OCEANS CANNOT PROTECT YOU."

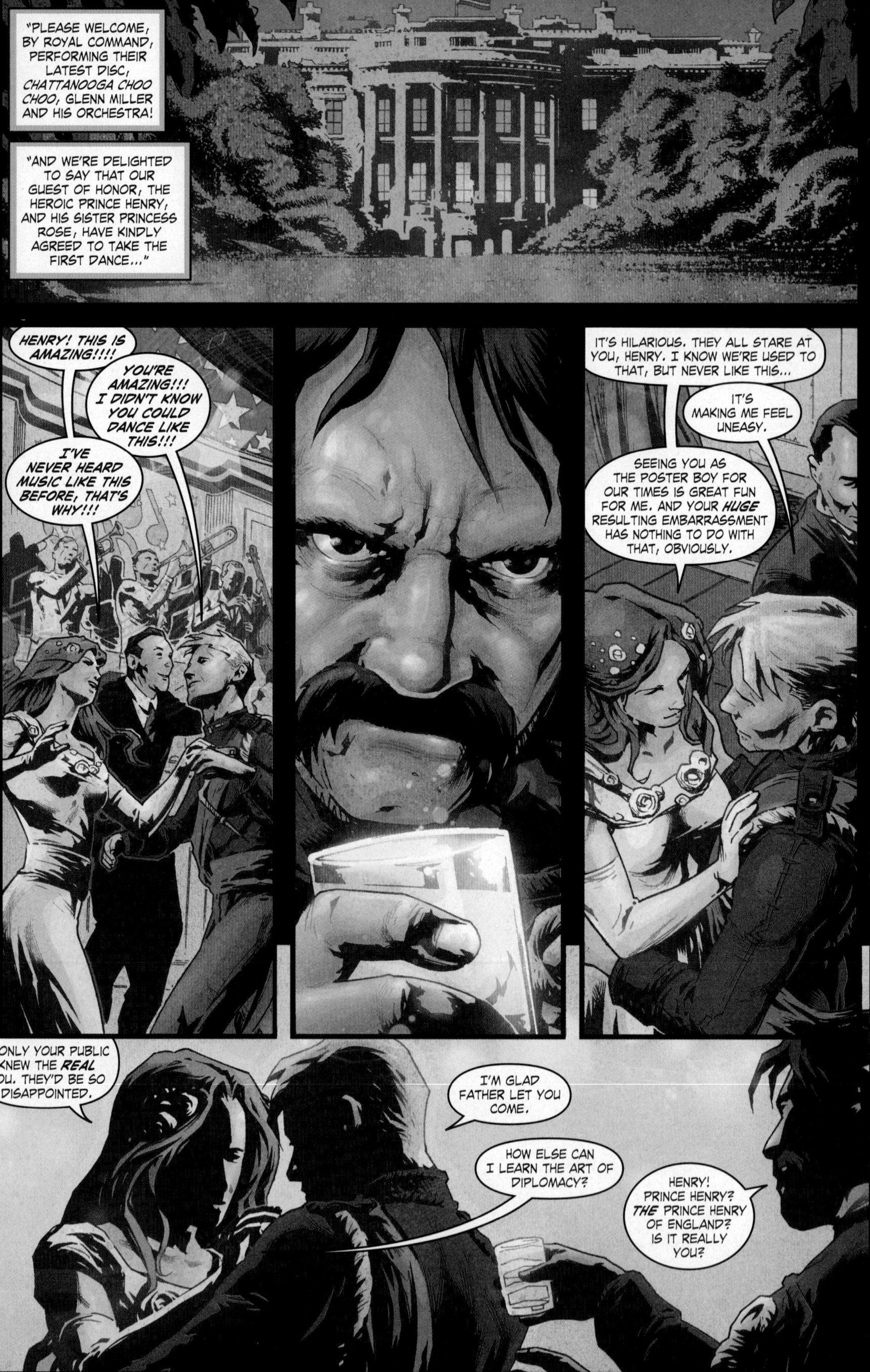
"PLEASE WELCOME, BY ROYAL COMMAND, PERFORMING THEIR LATEST DISC, CHATTANOOGA CHOO CHOO, GLENN MILLER AND HIS ORCHESTRA!
"AND WE'RE DELIGHTED TO SAY THAT OUR GUEST OF HONOR, THE HEROIC PRINCE HENRY, AND HIS SISTER PRINCESS ROSE, HAVE KINDLY AGREED TO TAKE THE FIRST DANCE..."
HENRY! THIS IS AMAZING!!!!
YOU'RE AMAZING!!! I DIDN'T KNOW YOU COULD DANCE LIKE THIS!!!
I'VE NEVER HEARD MUSIC LIKE THIS BEFORE, THAT'S WHY!!!
IT'S HILARIOUS. THEY ALL STARE AT YOU, HENRY. I KNOW WE'RE USED TO THAT, BUT NEVER LIKE THIS...
IT'S MAKING ME FEEL UNEASY.
SEEING YOU AS THE POSTER BOY FOR OUR TIMES IS GREAT FUN FOR ME. AND YOUR HUGE RESULTING EMBARRASSMENT HAS NOTHING TO DO WITH THAT, OBVIOUSLY.
IF ONLY YOUR PUBLIC KNEW THE REAL YOU. THEY'D BE SO DISAPPOINTED.
I'M GLAD FATHER LET YOU COME.
HOW ELSE CAN I LEARN THE ART OF DIPLOMACY?
HENRY! PRINCE HENRY? THE PRINCE HENRY OF ENGLAND? IS IT REALLY YOU?

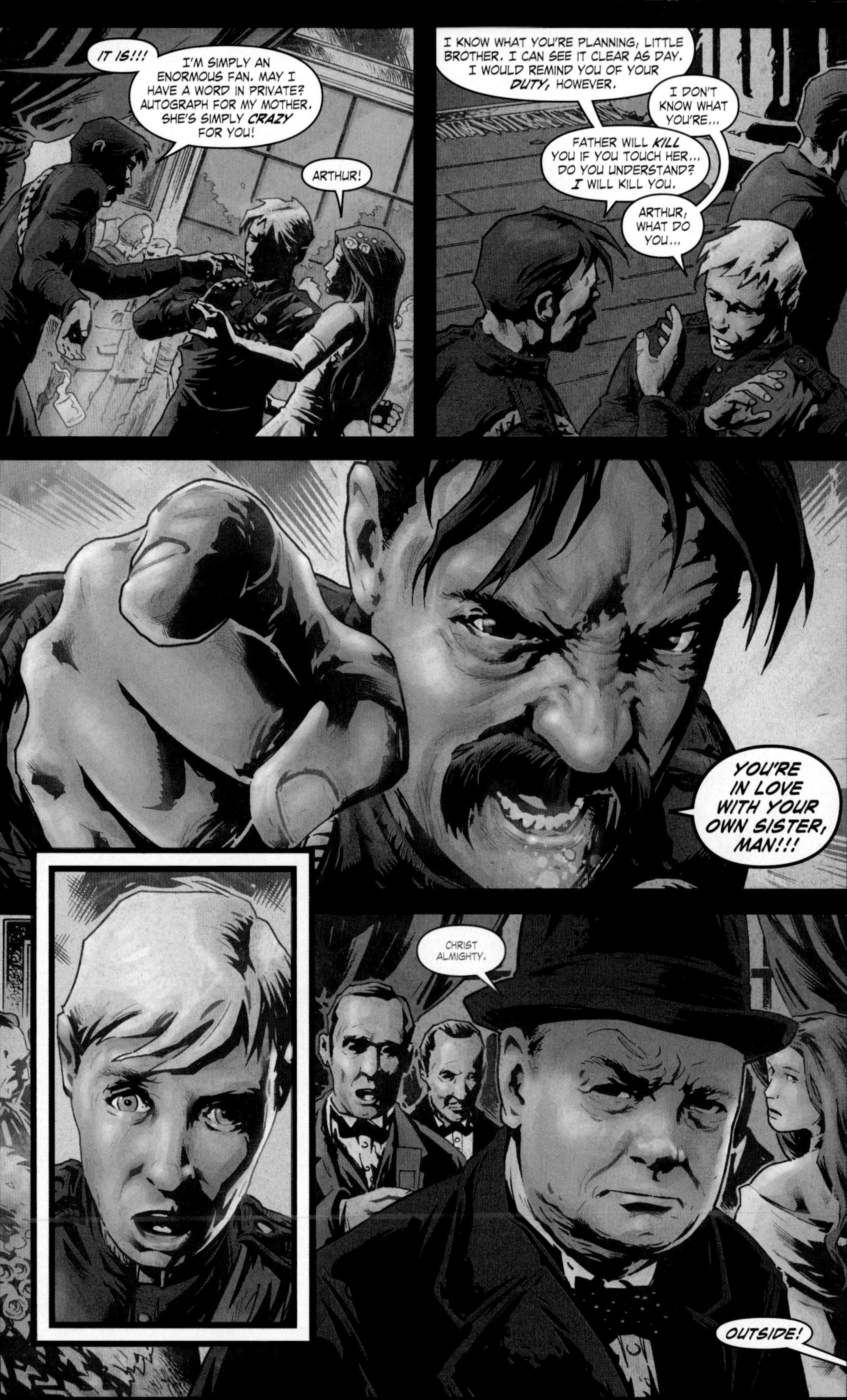
IT IS!!!
I'M SIMPLY AN ENORMOUS FAN. MAY I HAVE A WORD IN PRIVATE? AUTOGRAPH FOR MY MOTHER. SHE'S SIMPLY CRAZY FOR YOU!
ARTHUR!
I KNOW WHAT YOU'RE PLANNING, LITTLE BROTHER. I CAN SEE IT CLEAR AS DAY. I WOULD REMIND YOU OF YOUR DUTY, HOWEVER.
I DON'T KNOW WHAT YOU'RE...
FATHER WILL KILL YOU IF YOU TOUCH HER... DO YOU UNDERSTAND? I WILL KILL YOU.
ARTHUR, WHAT DO YOU...
YOU'RE IN LOVE WITH YOUR OWN SISTER, MAN!!!
CHRIST ALMIGHTY.
OUTSIDE!

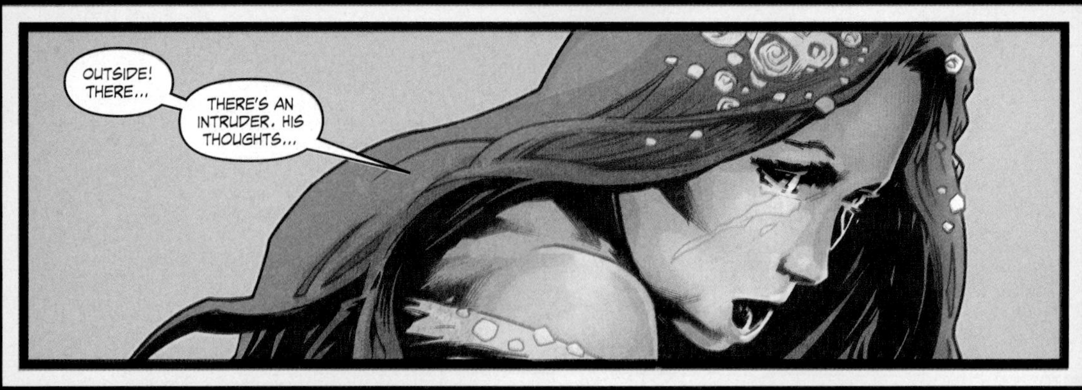
OUTSIDE! THERE...
THERE'S AN INTRUDER. HIS THOUGHTS...

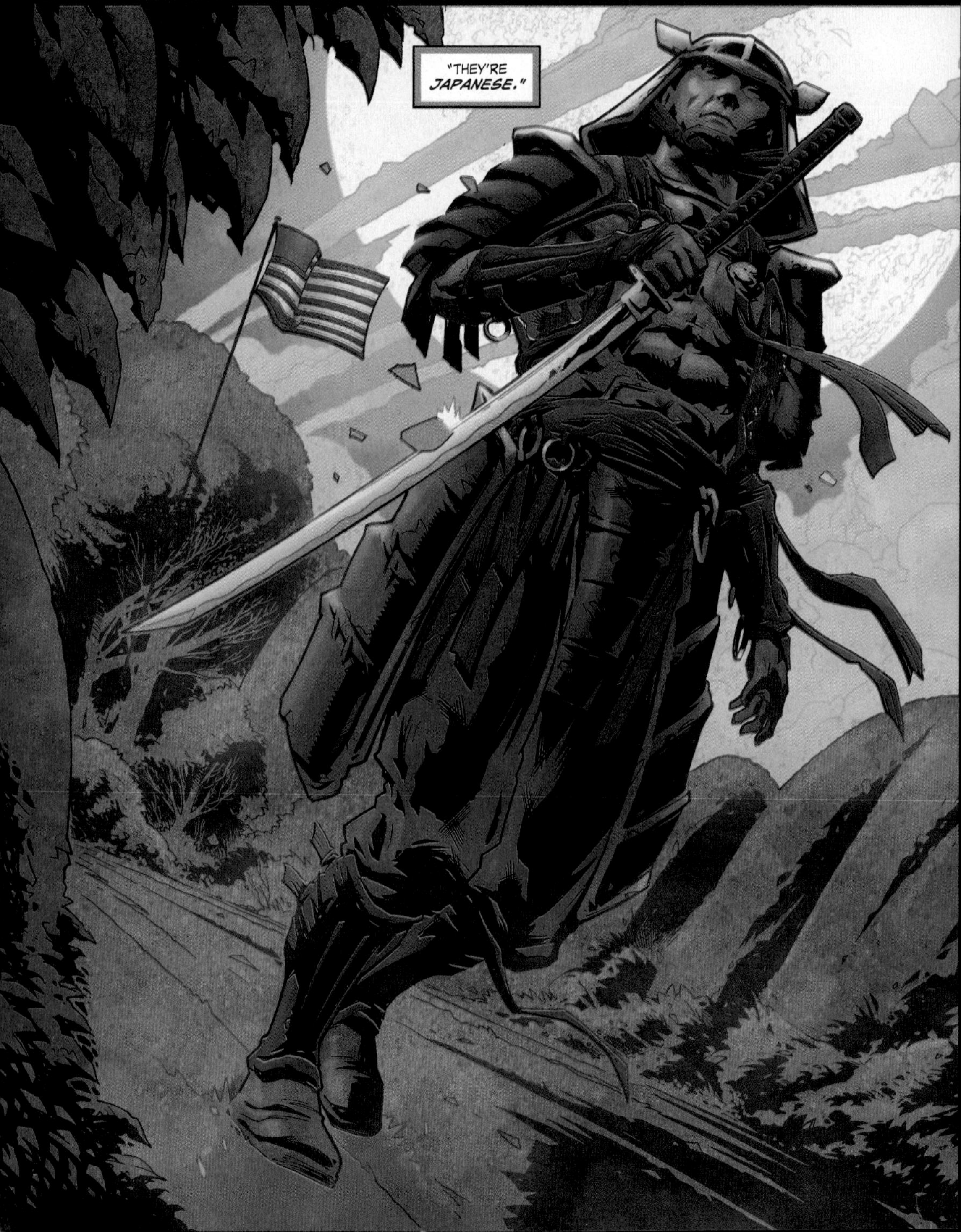
"THEY'RE *JAPANESE.*"

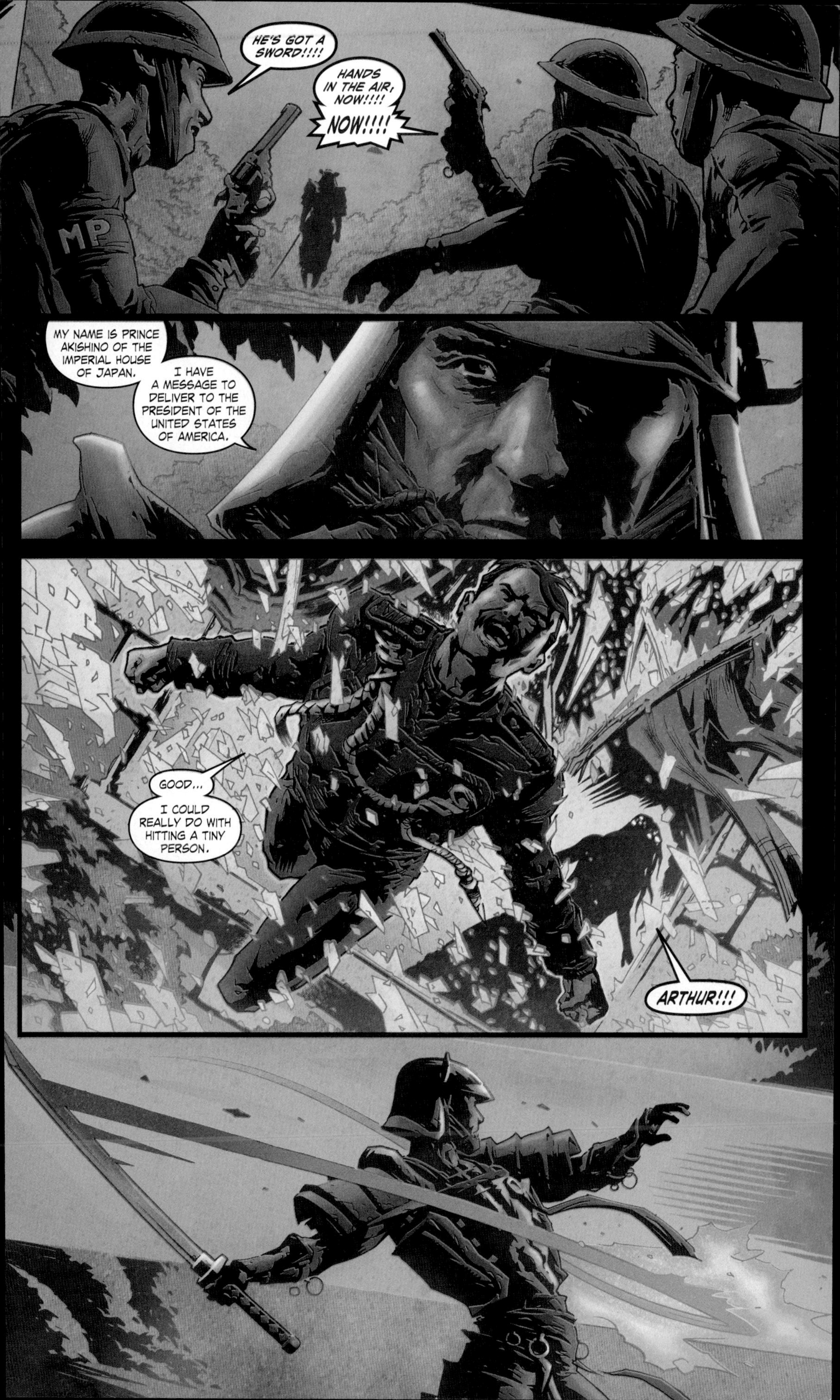
HE'S GOT A SWORD!!!!
HANDS IN THE AIR, NOW!!!!
NOW!!!!
MY NAME IS PRINCE AKISHINO OF THE IMPERIAL HOUSE OF JAPAN.
I HAVE A MESSAGE TO DELIVER TO THE PRESIDENT OF THE UNITED STATES OF AMERICA.
GOOD...
I COULD REALLY DO WITH HITTING A TINY PERSON.
ARTHUR!!!
MP

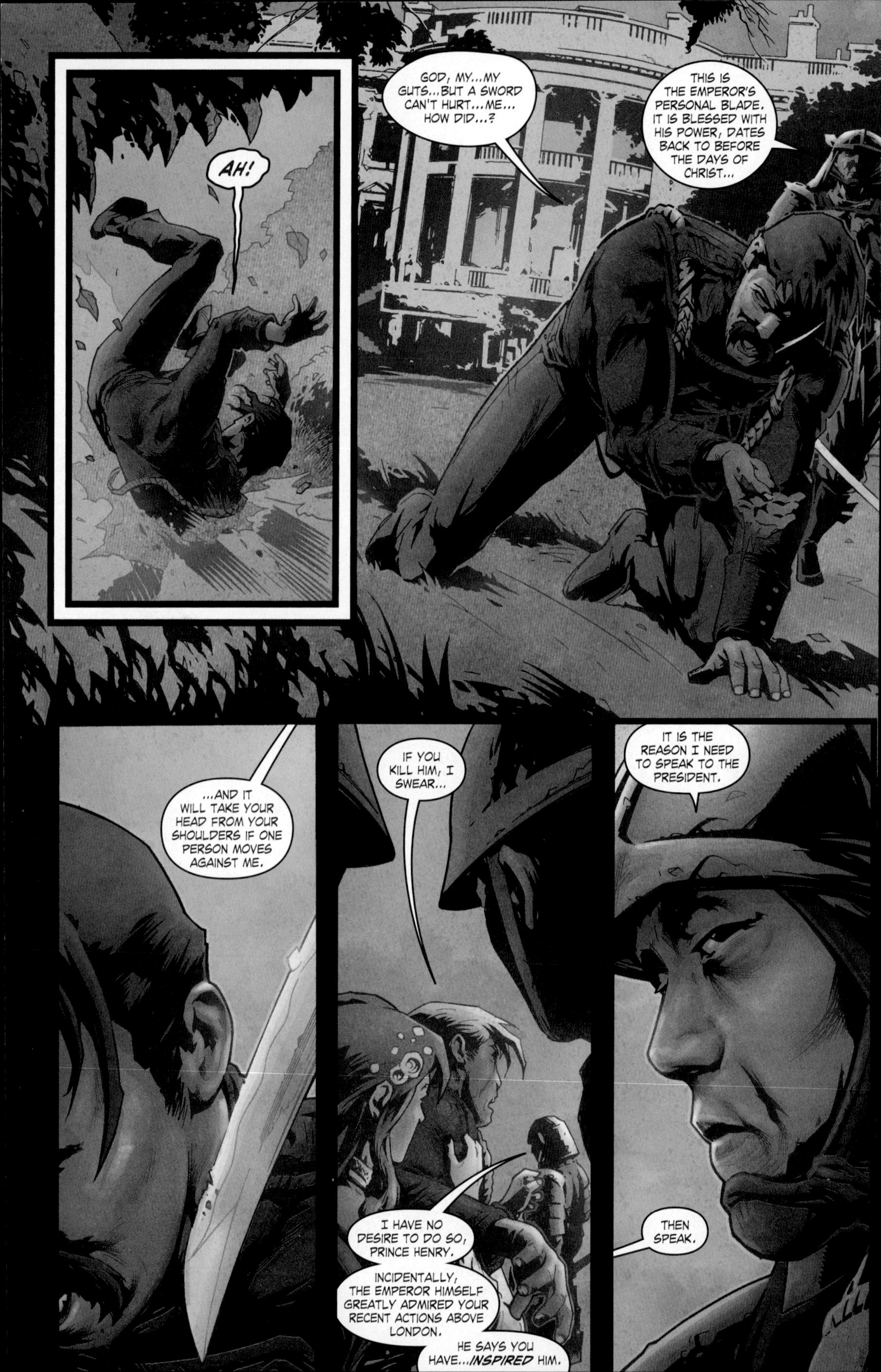
AH!
GOD, MY...MY GUTS...BUT A SWORD CAN'T HURT...ME... HOW DID...?
THIS IS THE EMPEROR'S PERSONAL BLADE. IT IS BLESSED WITH HIS POWER, DATES BACK TO BEFORE THE DAYS OF CHRIST...
...AND IT WILL TAKE YOUR HEAD FROM YOUR SHOULDERS IF ONE PERSON MOVES AGAINST ME.
IF YOU KILL HIM, I SWEAR...
I HAVE NO DESIRE TO DO SO, PRINCE HENRY.
INCIDENTALLY, THE EMPEROR HIMSELF GREATLY ADMIRED YOUR RECENT ACTIONS ABOVE LONDON.
HE SAYS YOU HAVE...INSPIRED HIM.
IT IS THE REASON I NEED TO SPEAK TO THE PRESIDENT.
THEN SPEAK.

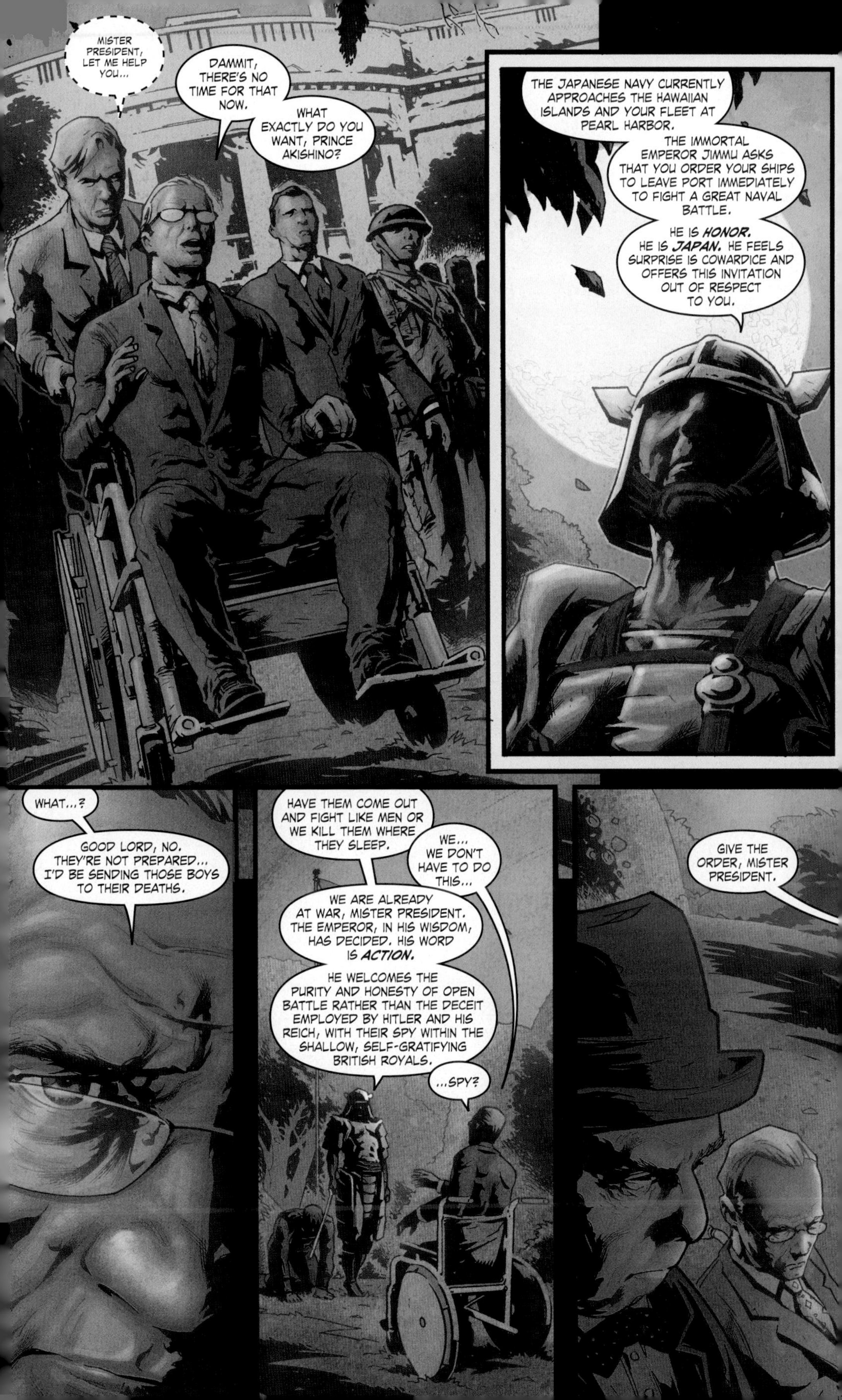

MISTER PRESIDENT, LET ME HELP YOU...
DAMMIT, THERE'S NO TIME FOR THAT NOW.
WHAT EXACTLY DO YOU WANT, PRINCE AKISHINO?
THE JAPANESE NAVY CURRENTLY APPROACHES THE HAWAIIAN ISLANDS AND YOUR FLEET AT PEARL HARBOR.
THE IMMORTAL EMPEROR JIMMU ASKS THAT YOU ORDER YOUR SHIPS TO LEAVE PORT IMMEDIATELY TO FIGHT A GREAT NAVAL BATTLE.
HE IS **HONOR.** HE IS **JAPAN.** HE FEELS SURPRISE IS COWARDICE AND OFFERS THIS INVITATION OUT OF RESPECT TO YOU.
WHAT...?
GOOD LORD, NO. THEY'RE NOT PREPARED... I'D BE SENDING THOSE BOYS TO THEIR DEATHS.
HAVE THEM COME OUT AND FIGHT LIKE MEN OR WE KILL THEM WHERE THEY SLEEP.
WE... WE DON'T HAVE TO DO THIS...
WE ARE ALREADY AT WAR, MISTER PRESIDENT. THE EMPEROR, IN HIS WISDOM, HAS DECIDED. HIS WORD IS **ACTION.**
HE WELCOMES THE PURITY AND HONESTY OF OPEN BATTLE RATHER THAN THE DECEIT EMPLOYED BY HITLER AND HIS REICH, WITH THEIR SPY WITHIN THE SHALLOW, SELF-GRATIFYING BRITISH ROYALS.
...SPY?
GIVE THE ORDER, MISTER PRESIDENT.

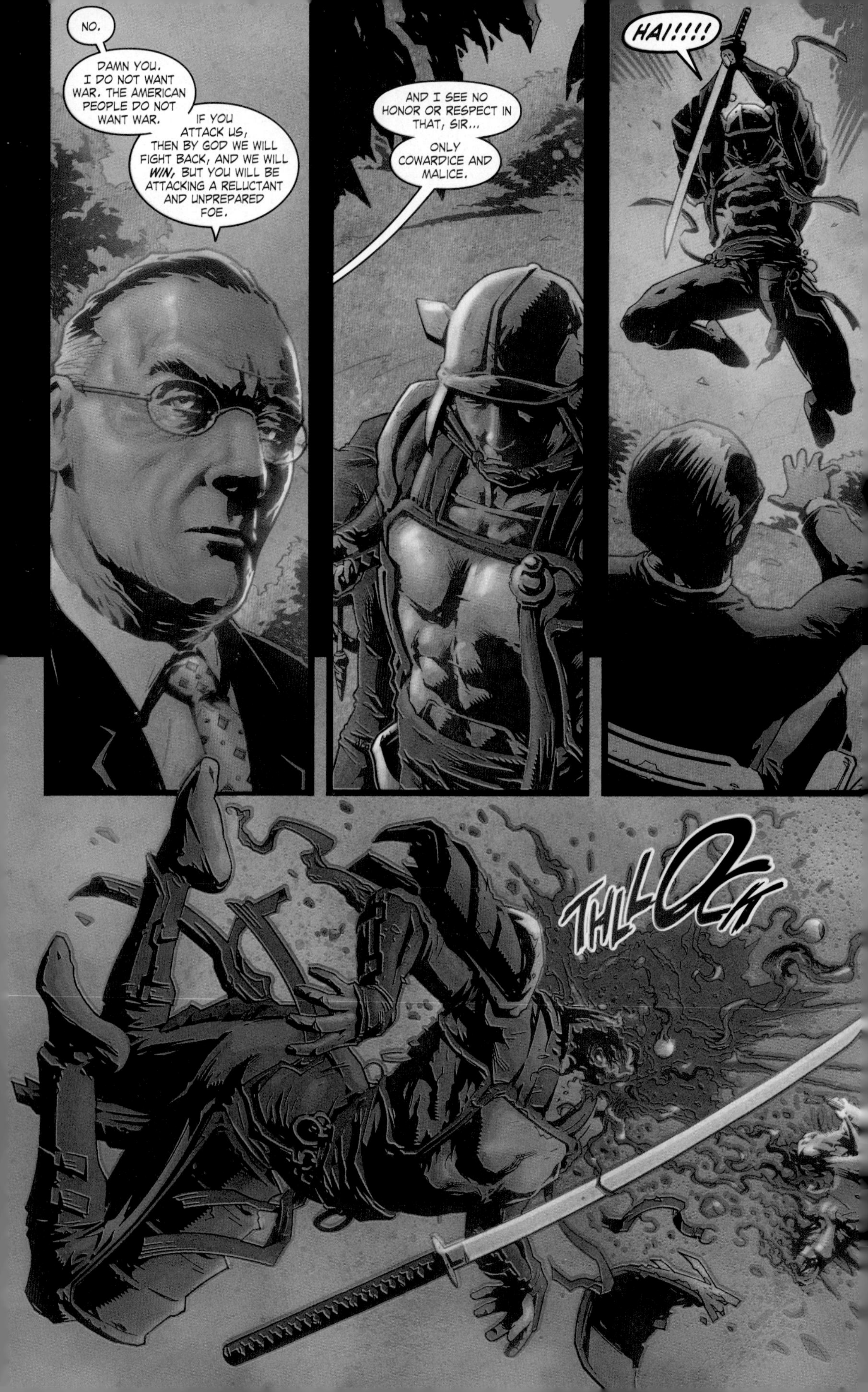
NO.
DAMN YOU. I DO NOT WANT WAR. THE AMERICAN PEOPLE DO NOT WANT WAR.
IF YOU ATTACK US, THEN BY GOD WE WILL FIGHT BACK, AND WE WILL WIN, BUT YOU WILL BE ATTACKING A RELUCTANT AND UNPREPARED FOE.
AND I SEE NO HONOR OR RESPECT IN THAT, SIR...
ONLY COWARDICE AND MALICE.
HAI!!!!
THLLOCK

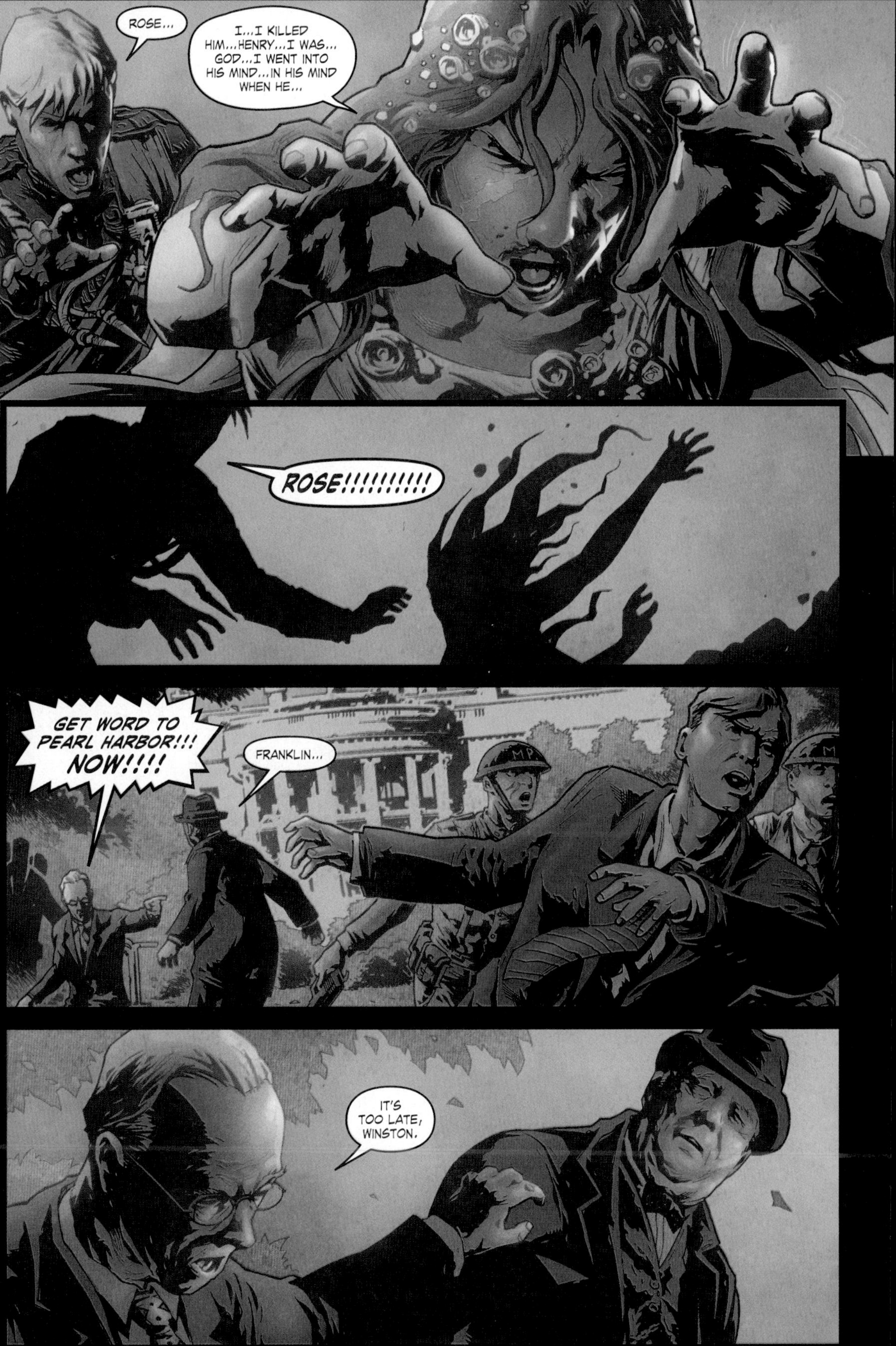
ROSE...
I...I KILLED HIM...HENRY...I WAS... GOD...I WENT INTO HIS MIND...IN HIS MIND WHEN HE...
ROSE!!!!!!!!!!
GET WORD TO PEARL HARBOR!!! NOW!!!!
FRANKLIN...
IT'S TOO LATE, WINSTON.

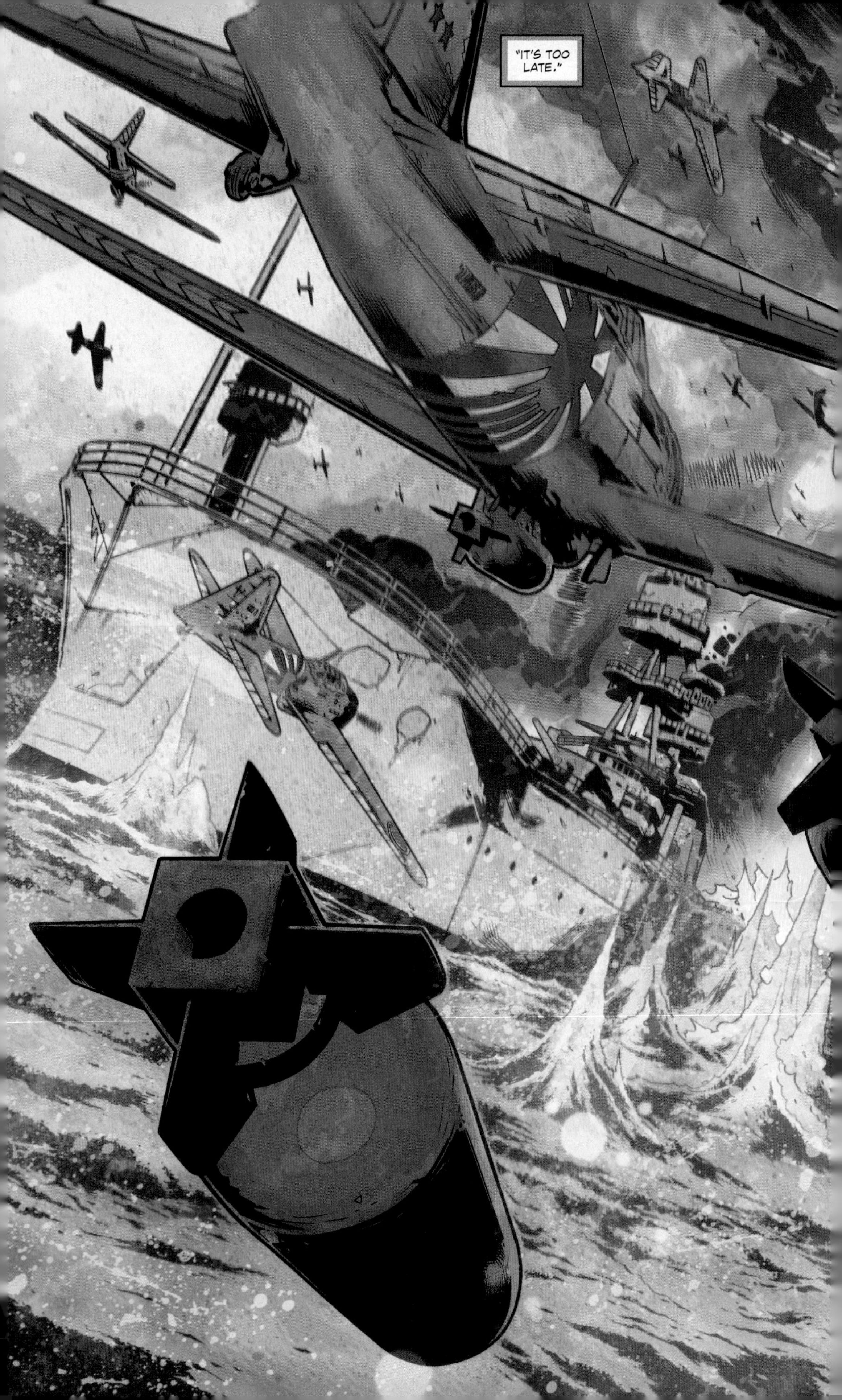
"IT'S TOO LATE."

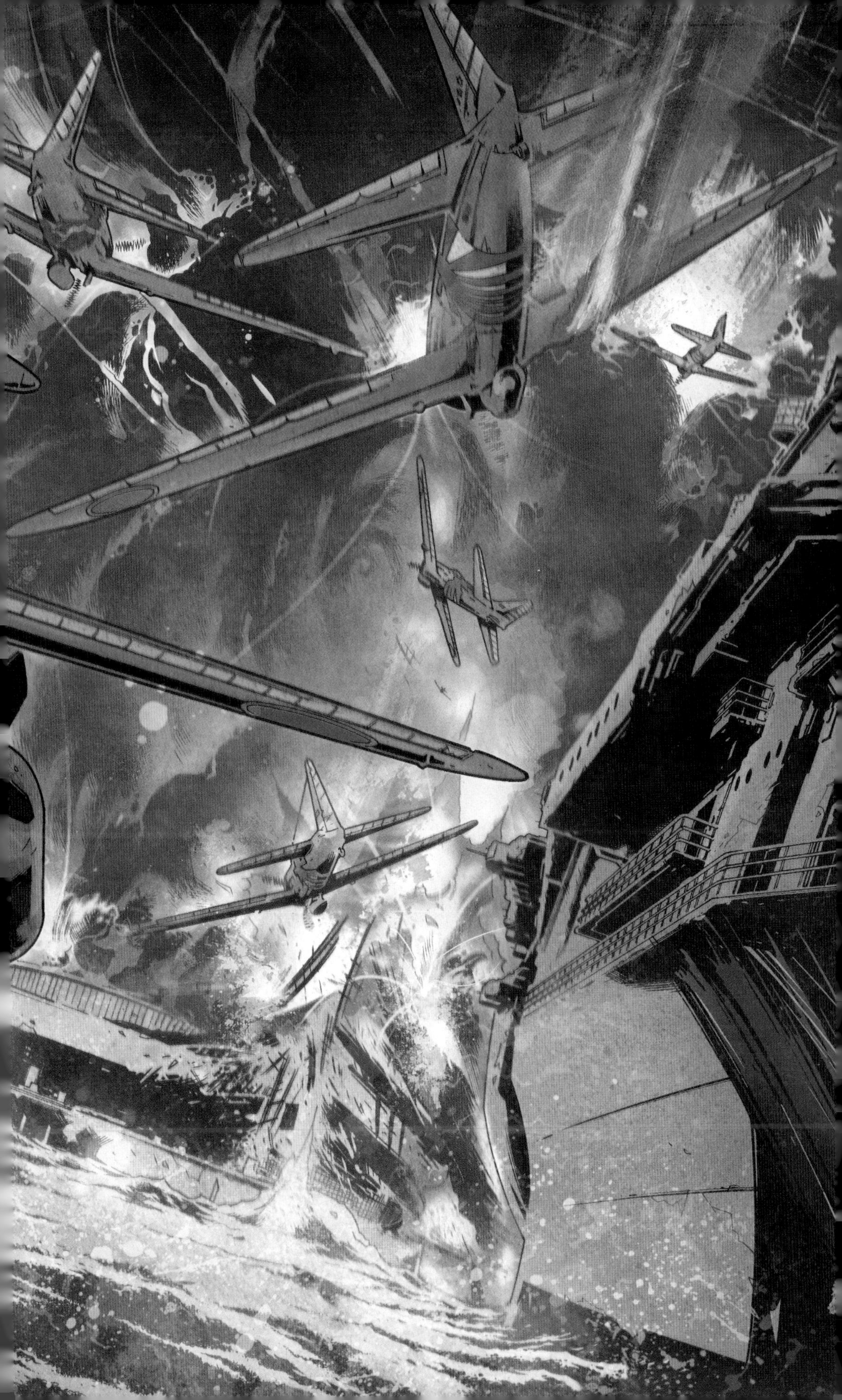

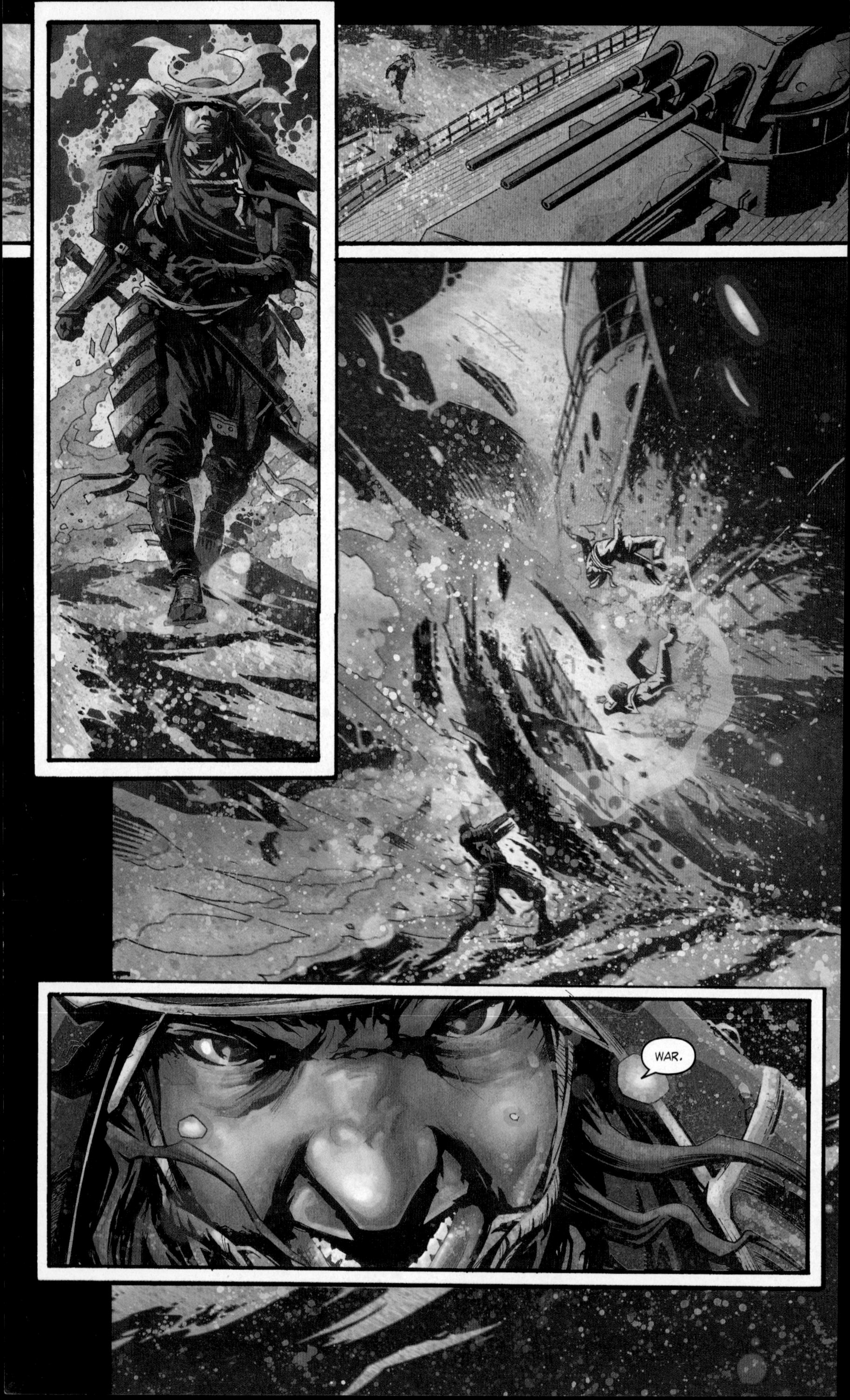
WAR.

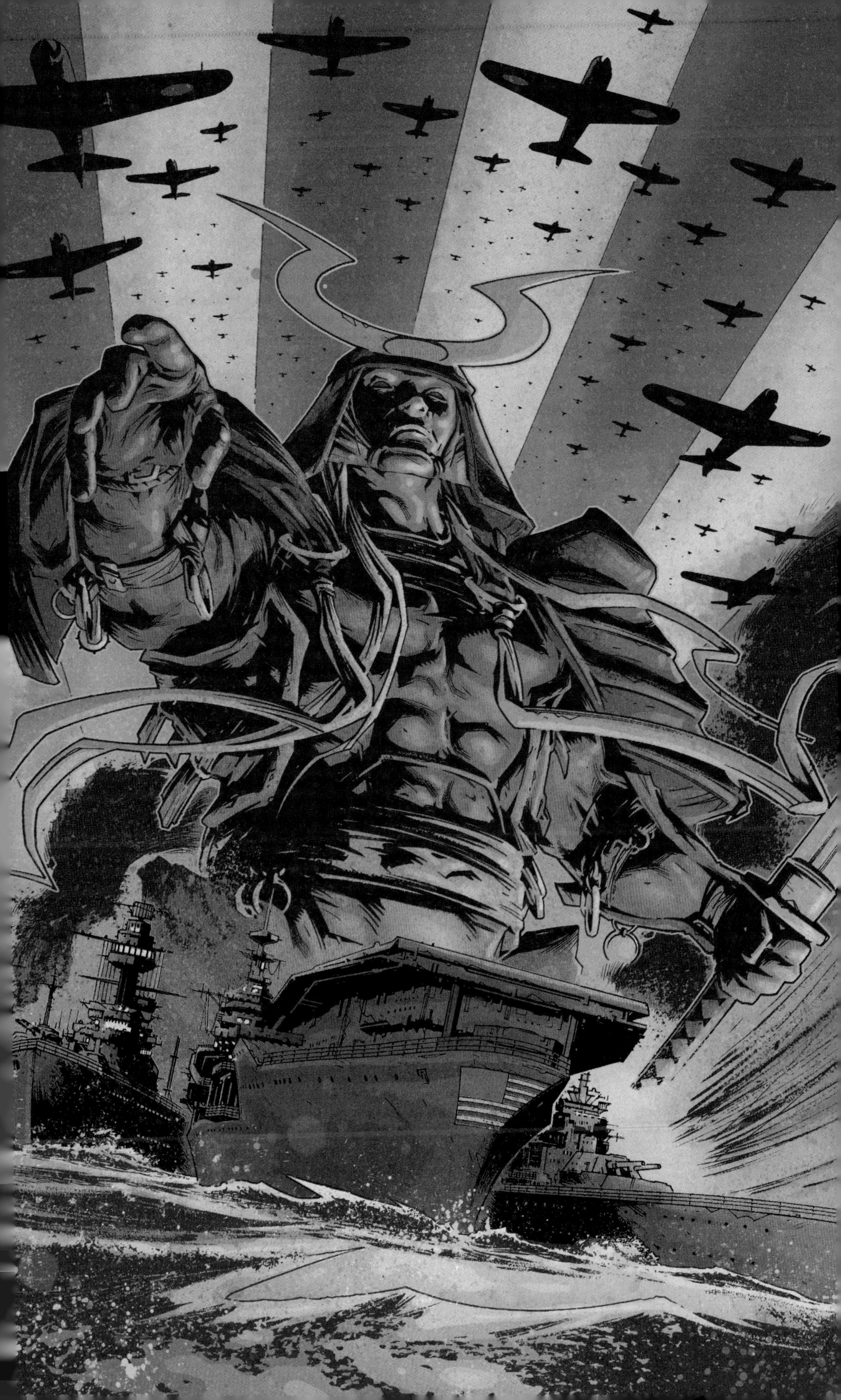

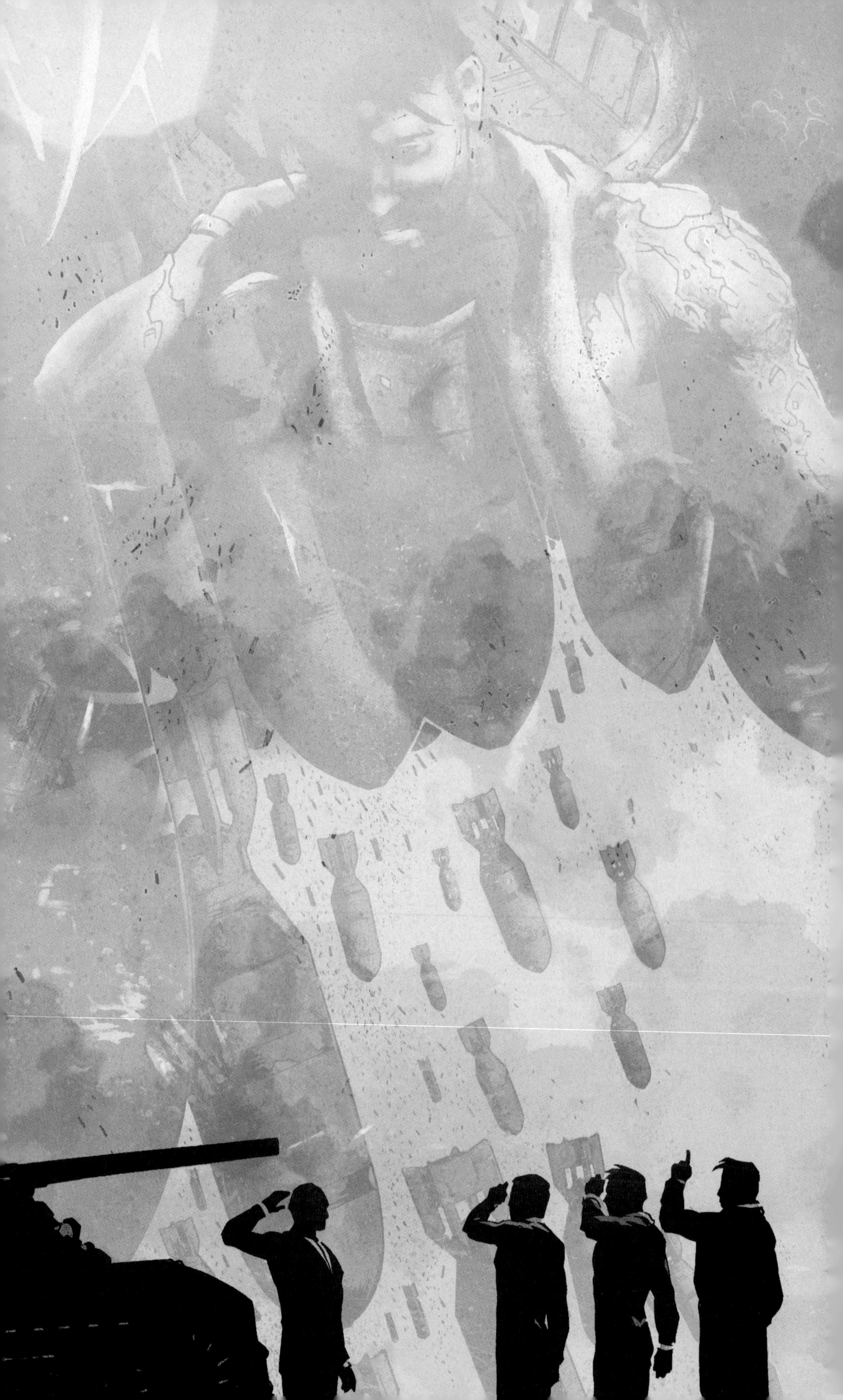

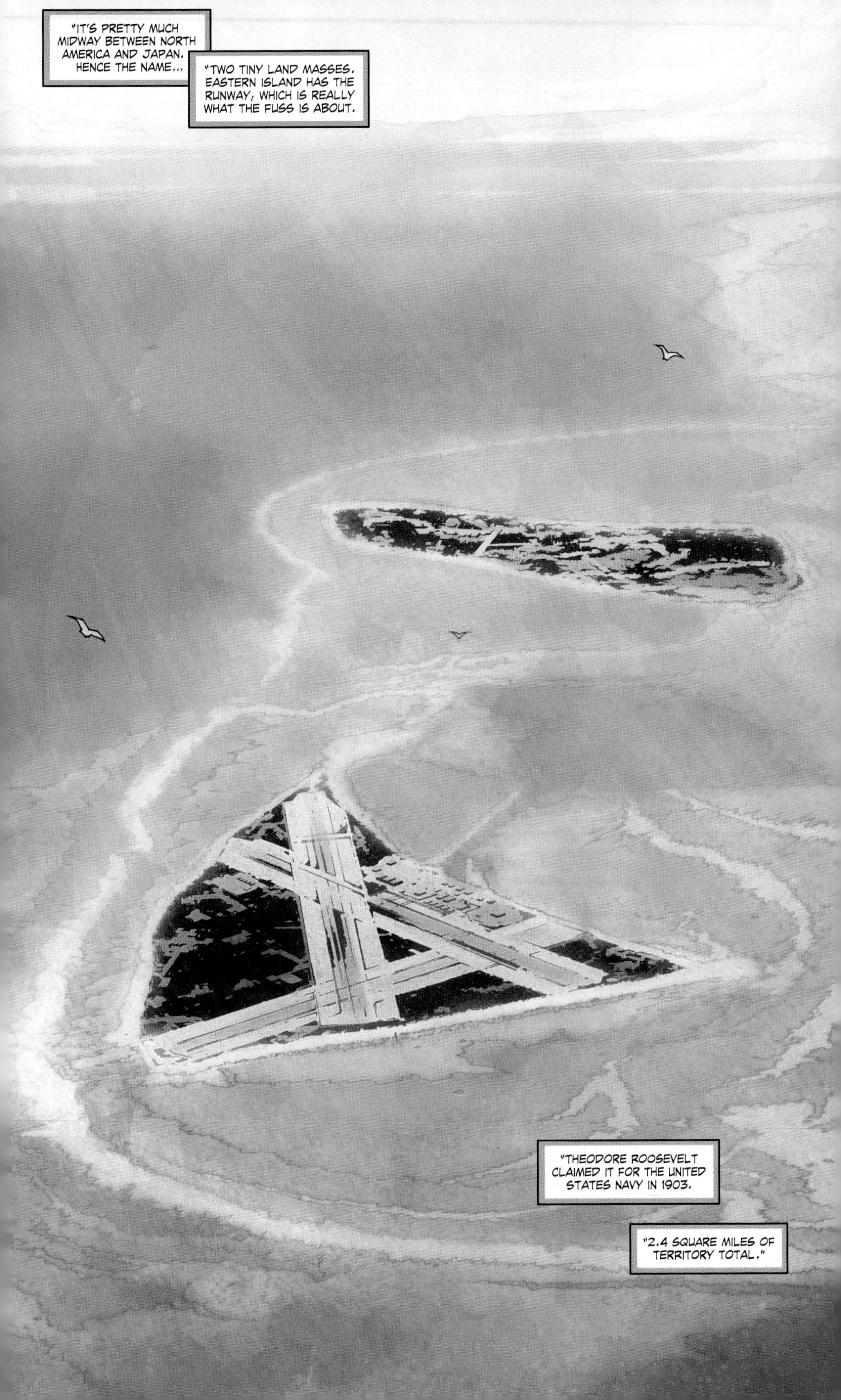
"IT'S PRETTY MUCH MIDWAY BETWEEN NORTH AMERICA AND JAPAN. HENCE THE NAME...
"TWO TINY LAND MASSES. EASTERN ISLAND HAS THE RUNWAY, WHICH IS REALLY WHAT THE FUSS IS ABOUT.
"THEODORE ROOSEVELT CLAIMED IT FOR THE UNITED STATES NAVY IN 1903.
"2.4 SQUARE MILES OF TERRITORY TOTAL."

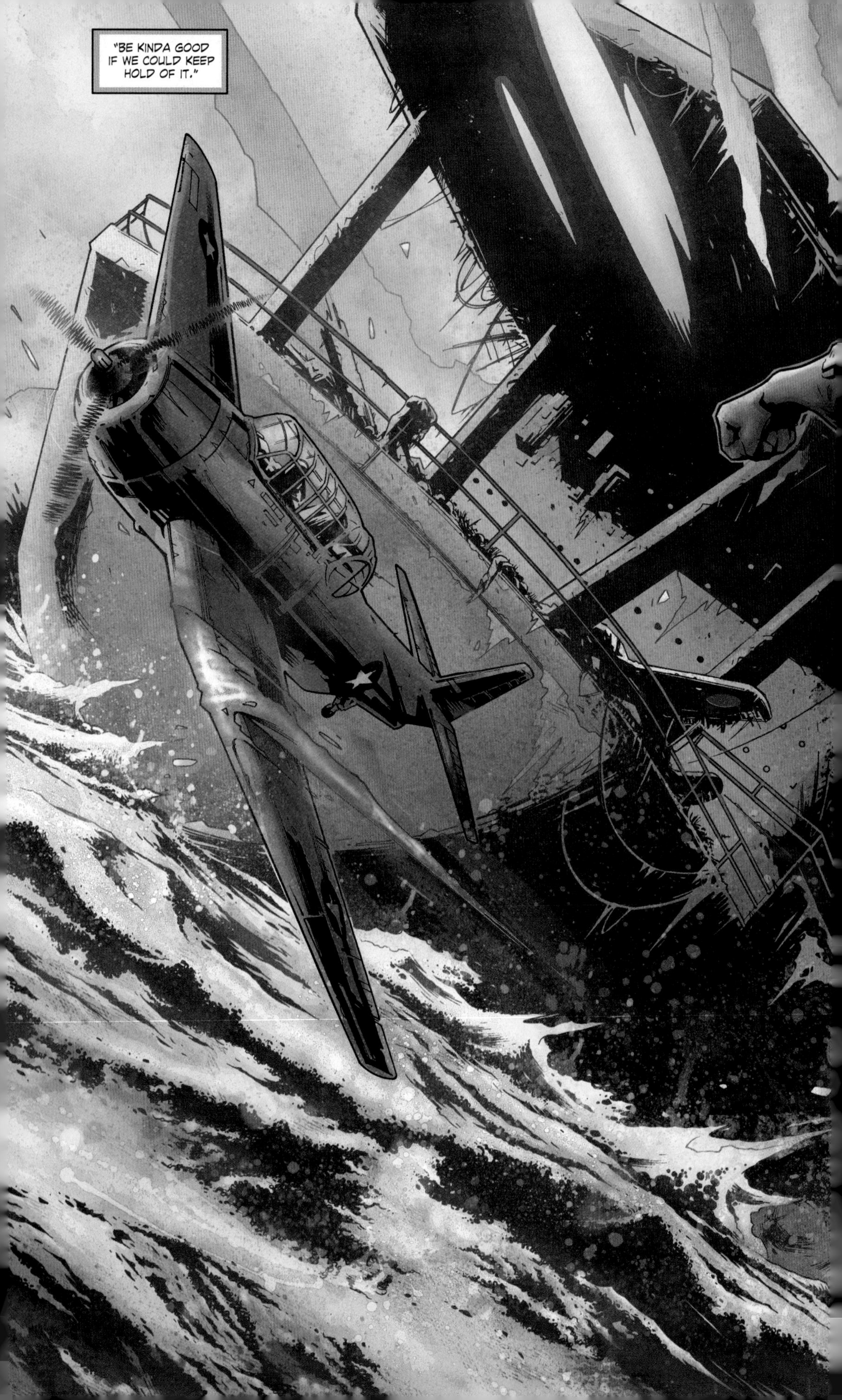
"BE KINDA GOOD IF WE COULD KEEP HOLD OF IT."

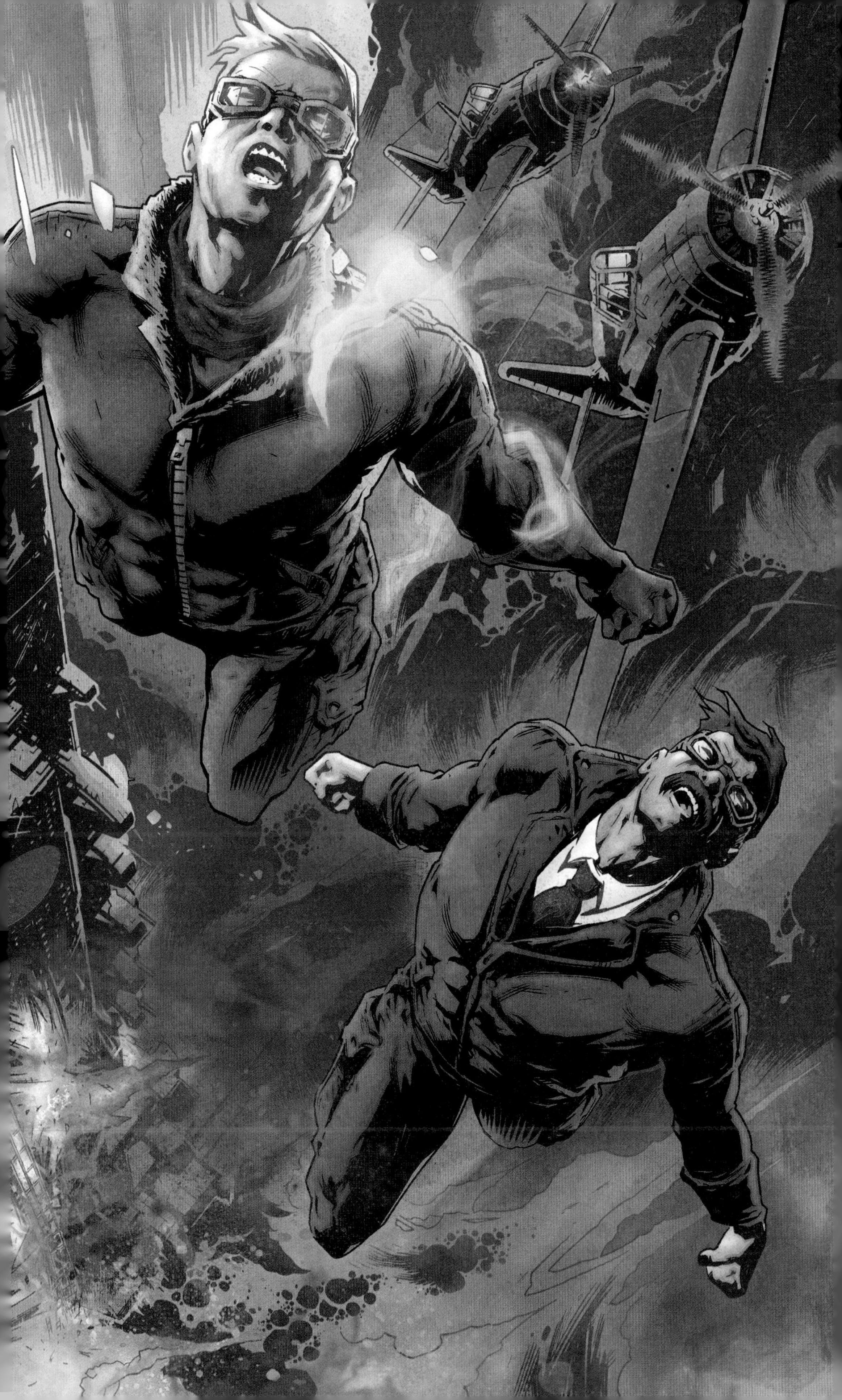

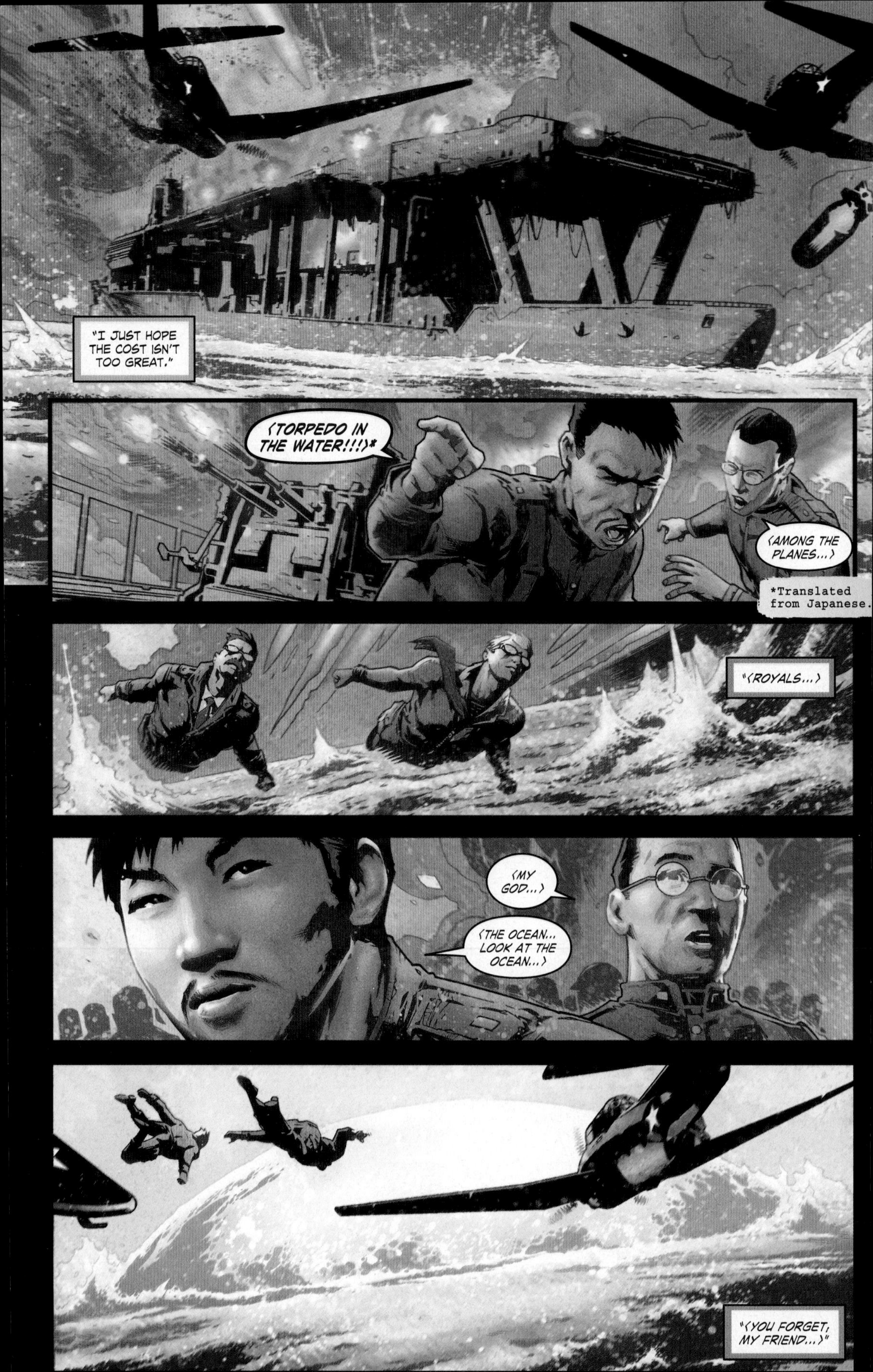
"I JUST HOPE THE COST ISN'T TOO GREAT."
<TORPEDO IN THE WATER!!!>*
<AMONG THE PLANES...>
*Translated from Japanese.
"<ROYALS...>
<MY GOD...>
<THE OCEAN... LOOK AT THE OCEAN...>
"<YOU FORGET, MY FRIEND...>"

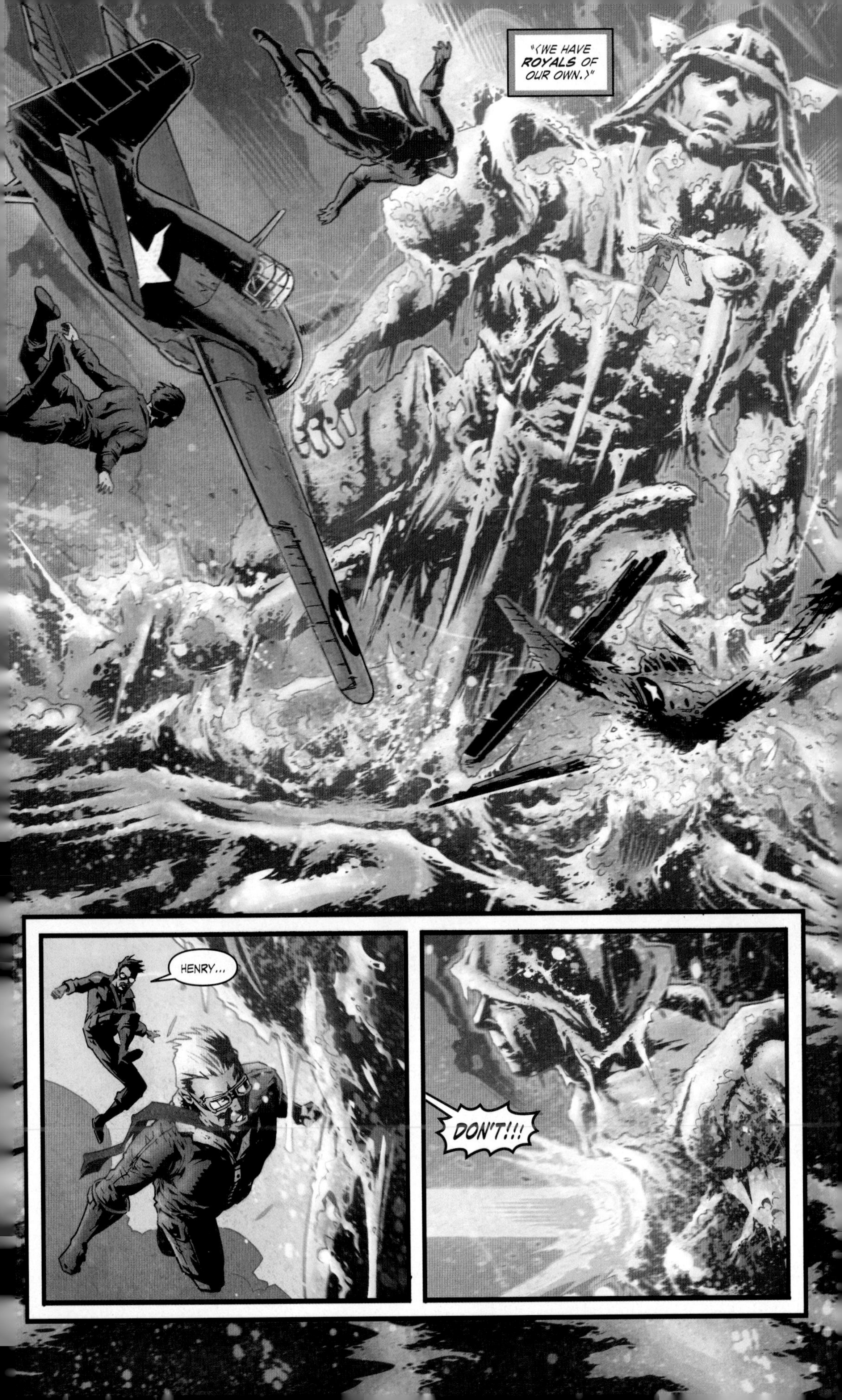
"‹WE HAVE ROYALS OF OUR OWN.›"
HENRY...
DON'T!!!

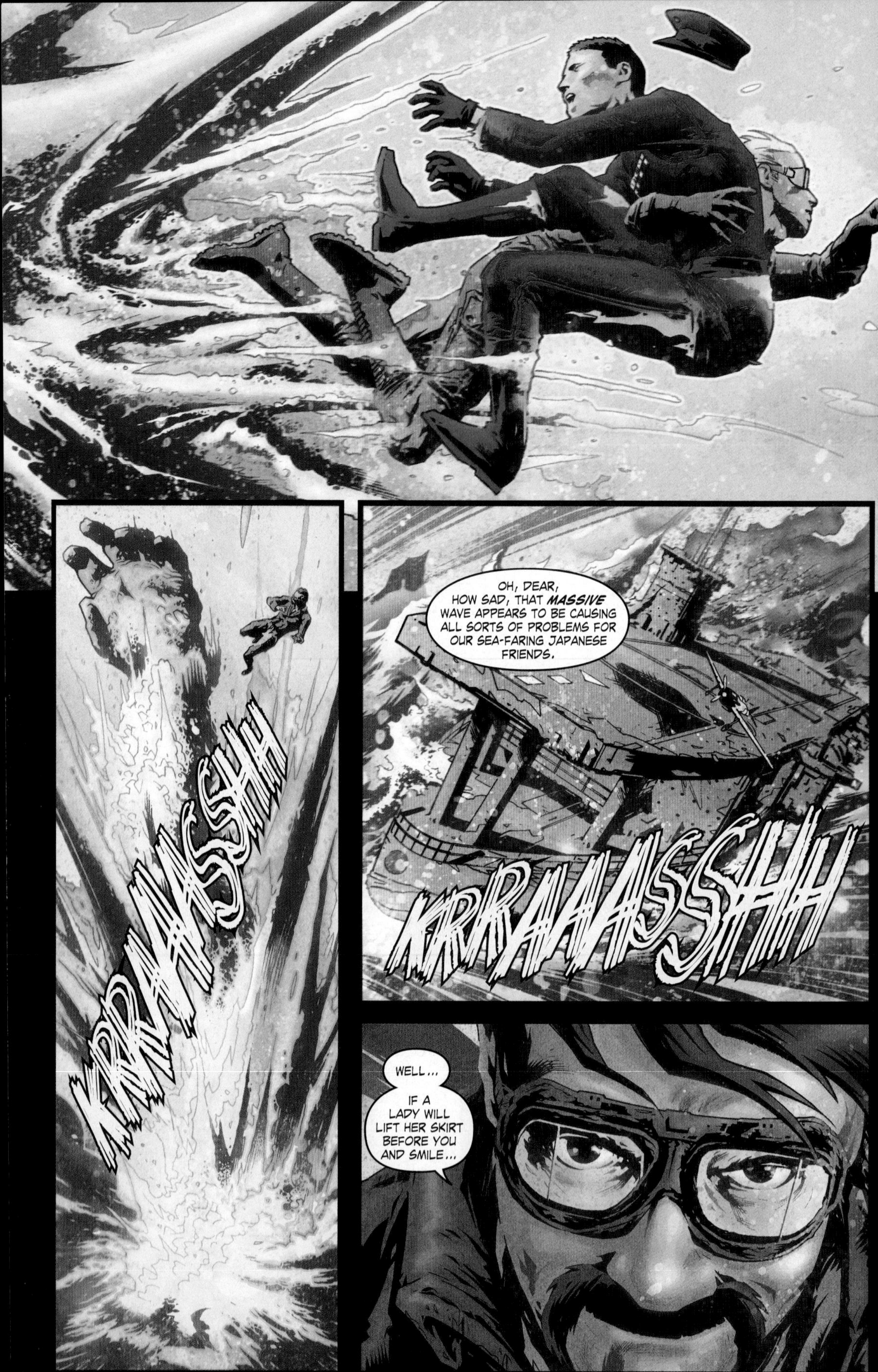

KRRAASSHH
OH, DEAR, HOW SAD, THAT MASSIVE WAVE APPEARS TO BE CAUSING ALL SORTS OF PROBLEMS FOR OUR SEA-FARING JAPANESE FRIENDS.
KRRAAASSHH
WELL...
IF A LADY WILL LIFT HER SKIRT BEFORE YOU AND SMILE...

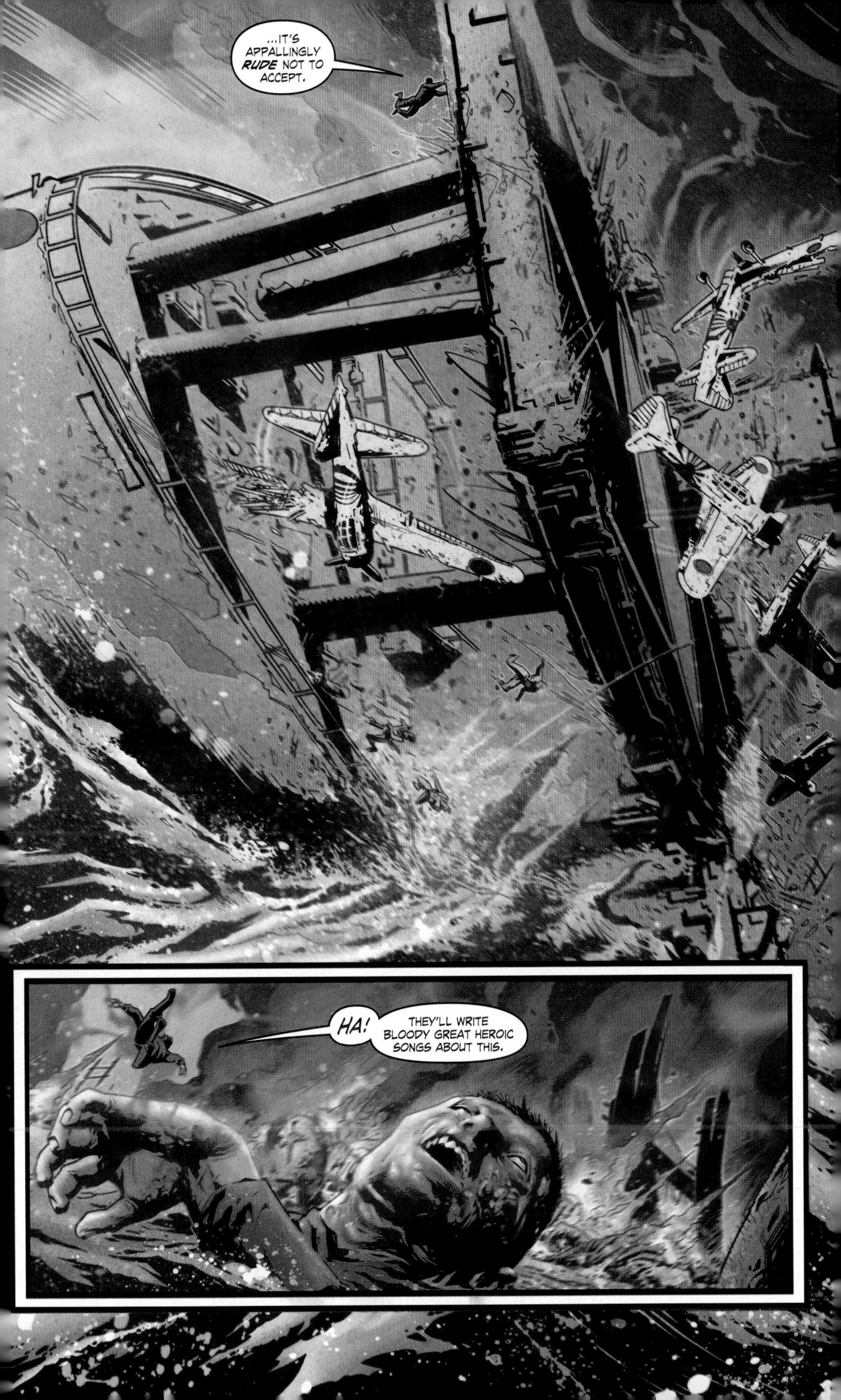
...IT'S APPALLINGLY RUDE NOT TO ACCEPT.
HA!
THEY'LL WRITE BLOODY GREAT HEROIC SONGS ABOUT THIS.

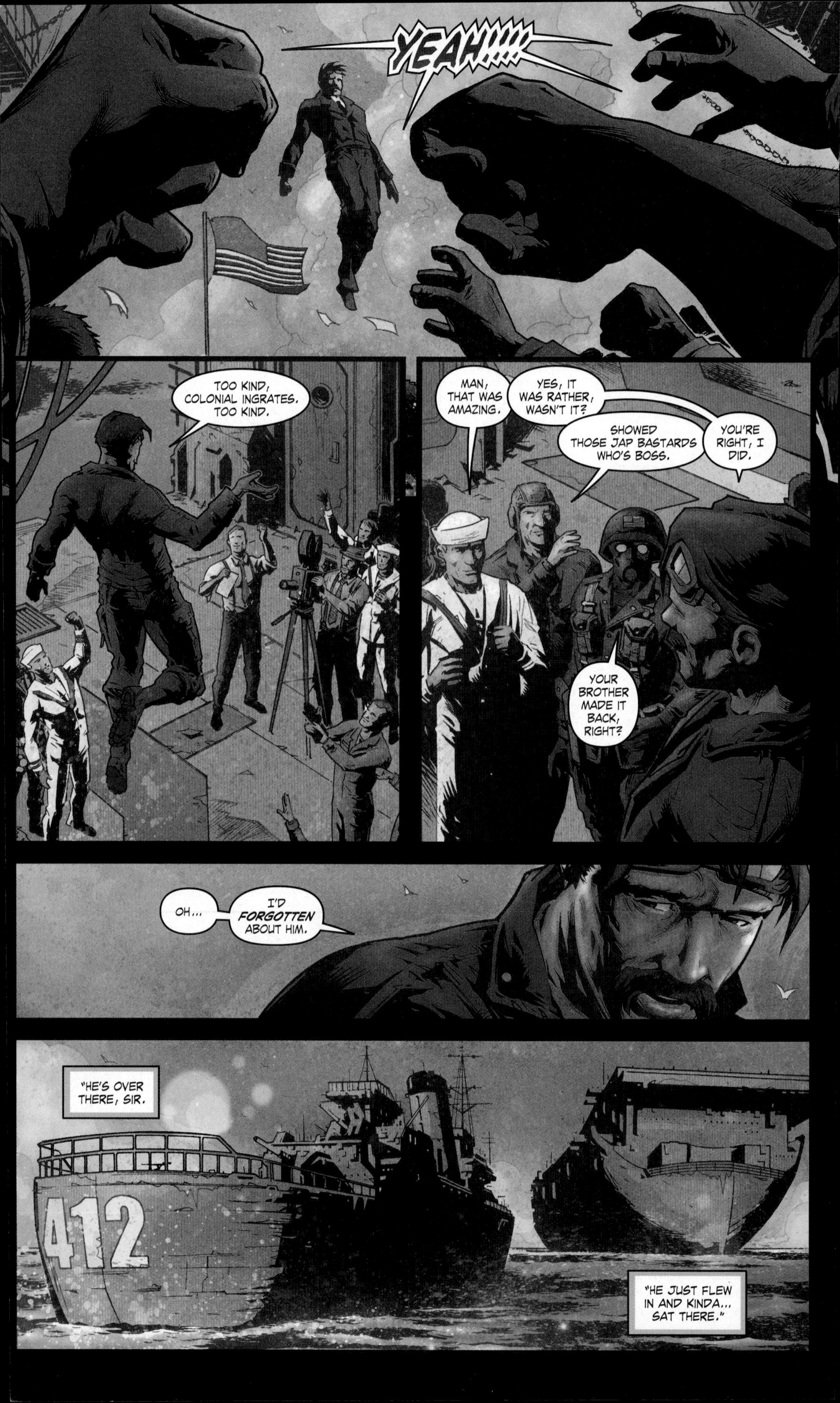

YEAH!!!!
TOO KIND, COLONIAL INGRATES. TOO KIND.
MAN, THAT WAS AMAZING.
YES, IT WAS RATHER, WASN'T IT?
SHOWED THOSE JAP BASTARDS WHO'S BOSS.
YOU'RE RIGHT, I DID.
YOUR BROTHER MADE IT BACK, RIGHT?
OH...
I'D FORGOTTEN ABOUT HIM.
"HE'S OVER THERE, SIR.
412
"HE JUST FLEW IN AND KINDA... SAT THERE."

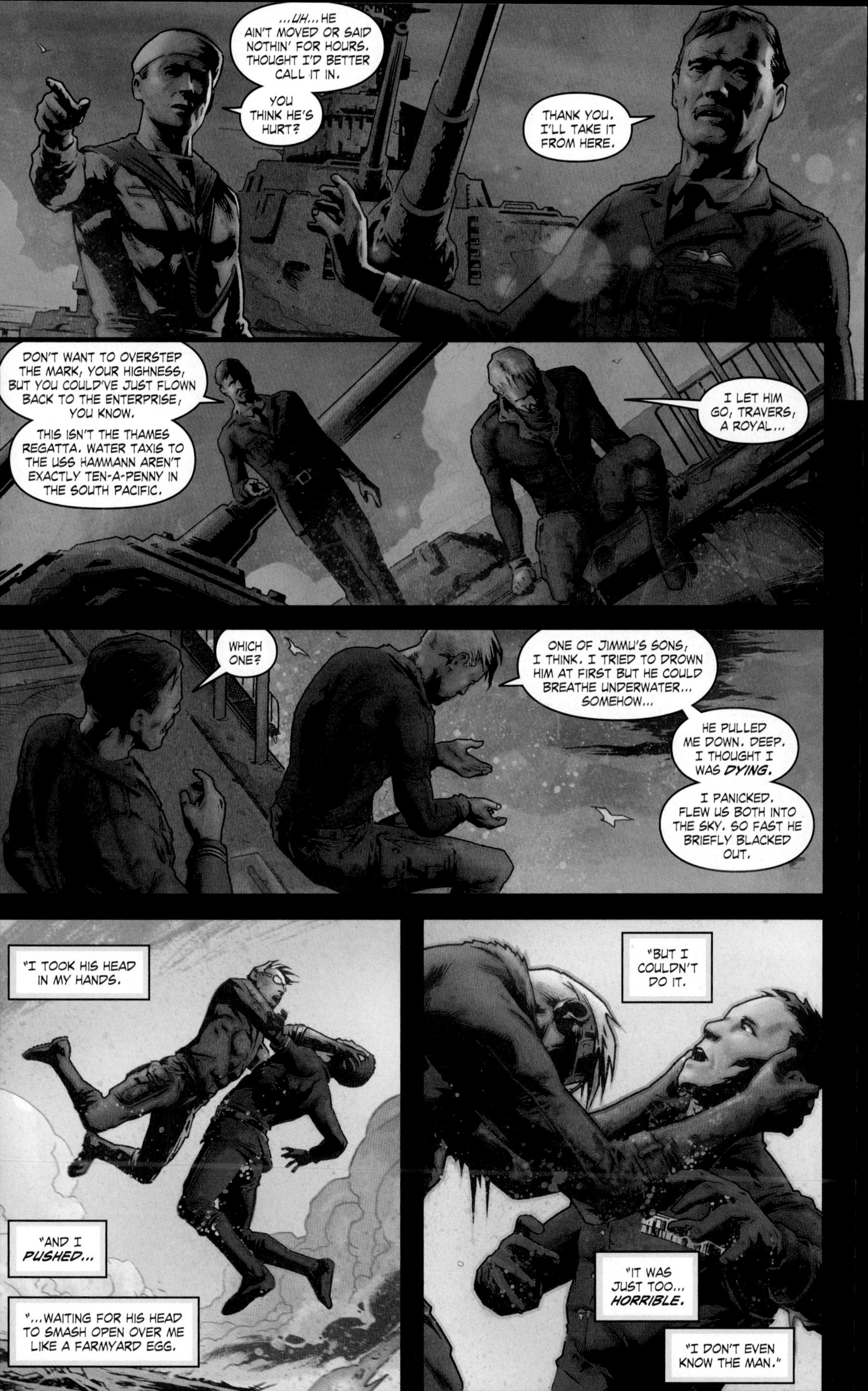
...UH... HE AIN'T MOVED OR SAID NOTHIN' FOR HOURS. THOUGHT I'D BETTER CALL IT IN.
YOU THINK HE'S HURT?
THANK YOU. I'LL TAKE IT FROM HERE.
DON'T WANT TO OVERSTEP THE MARK, YOUR HIGHNESS, BUT YOU COULD'VE JUST FLOWN BACK TO THE ENTERPRISE, YOU KNOW.
THIS ISN'T THE THAMES REGATTA. WATER TAXIS TO THE USS HAMMANN AREN'T EXACTLY TEN-A-PENNY IN THE SOUTH PACIFIC.
I LET HIM GO, TRAVERS, A ROYAL...
WHICH ONE?
ONE OF JIMMU'S SONS, I THINK. I TRIED TO DROWN HIM AT FIRST BUT HE COULD BREATHE UNDERWATER... SOMEHOW...
HE PULLED ME DOWN. DEEP. I THOUGHT I WAS DYING.
I PANICKED. FLEW US BOTH INTO THE SKY. SO FAST HE BRIEFLY BLACKED OUT.
"I TOOK HIS HEAD IN MY HANDS.
"AND I PUSHED...
"...WAITING FOR HIS HEAD TO SMASH OPEN OVER ME LIKE A FARMYARD EGG.
"BUT I COULDN'T DO IT.
"IT WAS JUST TOO... HORRIBLE.
"I DON'T EVEN KNOW THE MAN."

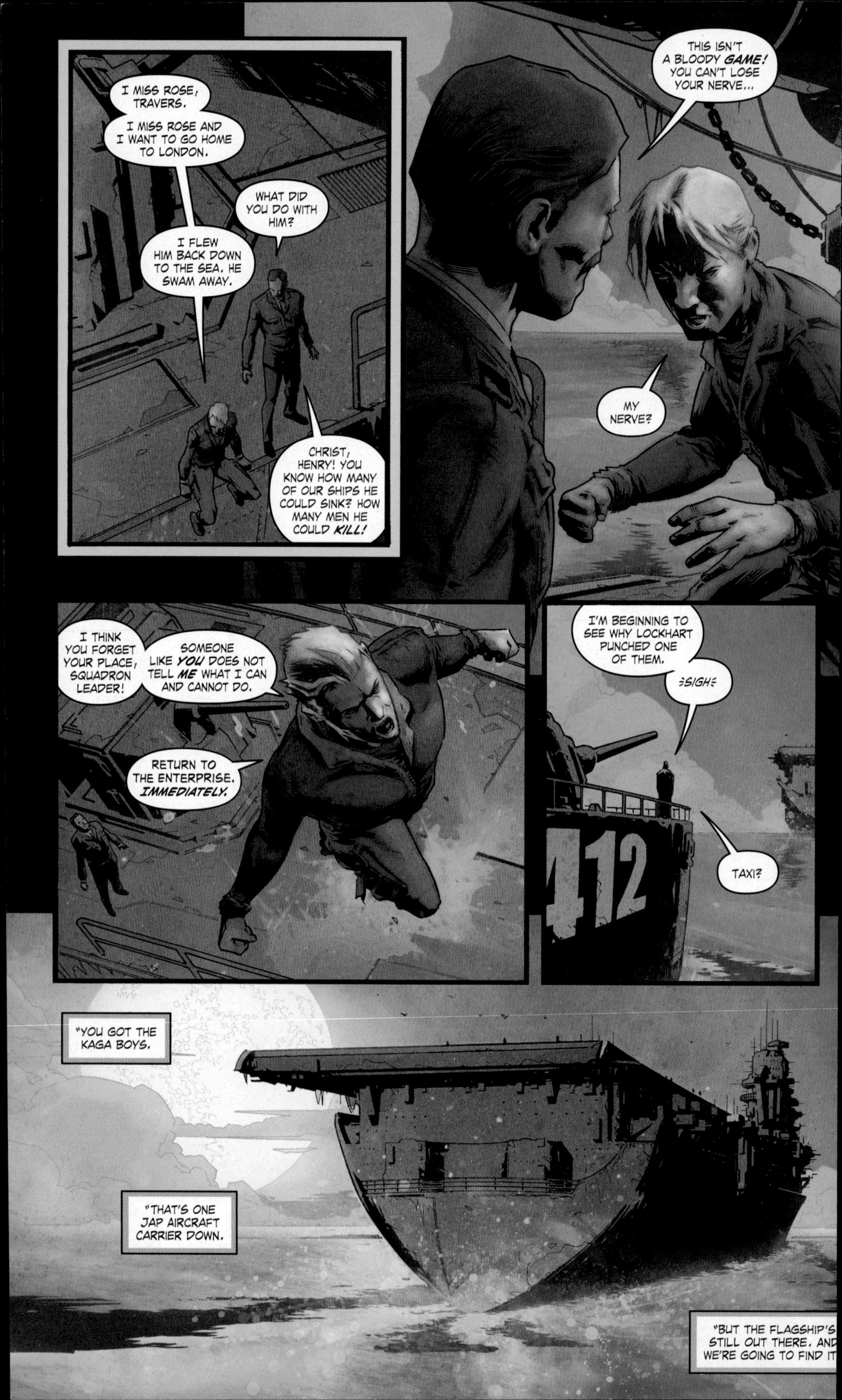

I MISS ROSE, TRAVERS.
I MISS ROSE AND I WANT TO GO HOME TO LONDON.
WHAT DID YOU DO WITH HIM?
I FLEW HIM BACK DOWN TO THE SEA. HE SWAM AWAY.
CHRIST, HENRY! YOU KNOW HOW MANY OF OUR SHIPS HE COULD SINK? HOW MANY MEN HE COULD KILL!
THIS ISN'T A BLOODY GAME! YOU CAN'T LOSE YOUR NERVE...
MY NERVE?
I THINK YOU FORGET YOUR PLACE, SQUADRON LEADER!
SOMEONE LIKE YOU DOES NOT TELL ME WHAT I CAN AND CANNOT DO.
RETURN TO THE ENTERPRISE. IMMEDIATELY.
I'M BEGINNING TO SEE WHY LOCKHART PUNCHED ONE OF THEM.
SIGH
412
TAXI?
"YOU GOT THE KAGA BOYS.
"THAT'S ONE JAP AIRCRAFT CARRIER DOWN.
"BUT THE FLAGSHIP'S STILL OUT THERE. AND WE'RE GOING TO FIND IT

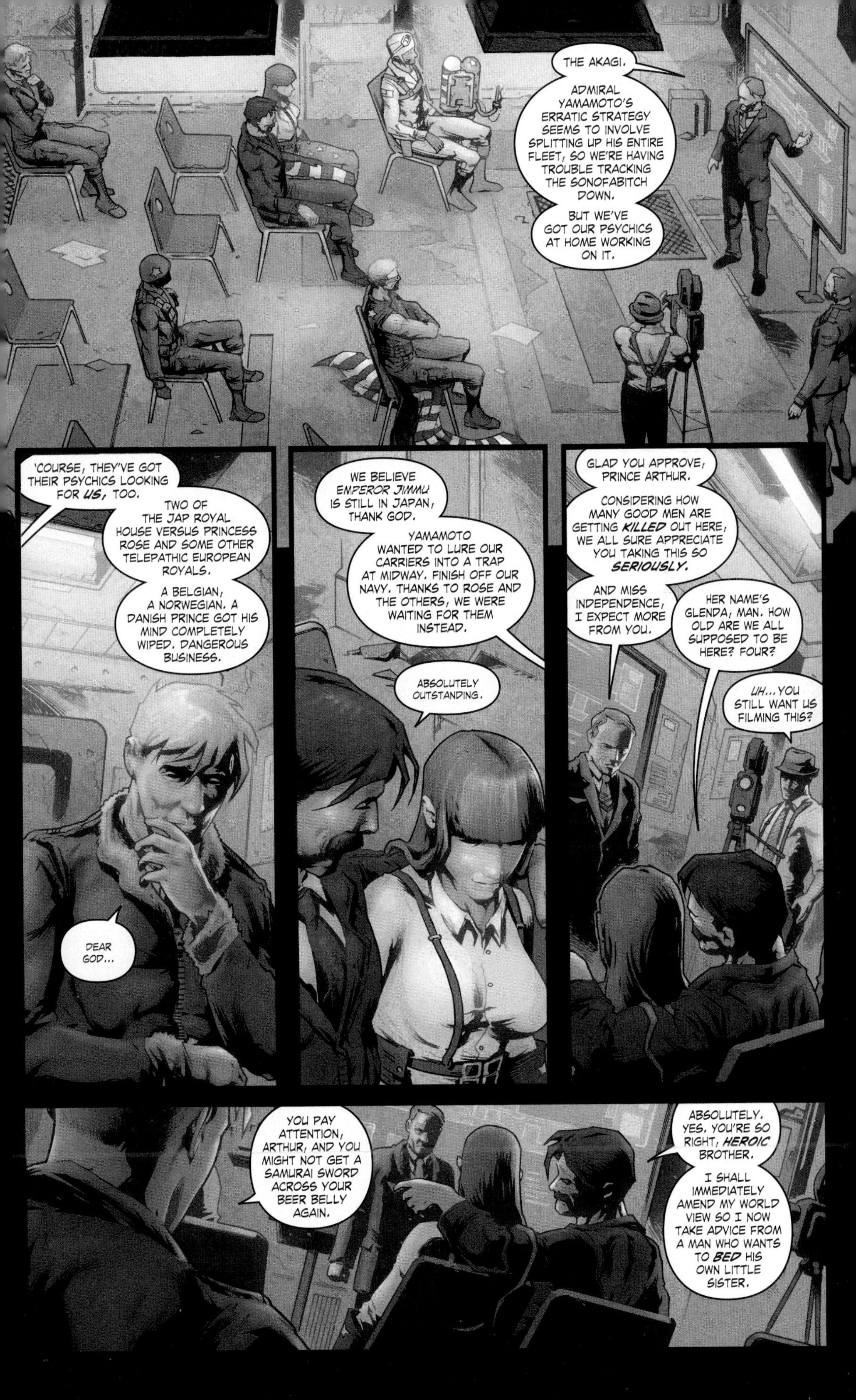
THE AKAGI.
ADMIRAL YAMAMOTO'S ERRATIC STRATEGY SEEMS TO INVOLVE SPLITTING UP HIS ENTIRE FLEET, SO WE'RE HAVING TROUBLE TRACKING THE SONOFABITCH DOWN.
BUT WE'VE GOT OUR PSYCHICS AT HOME WORKING ON IT.
'COURSE, THEY'VE GOT THEIR PSYCHICS LOOKING FOR *US*, TOO.
TWO OF THE JAP ROYAL HOUSE VERSUS PRINCESS ROSE AND SOME OTHER TELEPATHIC EUROPEAN ROYALS.
A BELGIAN, A NORWEGIAN. A DANISH PRINCE GOT HIS MIND COMPLETELY WIPED. DANGEROUS BUSINESS.
DEAR GOD...
WE BELIEVE *EMPEROR JIMMU* IS STILL IN JAPAN, THANK GOD.
YAMAMOTO WANTED TO LURE OUR CARRIERS INTO A TRAP AT MIDWAY. FINISH OFF OUR NAVY. THANKS TO ROSE AND THE OTHERS, WE WERE WAITING FOR THEM INSTEAD.
ABSOLUTELY OUTSTANDING.
GLAD YOU APPROVE, PRINCE ARTHUR.
CONSIDERING HOW MANY GOOD MEN ARE GETTING **KILLED** OUT HERE, WE ALL SURE APPRECIATE YOU TAKING THIS SO **SERIOUSLY.**
AND MISS INDEPENDENCE, I EXPECT MORE FROM YOU.
HER NAME'S GLENDA, MAN. HOW OLD ARE WE ALL SUPPOSED TO BE HERE? FOUR?
UH...YOU STILL WANT US FILMING THIS?
YOU PAY ATTENTION, ARTHUR, AND YOU MIGHT NOT GET A SAMURAI SWORD ACROSS YOUR BEER BELLY AGAIN.
ABSOLUTELY. YES. YOU'RE SO RIGHT, ***HEROIC*** BROTHER.
I SHALL IMMEDIATELY AMEND MY WORLD VIEW SO I NOW TAKE ADVICE FROM A MAN WHO WANTS TO ***BED*** HIS OWN LITTLE SISTER.

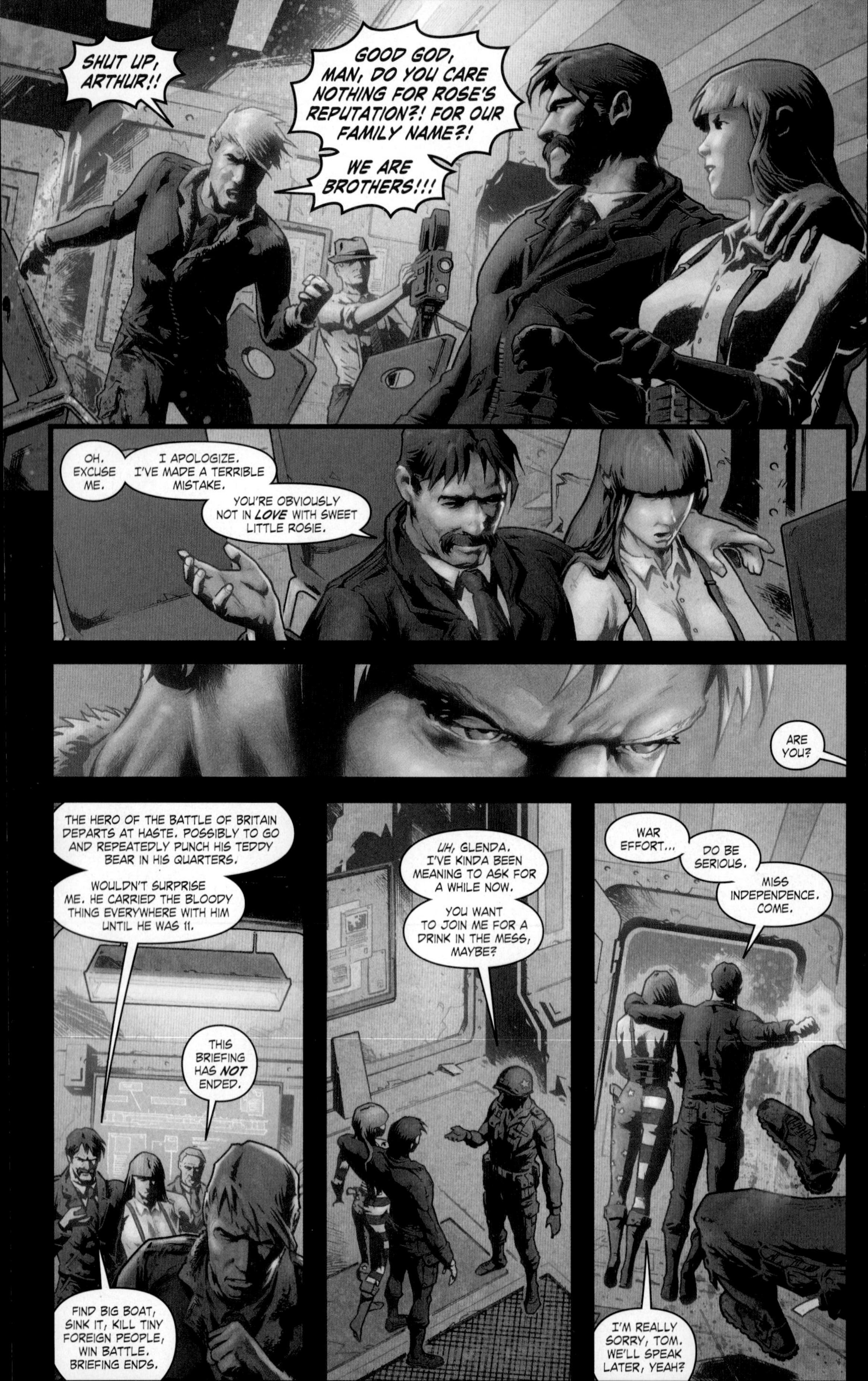
SHUT UP, ARTHUR!!
GOOD GOD, MAN, DO YOU CARE NOTHING FOR ROSE'S REPUTATION?! FOR OUR FAMILY NAME?!
WE ARE BROTHERS!!!
OH. EXCUSE ME.
I APOLOGIZE. I'VE MADE A TERRIBLE MISTAKE.
YOU'RE OBVIOUSLY NOT IN LOVE WITH SWEET LITTLE ROSIE.
ARE YOU?
THE HERO OF THE BATTLE OF BRITAIN DEPARTS AT HASTE. POSSIBLY TO GO AND REPEATEDLY PUNCH HIS TEDDY BEAR IN HIS QUARTERS.
WOULDN'T SURPRISE ME. HE CARRIED THE BLOODY THING EVERYWHERE WITH HIM UNTIL HE WAS 11.
THIS BRIEFING HAS NOT ENDED.
FIND BIG BOAT, SINK IT, KILL TINY FOREIGN PEOPLE, WIN BATTLE. BRIEFING ENDS.
UH, GLENDA. I'VE KINDA BEEN MEANING TO ASK FOR A WHILE NOW.
YOU WANT TO JOIN ME FOR A DRINK IN THE MESS, MAYBE?
WAR EFFORT...
DO BE SERIOUS.
MISS INDEPENDENCE. COME.
I'M REALLY SORRY, TOM. WE'LL SPEAK LATER, YEAH?

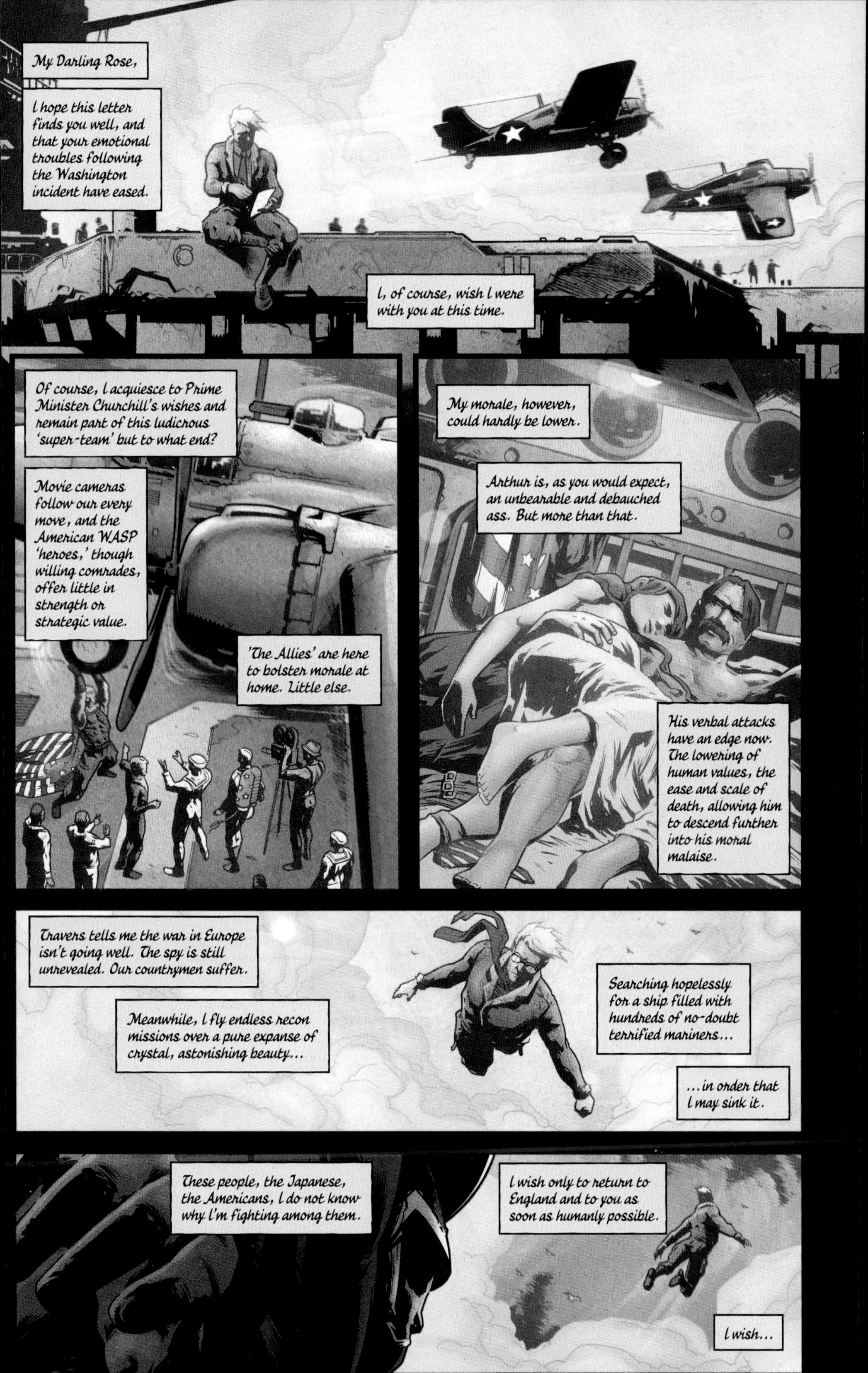
My Darling Rose,
I hope this letter finds you well, and that your emotional troubles following the Washington incident have eased.
I, of course, wish I were with you at this time.
Of course, I acquiesce to Prime Minister Churchill's wishes and remain part of this ludicrous 'super-team' but to what end?
Movie cameras follow our every move, and the American WASP 'heroes,' though willing comrades, offer little in strength or strategic value.
'The Allies' are here to bolster morale at home. Little else.
My morale, however, could hardly be lower.
Arthur is, as you would expect, an unbearable and debauched ass. But more than that.
His verbal attacks have an edge now. The lowering of human values, the ease and scale of death, allowing him to descend further into his moral malaise.
Travers tells me the war in Europe isn't going well. The spy is still unrevealed. Our countrymen suffer.
Meanwhile, I fly endless recon missions over a pure expanse of crystal, astonishing beauty...
Searching hopelessly for a ship filled with hundreds of no-doubt terrified mariners...
...in order that I may sink it.
These people, the Japanese, the Americans, I do not know why I'm fighting among them.
I wish only to return to England and to you as soon as humanly possible.
I wish...

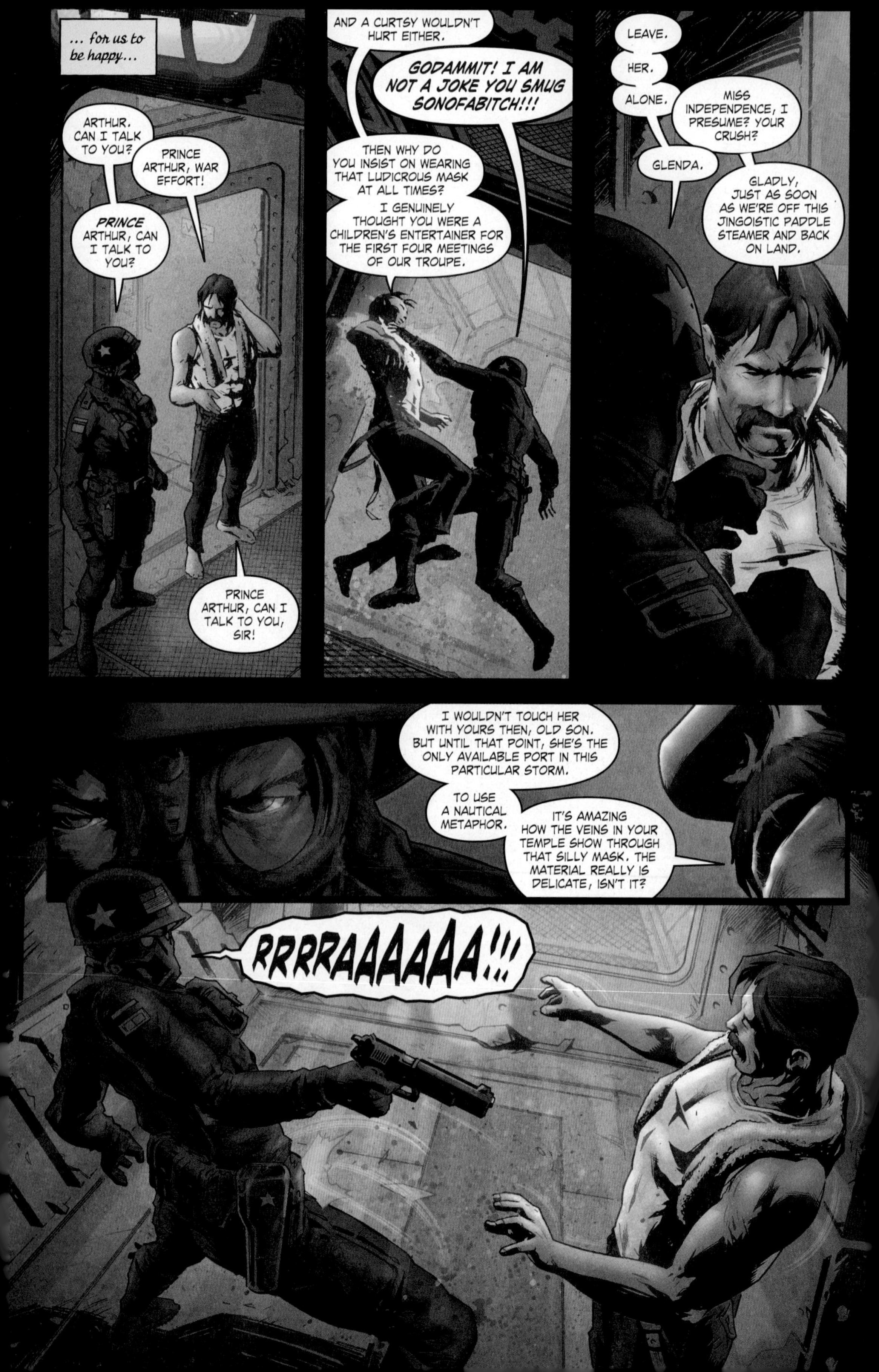
... for us to be happy...
ARTHUR. CAN I TALK TO YOU?
PRINCE ARTHUR, WAR EFFORT!
PRINCE ARTHUR, CAN I TALK TO YOU?
PRINCE ARTHUR, CAN I TALK TO YOU, SIR!
AND A CURTSY WOULDN'T HURT EITHER.
GODAMMIT! I AM NOT A JOKE YOU SMUG SONOFABITCH!!!
THEN WHY DO YOU INSIST ON WEARING THAT LUDICROUS MASK AT ALL TIMES?
I GENUINELY THOUGHT YOU WERE A CHILDREN'S ENTERTAINER FOR THE FIRST FOUR MEETINGS OF OUR TROUPE.
LEAVE.
HER.
ALONE.
MISS INDEPENDENCE, I PRESUME? YOUR CRUSH?
GLENDA.
GLADLY, JUST AS SOON AS WE'RE OFF THIS JINGOISTIC PADDLE STEAMER AND BACK ON LAND.
I WOULDN'T TOUCH HER WITH YOURS THEN, OLD SON. BUT UNTIL THAT POINT, SHE'S THE ONLY AVAILABLE PORT IN THIS PARTICULAR STORM.
TO USE A NAUTICAL METAPHOR.
IT'S AMAZING HOW THE VEINS IN YOUR TEMPLE SHOW THROUGH THAT SILLY MASK. THE MATERIAL REALLY IS DELICATE, ISN'T IT?
RRRRAAAAAA!!!

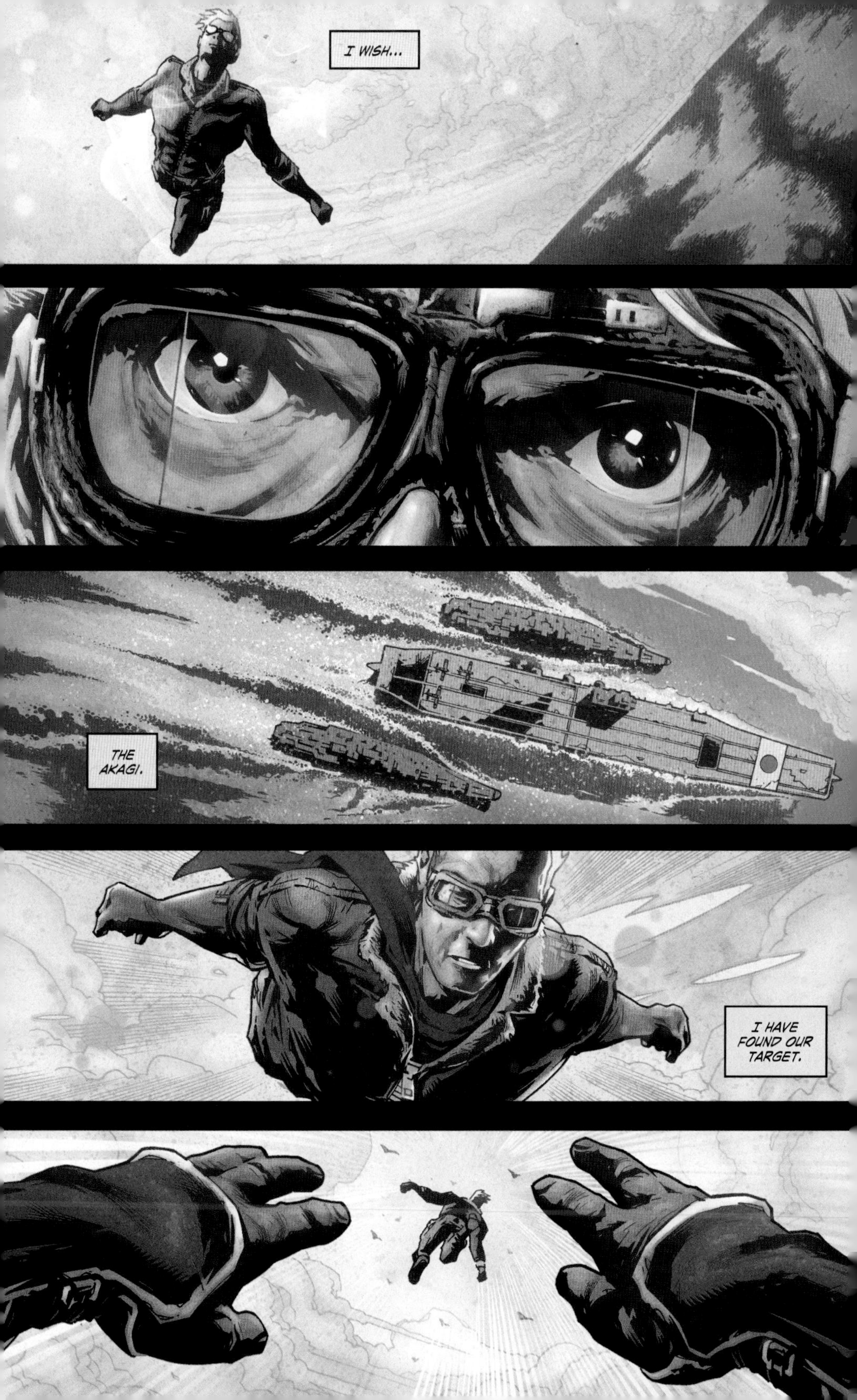
I WISH...
THE AKAGI.
I HAVE FOUND OUR TARGET.

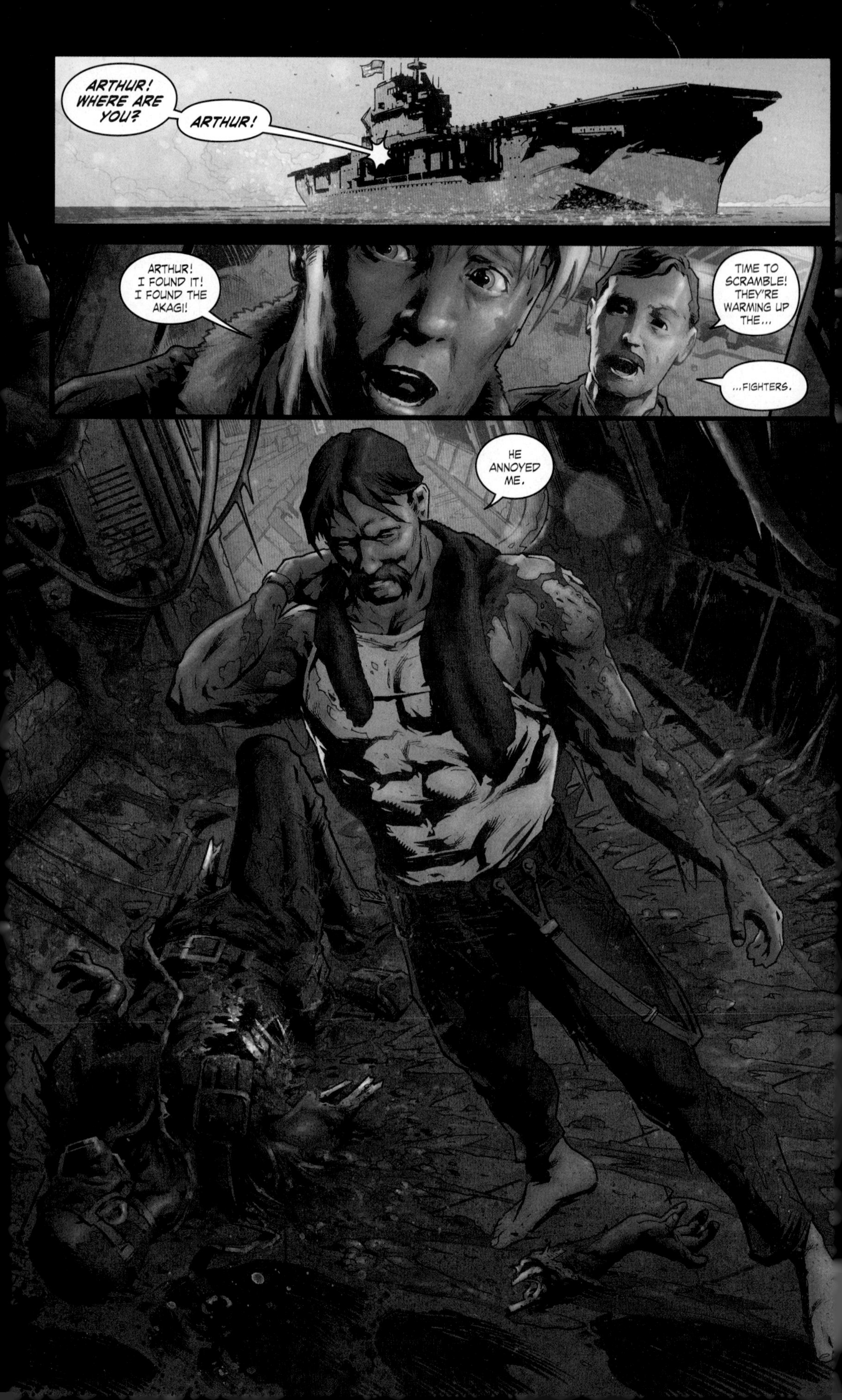
ARTHUR! WHERE ARE YOU?
ARTHUR!
ARTHUR! I FOUND IT! I FOUND THE AKAGI!
TIME TO SCRAMBLE! THEY'RE WARMING UP THE...
...FIGHTERS.
HE ANNOYED ME.

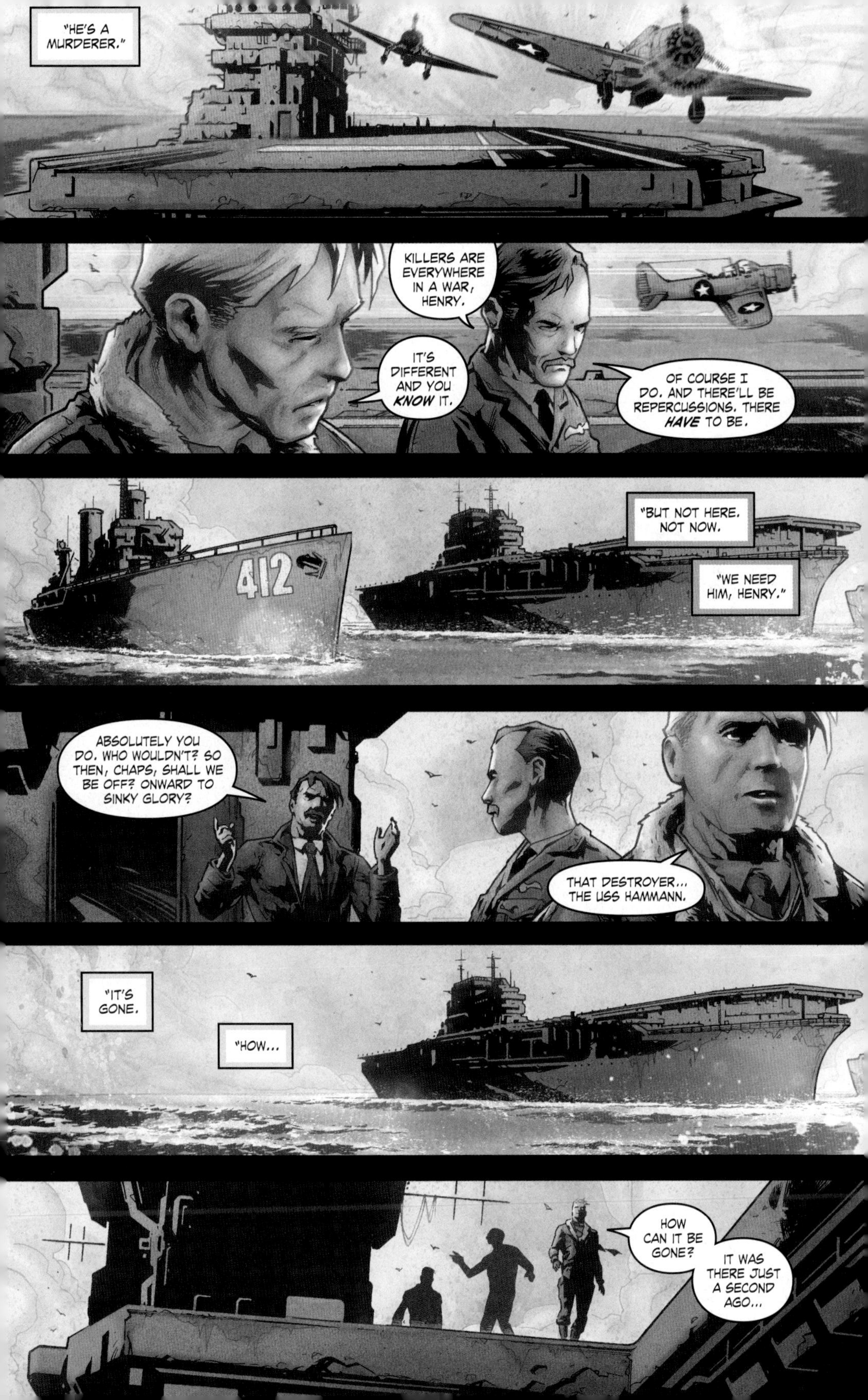
"HE'S A MURDERER."
KILLERS ARE EVERYWHERE IN A WAR, HENRY.
IT'S DIFFERENT AND YOU KNOW IT.
OF COURSE I DO. AND THERE'LL BE REPERCUSSIONS. THERE HAVE TO BE.
"BUT NOT HERE. NOT NOW.
"WE NEED HIM, HENRY."
412
ABSOLUTELY YOU DO. WHO WOULDN'T? SO THEN, CHAPS, SHALL WE BE OFF? ONWARD TO SINKY GLORY?
THAT DESTROYER... THE USS HAMMANN.
"IT'S GONE.
"HOW...
HOW CAN IT BE GONE?
IT WAS THERE JUST A SECOND AGO...

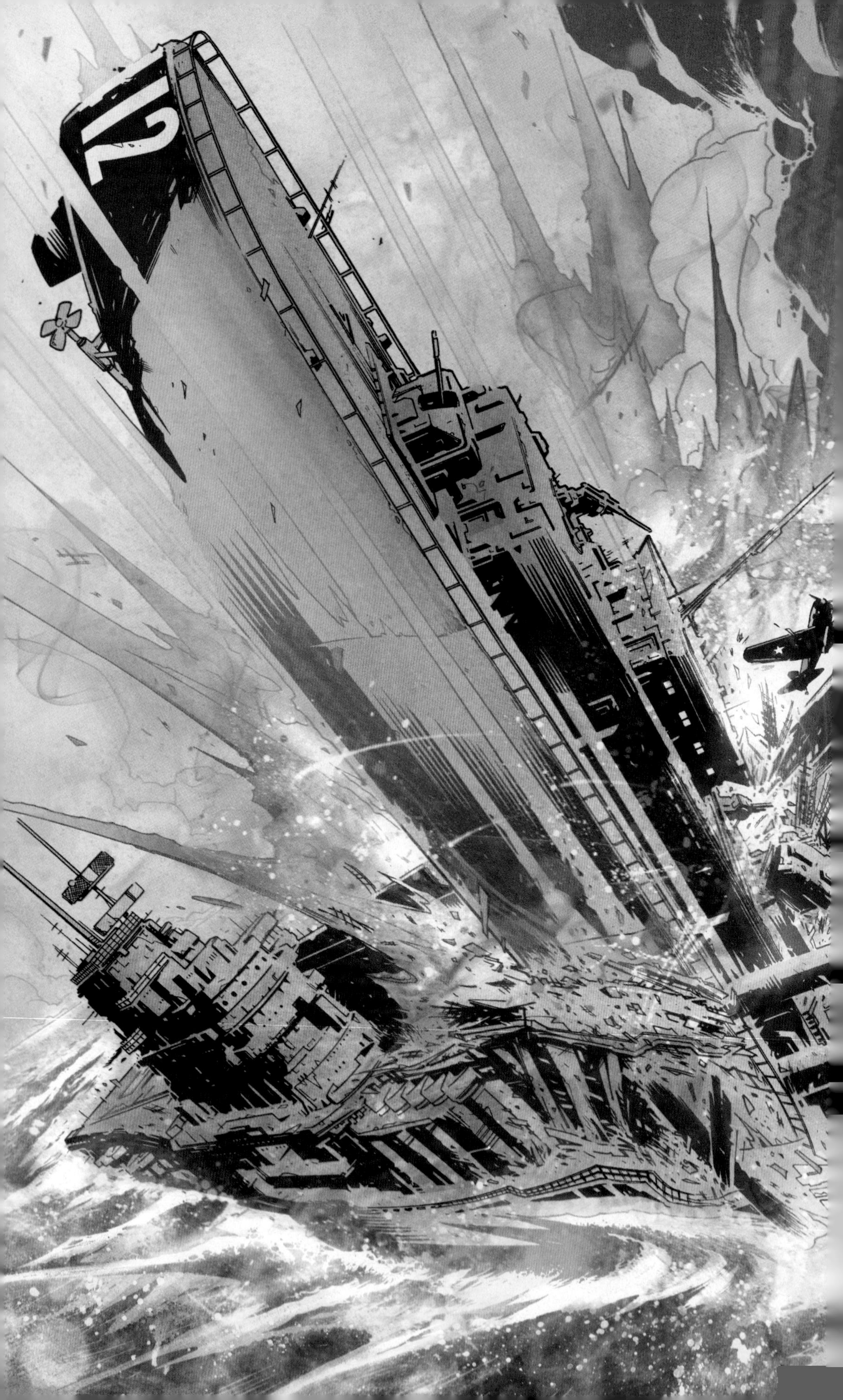

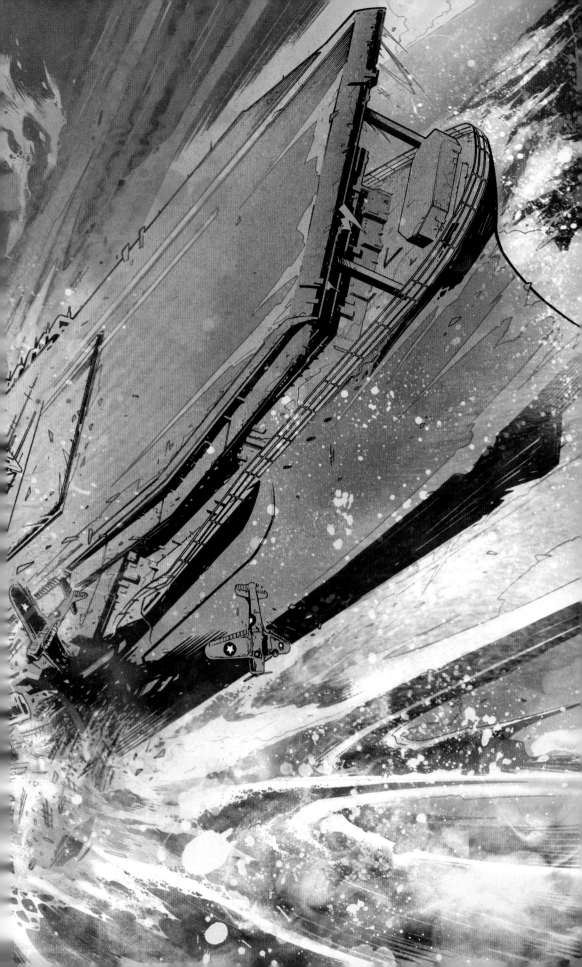

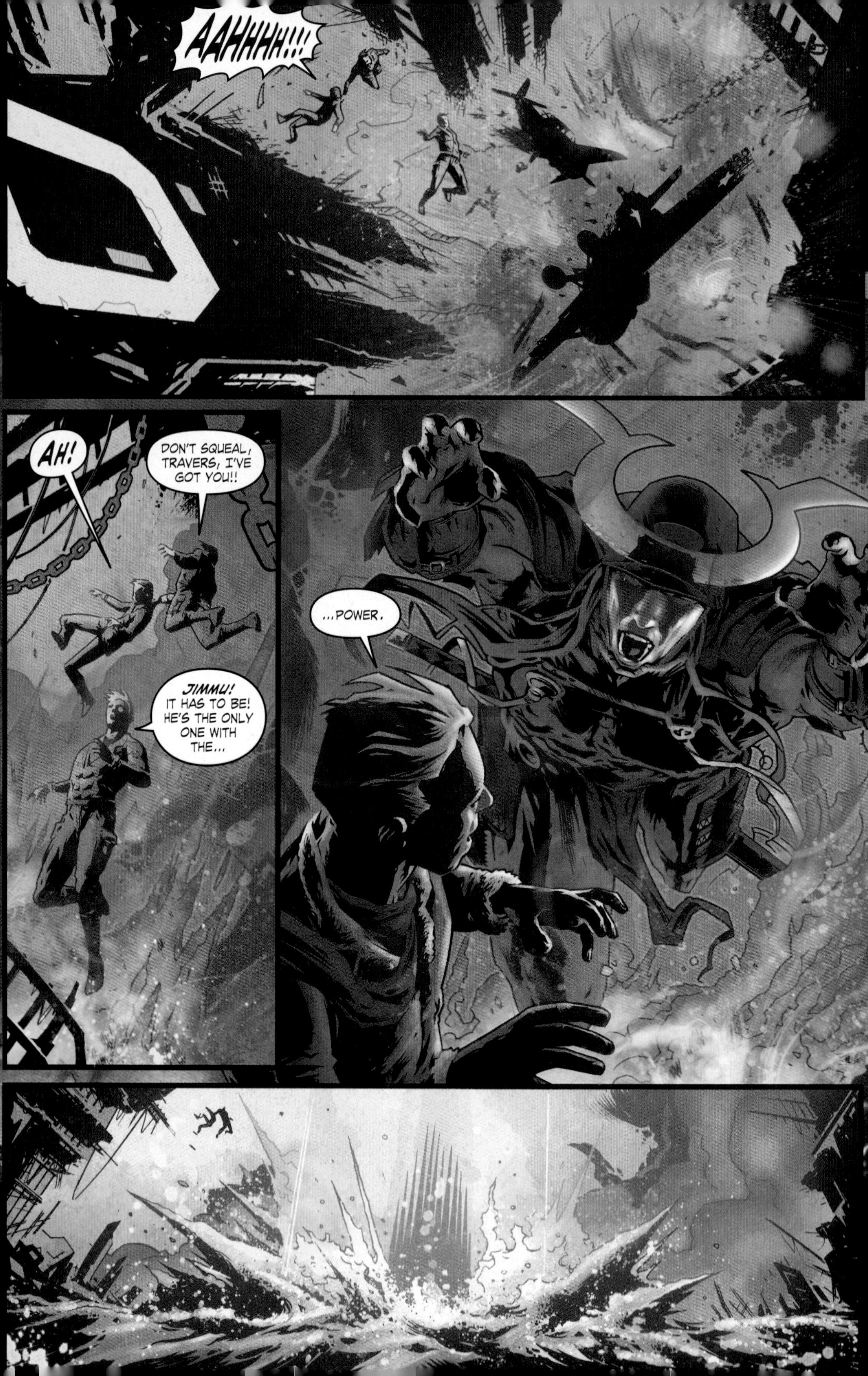
AAHHHH!!!
AH!
DON'T SQUEAL, TRAVERS, I'VE GOT YOU!!
JIMMU! IT HAS TO BE! HE'S THE ONLY ONE WITH THE...
...POWER.

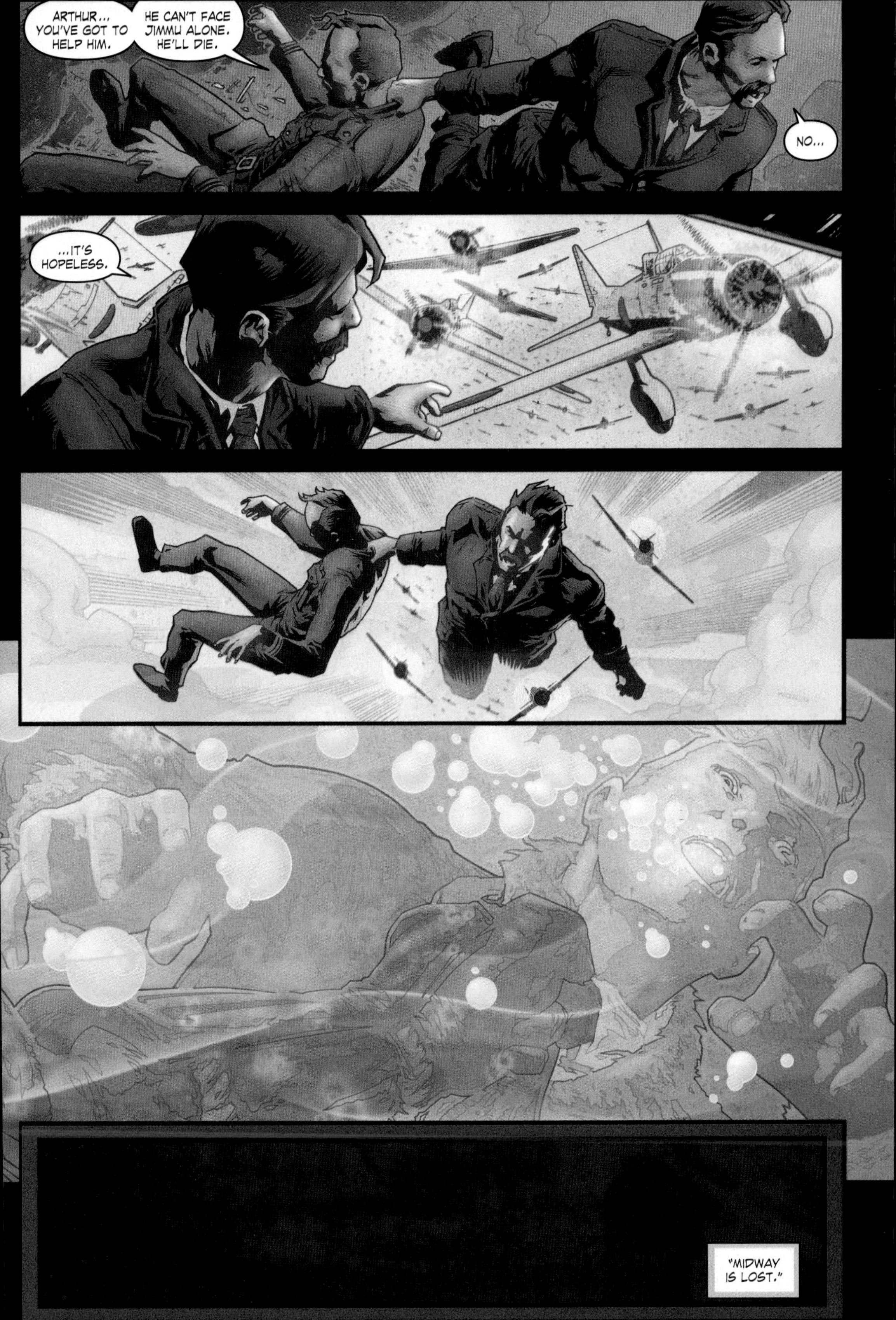
ARTHUR... YOU'VE GOT TO HELP HIM.
HE CAN'T FACE JIMMU ALONE. HE'LL DIE.
NO...
...IT'S HOPELESS.
"MIDWAY IS LOST."

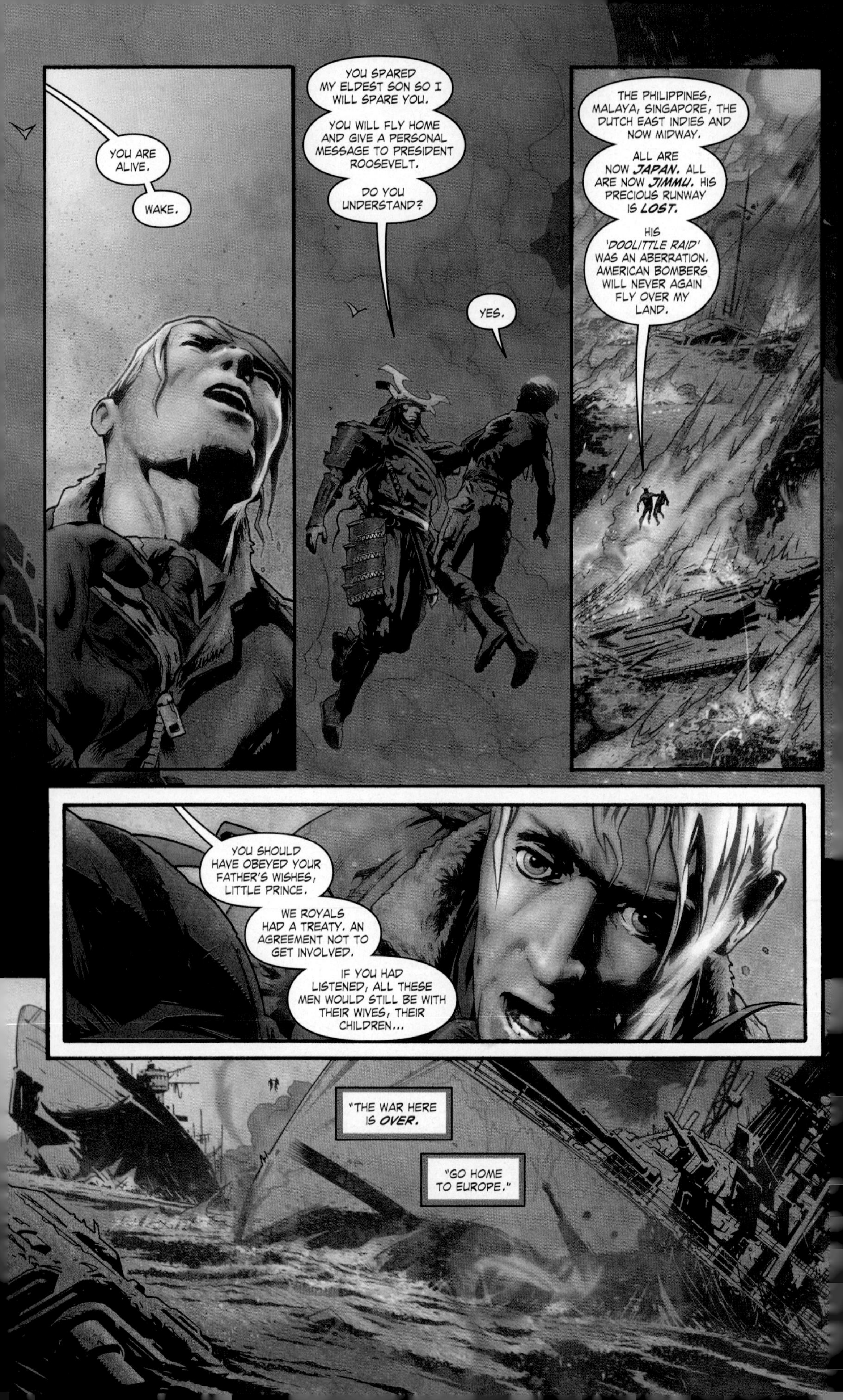
YOU ARE ALIVE.
WAKE.
YOU SPARED MY ELDEST SON SO I WILL SPARE YOU.
YOU WILL FLY HOME AND GIVE A PERSONAL MESSAGE TO PRESIDENT ROOSEVELT.
DO YOU UNDERSTAND?
YES.
THE PHILIPPINES, MALAYA, SINGAPORE, THE DUTCH EAST INDIES AND NOW MIDWAY.
ALL ARE NOW *JAPAN.* ALL ARE NOW *JIMMU.* HIS PRECIOUS RUNWAY IS *LOST.*
HIS *'DOOLITTLE RAID'* WAS AN ABERRATION. AMERICAN BOMBERS WILL NEVER AGAIN FLY OVER MY LAND.
YOU SHOULD HAVE OBEYED YOUR FATHER'S WISHES, LITTLE PRINCE.
WE ROYALS HAD A TREATY. AN AGREEMENT NOT TO GET INVOLVED.
IF YOU HAD LISTENED, ALL THESE MEN WOULD STILL BE WITH THEIR WIVES, THEIR CHILDREN...
"THE WAR HERE IS *OVER.*
"GO HOME TO EUROPE."

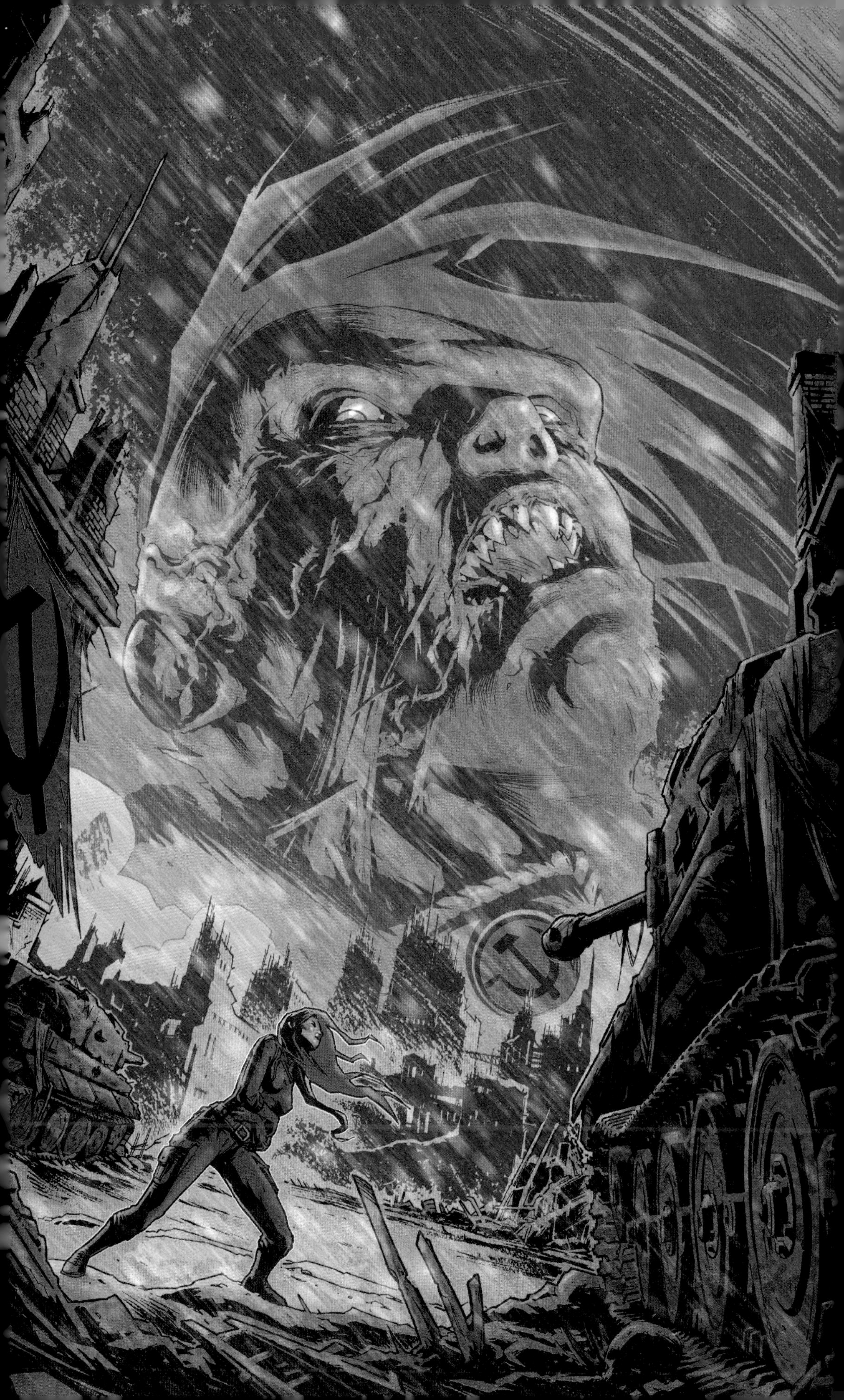

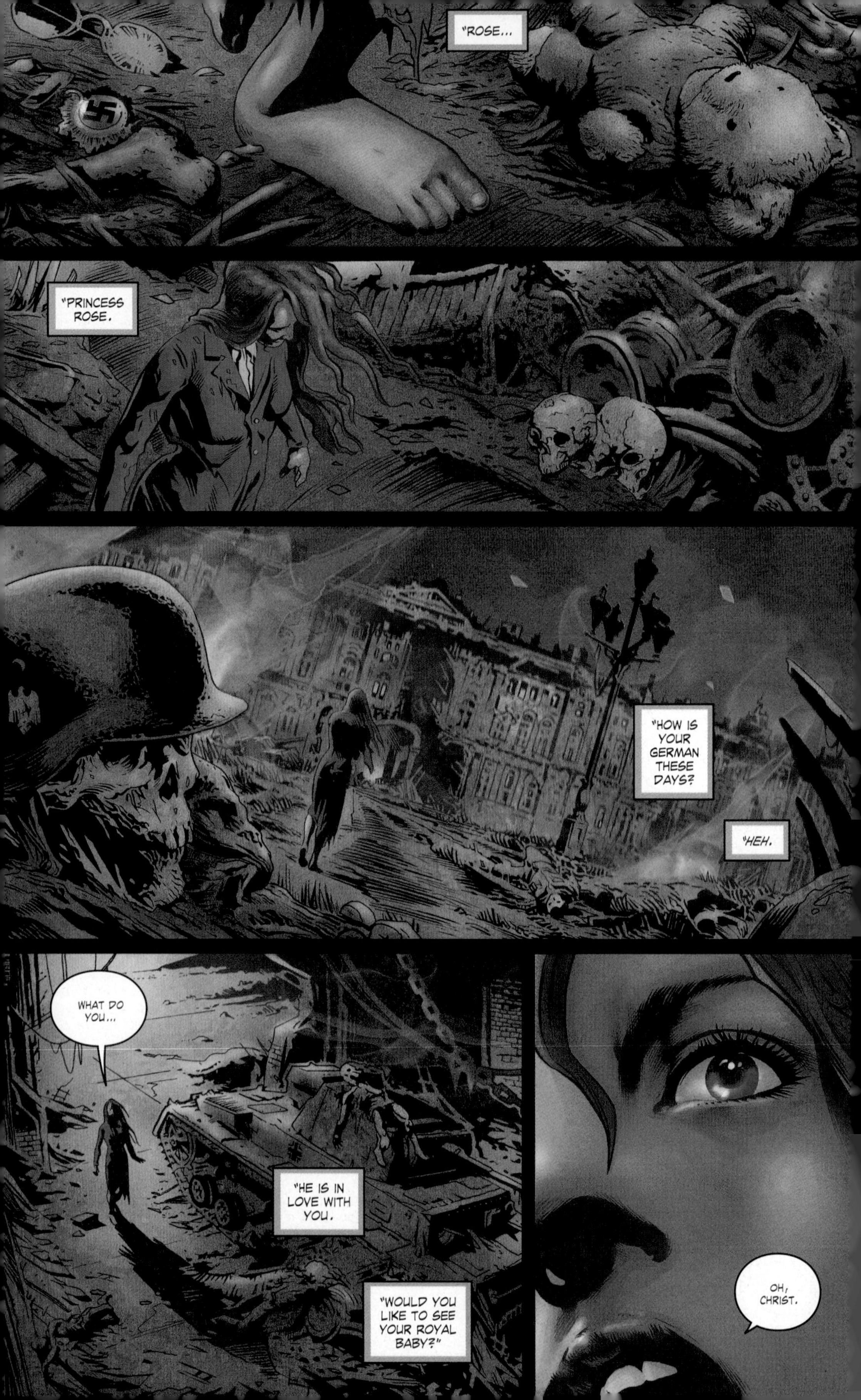
"ROSE...
"PRINCESS ROSE.
"HOW IS YOUR GERMAN THESE DAYS?
"HEH.
WHAT DO YOU...
"HE IS IN LOVE WITH YOU.
"WOULD YOU LIKE TO SEE YOUR ROYAL BABY?"
OH, CHRIST.

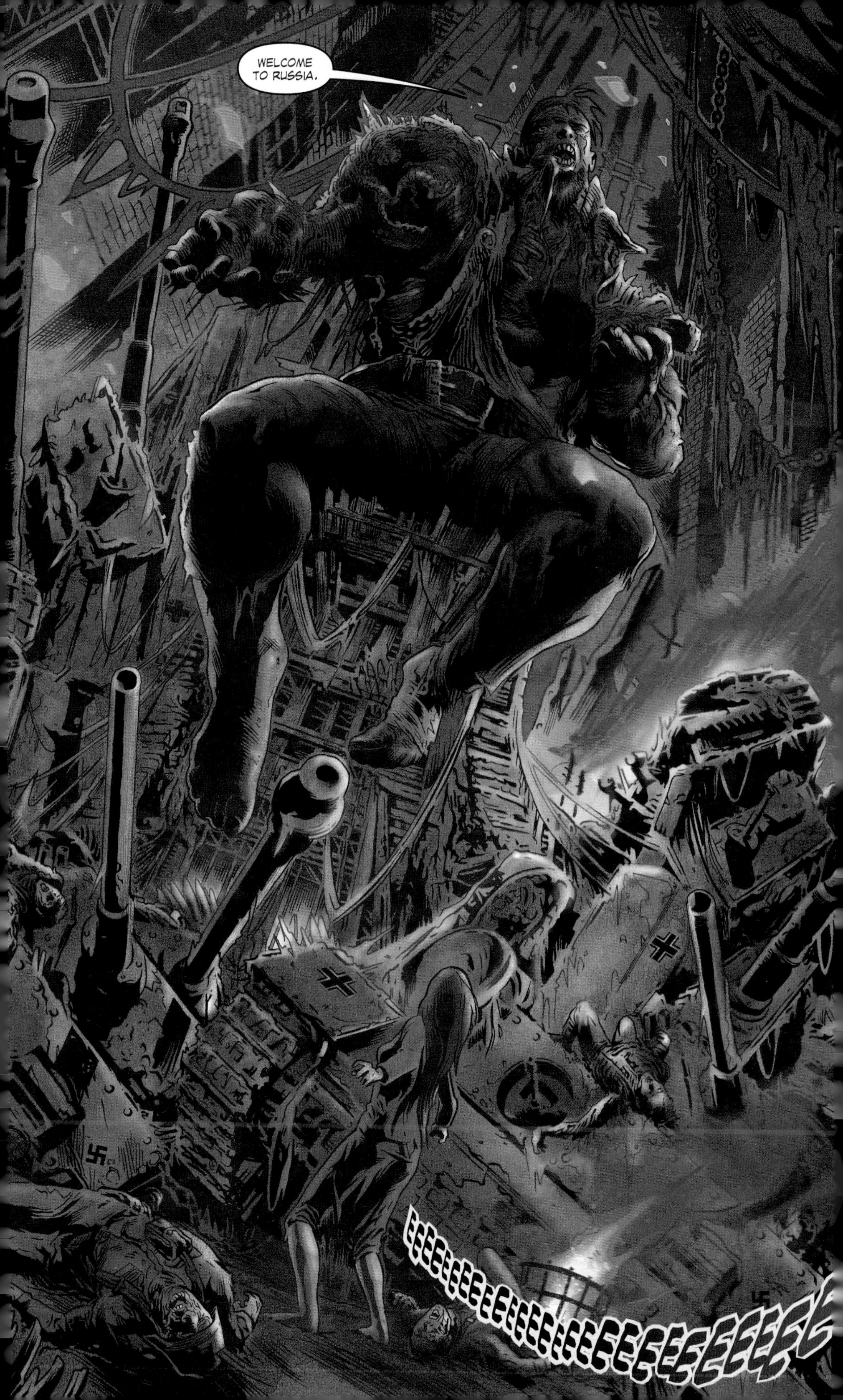
WELCOME TO RUSSIA.
EEEEEEEEEEEEEEEEEEEEEEEEEEEEK

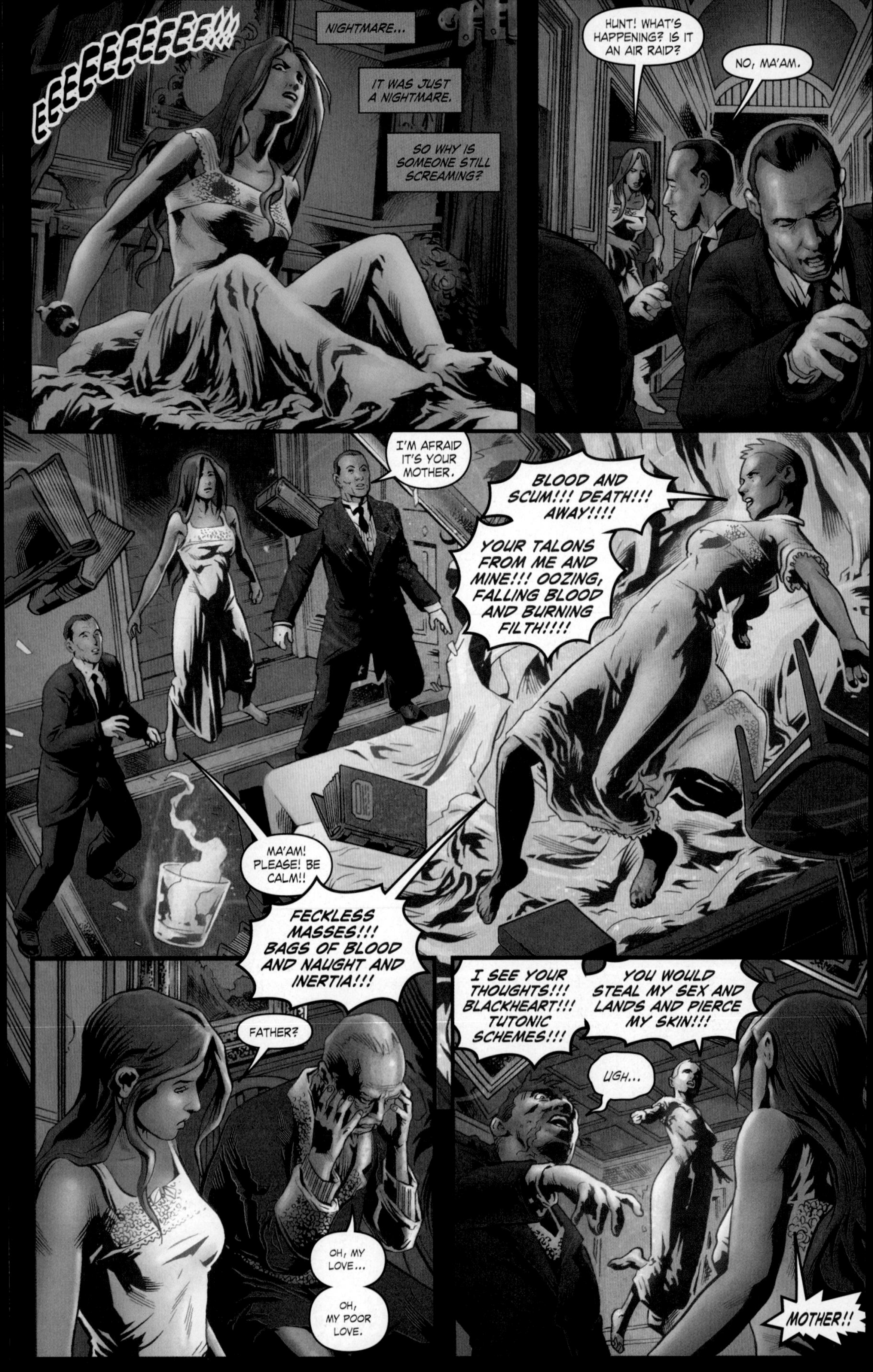
EEEEEEEEEEEE!!!
NIGHTMARE...
IT WAS JUST A NIGHTMARE.
SO WHY IS SOMEONE STILL SCREAMING?
HUNT! WHAT'S HAPPENING? IS IT AN AIR RAID?
NO, MA'AM.
I'M AFRAID IT'S YOUR MOTHER.
BLOOD AND SCUM!!! DEATH!!! AWAY!!!!
YOUR TALONS FROM ME AND MINE!!! OOZING, FALLING BLOOD AND BURNING FILTH!!!!
MA'AM! PLEASE! BE CALM!!
FECKLESS MASSES!!! BAGS OF BLOOD AND NAUGHT AND INERTIA!!!
FATHER?
OH, MY LOVE...
OH, MY POOR LOVE.
I SEE YOUR THOUGHTS!!! BLACKHEART!!! TUTONIC SCHEMES!!!
YOU WOULD STEAL MY SEX AND LANDS AND PIERCE MY SKIN!!!
UGH...
MOTHER!!

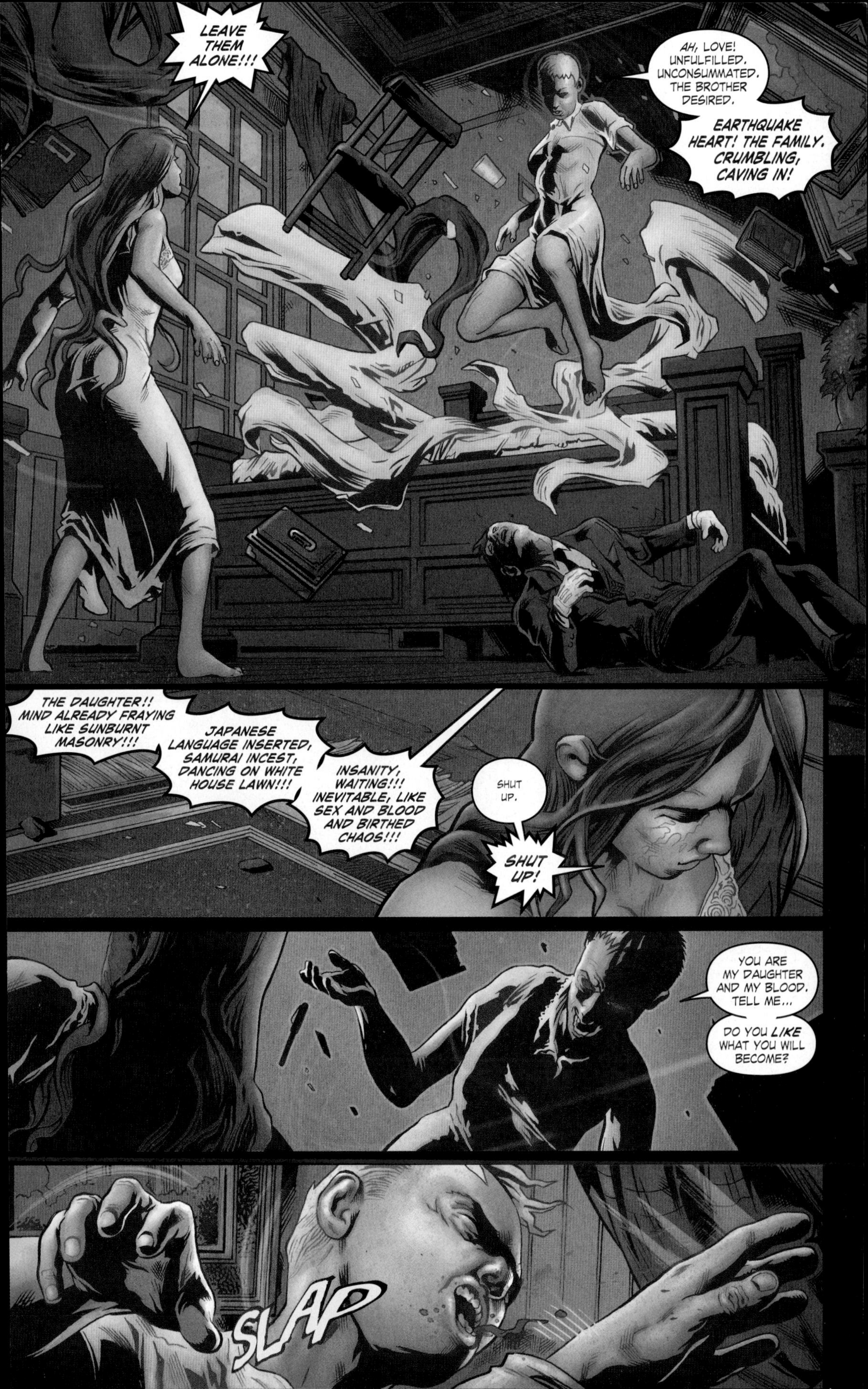

LEAVE THEM ALONE!!!
AH, LOVE! UNFULFILLED. UNCONSUMMATED. THE BROTHER DESIRED.
EARTHQUAKE HEART! THE FAMILY. CRUMBLING, CAVING IN!
THE DAUGHTER!! MIND ALREADY FRAYING LIKE SUNBURNT MASONRY!!!
JAPANESE LANGUAGE INSERTED, SAMURAI INCEST, DANCING ON WHITE HOUSE LAWN!!!
INSANITY, WAITING!!! INEVITABLE, LIKE SEX AND BLOOD AND BIRTHED CHAOS!!!
SHUT UP.
SHUT UP!
YOU ARE MY DAUGHTER AND MY BLOOD. TELL ME...
DO YOU LIKE WHAT YOU WILL BECOME?
SLAP

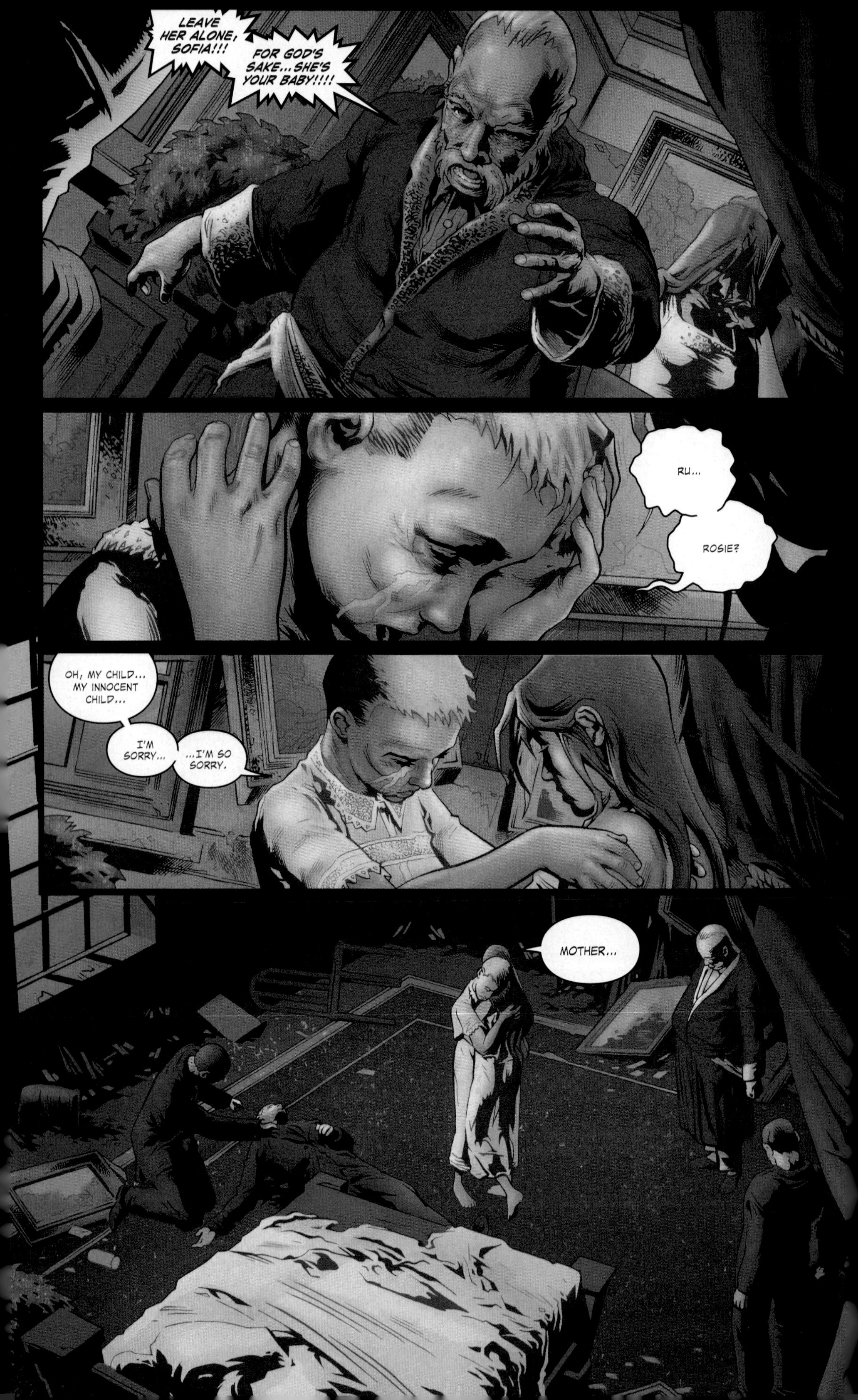

LEAVE HER ALONE, SOFIA!!!
FOR GOD'S SAKE...SHE'S YOUR BABY!!!!
RU...
ROSIE?
OH, MY CHILD... MY INNOCENT CHILD...
I'M SORRY...
...I'M SO SORRY.
MOTHER...

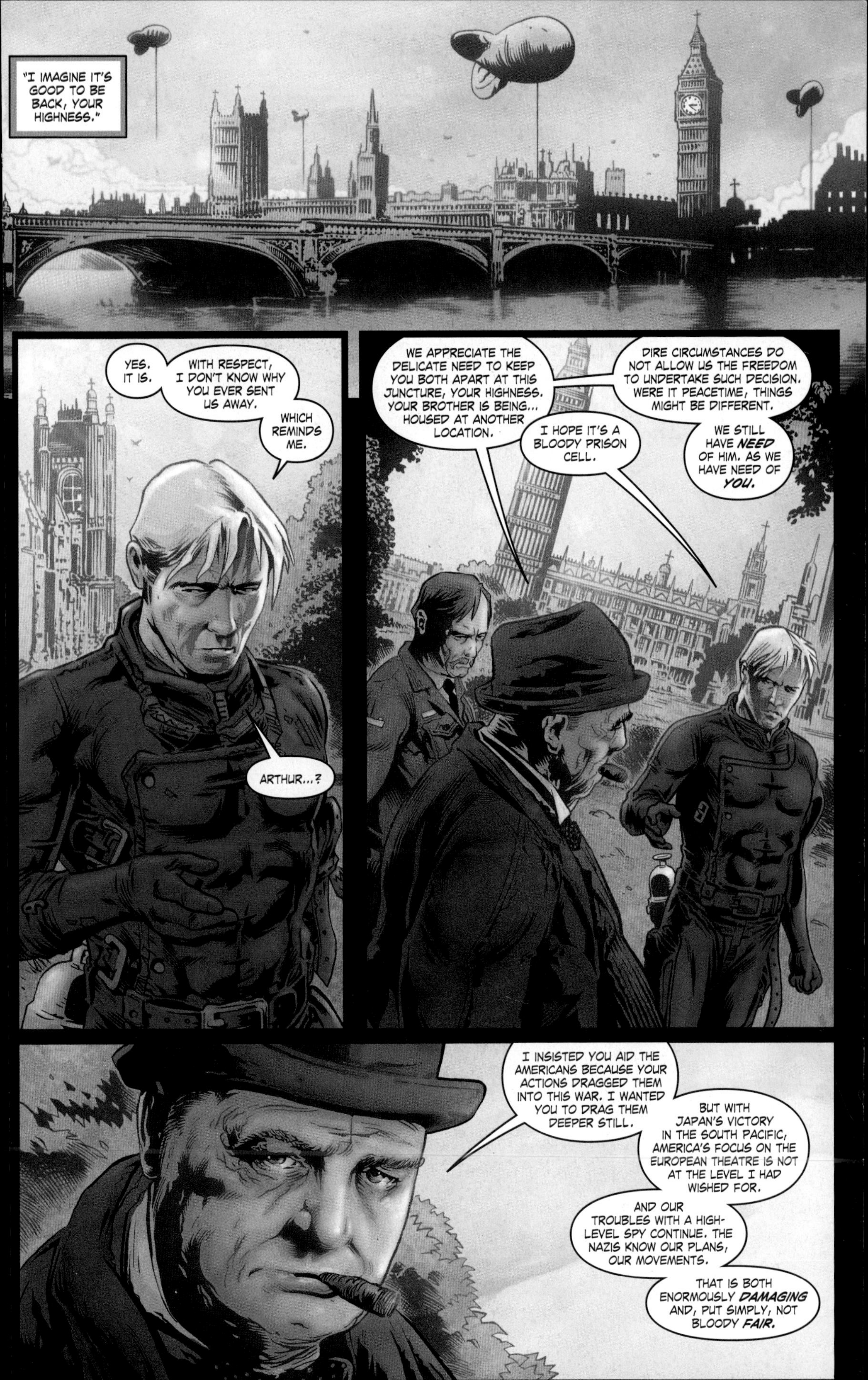
"I IMAGINE IT'S GOOD TO BE BACK, YOUR HIGHNESS."
YES. IT IS.
WITH RESPECT, I DON'T KNOW WHY YOU EVER SENT US AWAY.
WHICH REMINDS ME.
ARTHUR...?
WE APPRECIATE THE DELICATE NEED TO KEEP YOU BOTH APART AT THIS JUNCTURE, YOUR HIGHNESS. YOUR BROTHER IS BEING... HOUSED AT ANOTHER LOCATION.
I HOPE IT'S A BLOODY PRISON CELL.
DIRE CIRCUMSTANCES DO NOT ALLOW US THE FREEDOM TO UNDERTAKE SUCH DECISION. WERE IT PEACETIME, THINGS MIGHT BE DIFFERENT.
WE STILL HAVE NEED OF HIM. AS WE HAVE NEED OF YOU.
I INSISTED YOU AID THE AMERICANS BECAUSE YOUR ACTIONS DRAGGED THEM INTO THIS WAR. I WANTED YOU TO DRAG THEM DEEPER STILL.
BUT WITH JAPAN'S VICTORY IN THE SOUTH PACIFIC, AMERICA'S FOCUS ON THE EUROPEAN THEATRE IS NOT AT THE LEVEL I HAD WISHED FOR.
AND OUR TROUBLES WITH A HIGH-LEVEL SPY CONTINUE. THE NAZIS KNOW OUR PLANS, OUR MOVEMENTS.
THAT IS BOTH ENORMOUSLY DAMAGING AND, PUT SIMPLY, NOT BLOODY FAIR.

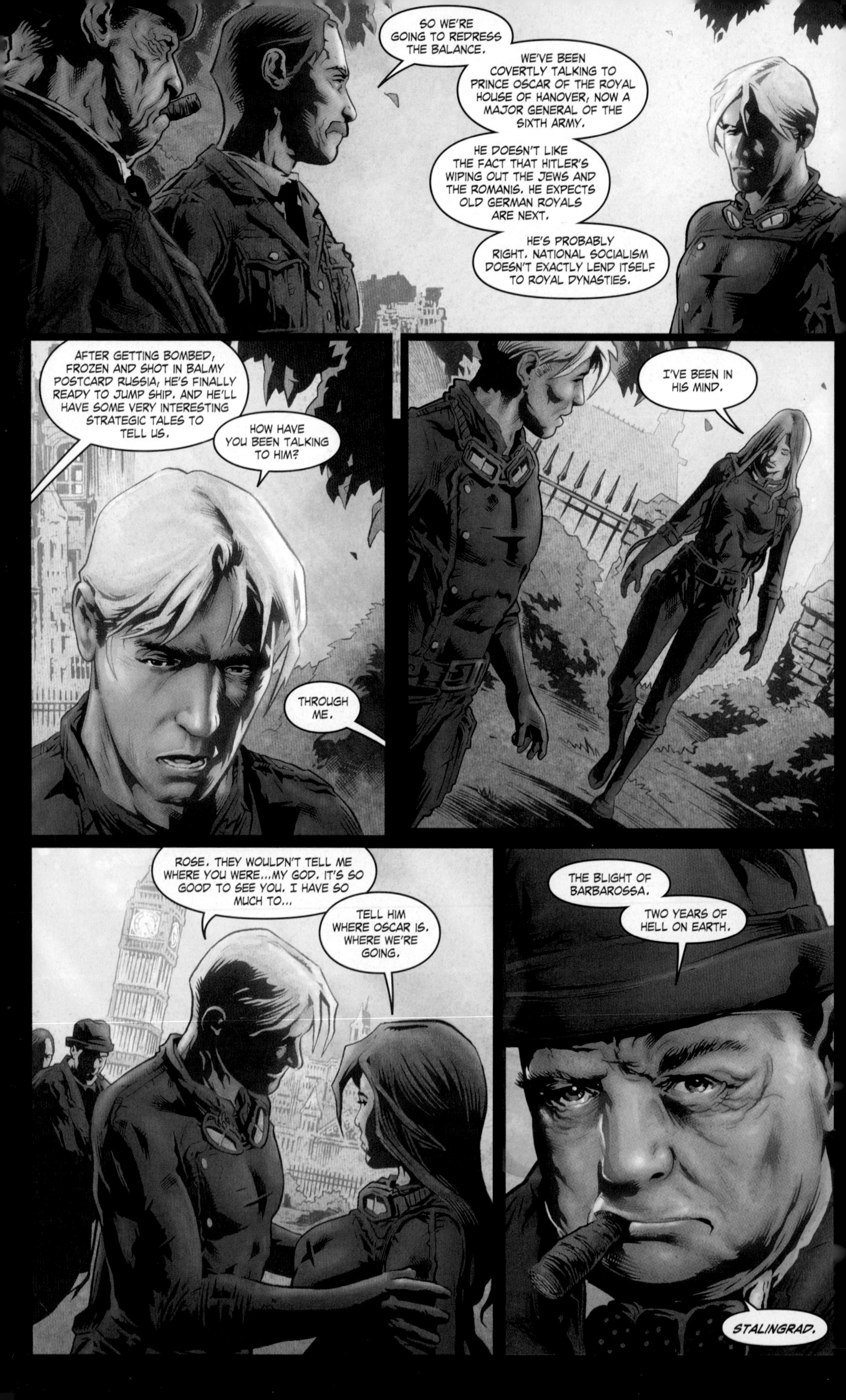

SO WE'RE GOING TO REDRESS THE BALANCE.
WE'VE BEEN COVERTLY TALKING TO PRINCE OSCAR OF THE ROYAL HOUSE OF HANOVER, NOW A MAJOR GENERAL OF THE SIXTH ARMY.
HE DOESN'T LIKE THE FACT THAT HITLER'S WIPING OUT THE JEWS AND THE ROMANIS. HE EXPECTS OLD GERMAN ROYALS ARE NEXT.
HE'S PROBABLY RIGHT. NATIONAL SOCIALISM DOESN'T EXACTLY LEND ITSELF TO ROYAL DYNASTIES.
AFTER GETTING BOMBED, FROZEN AND SHOT IN BALMY POSTCARD RUSSIA, HE'S FINALLY READY TO JUMP SHIP. AND HE'LL HAVE SOME VERY INTERESTING STRATEGIC TALES TO TELL US.
HOW HAVE YOU BEEN TALKING TO HIM?
THROUGH ME.
I'VE BEEN IN HIS MIND.
ROSE. THEY WOULDN'T TELL ME WHERE YOU WERE...MY GOD. IT'S SO GOOD TO SEE YOU. I HAVE SO MUCH TO...
TELL HIM WHERE OSCAR IS. WHERE WE'RE GOING.
THE BLIGHT OF BARBAROSSA.
TWO YEARS OF HELL ON EARTH.
STALINGRAD.

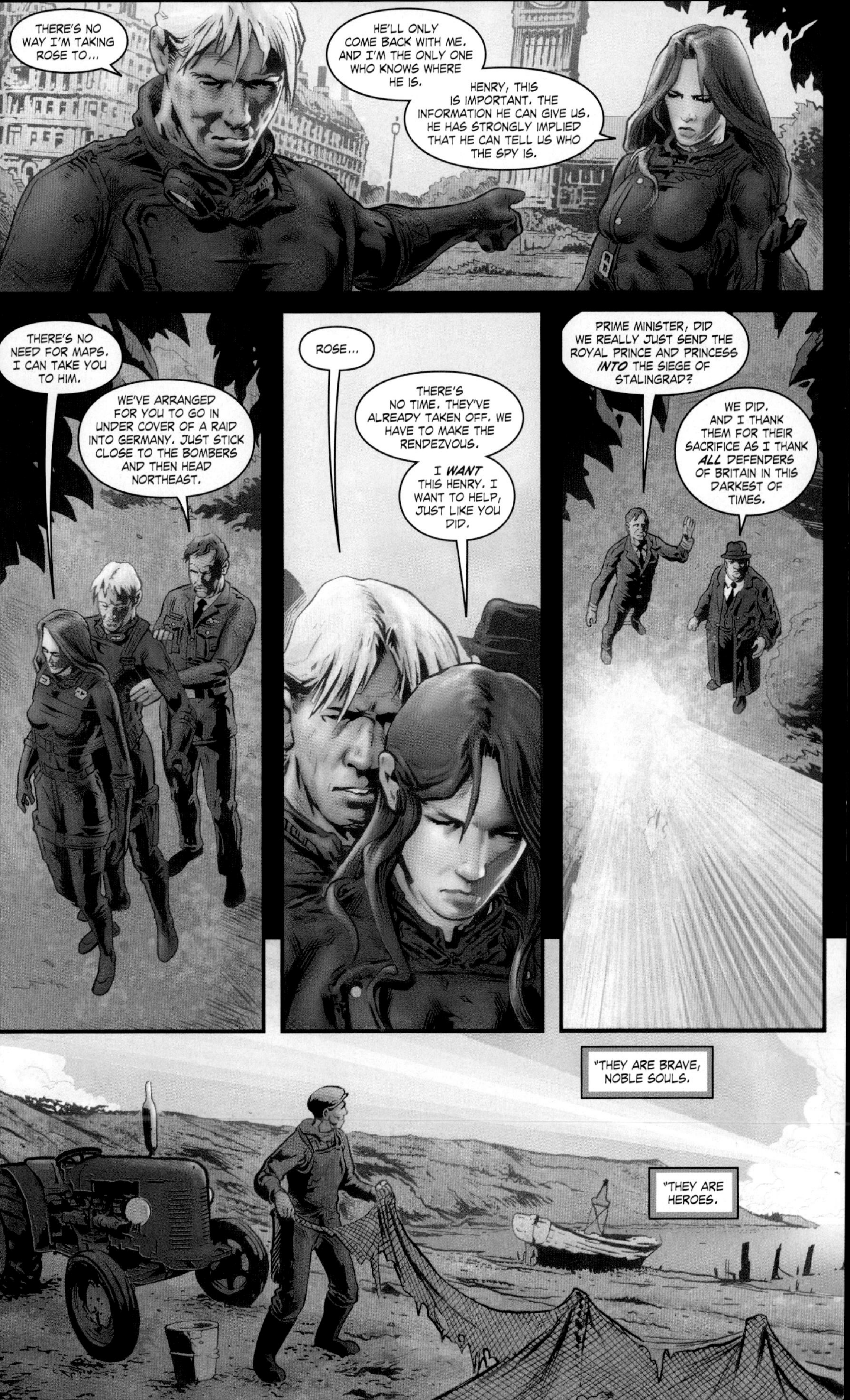
THERE'S NO WAY I'M TAKING ROSE TO...
HE'LL ONLY COME BACK WITH ME. AND I'M THE ONLY ONE WHO KNOWS WHERE HE IS.
HENRY, THIS IS IMPORTANT. THE INFORMATION HE CAN GIVE US. HE HAS STRONGLY IMPLIED THAT HE CAN TELL US WHO THE SPY IS.
THERE'S NO NEED FOR MAPS. I CAN TAKE YOU TO HIM.
WE'VE ARRANGED FOR YOU TO GO IN UNDER COVER OF A RAID INTO GERMANY. JUST STICK CLOSE TO THE BOMBERS AND THEN HEAD NORTHEAST.
ROSE...
THERE'S NO TIME. THEY'VE ALREADY TAKEN OFF. WE HAVE TO MAKE THE RENDEZVOUS.
I WANT THIS HENRY. I WANT TO HELP, JUST LIKE YOU DID.
PRIME MINISTER, DID WE REALLY JUST SEND THE ROYAL PRINCE AND PRINCESS INTO THE SIEGE OF STALINGRAD?
WE DID. AND I THANK THEM FOR THEIR SACRIFICE AS I THANK ALL DEFENDERS OF BRITAIN IN THIS DARKEST OF TIMES.
"THEY ARE BRAVE, NOBLE SOULS.
"THEY ARE HEROES.

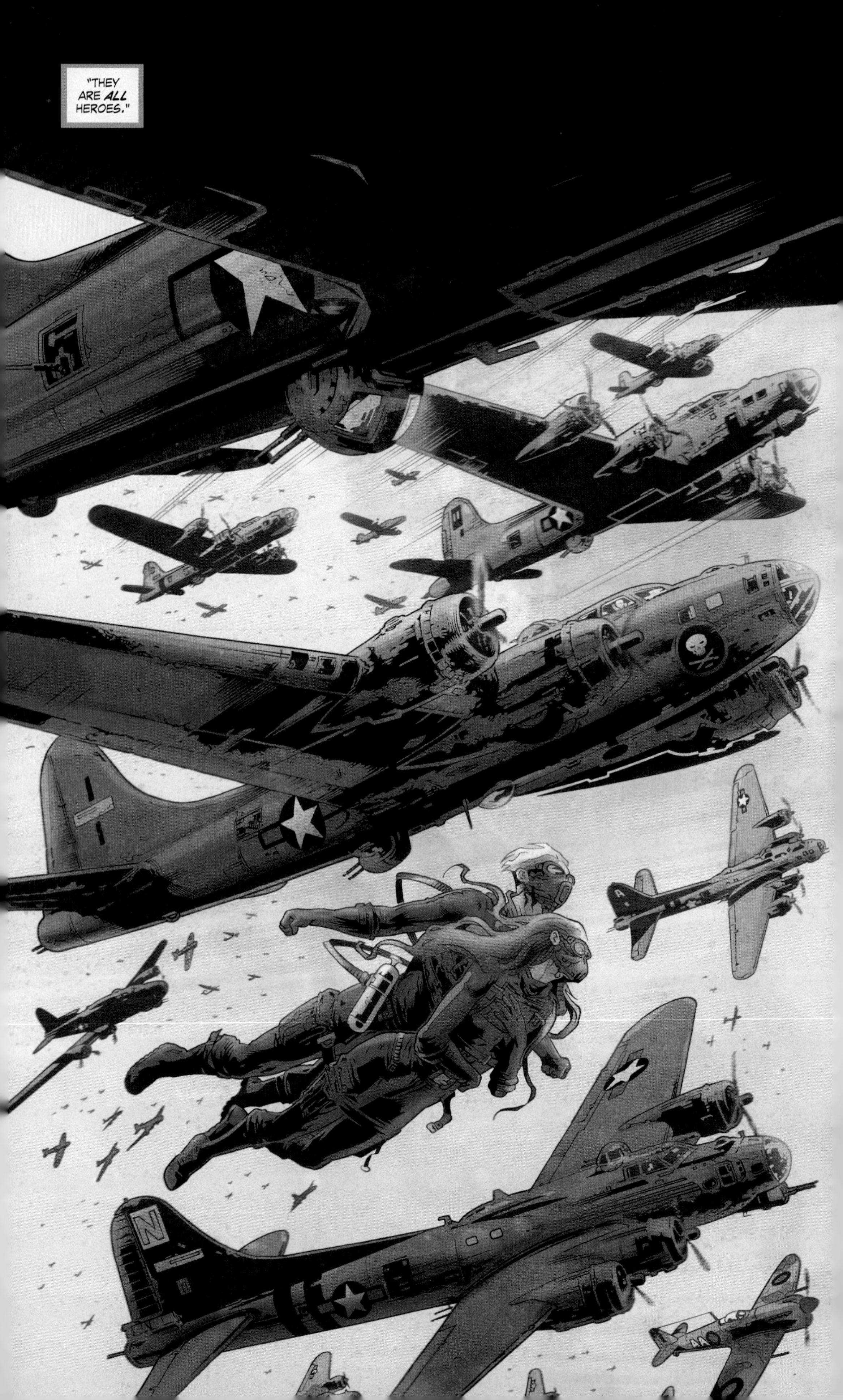
"THEY ARE ALL HEROES."

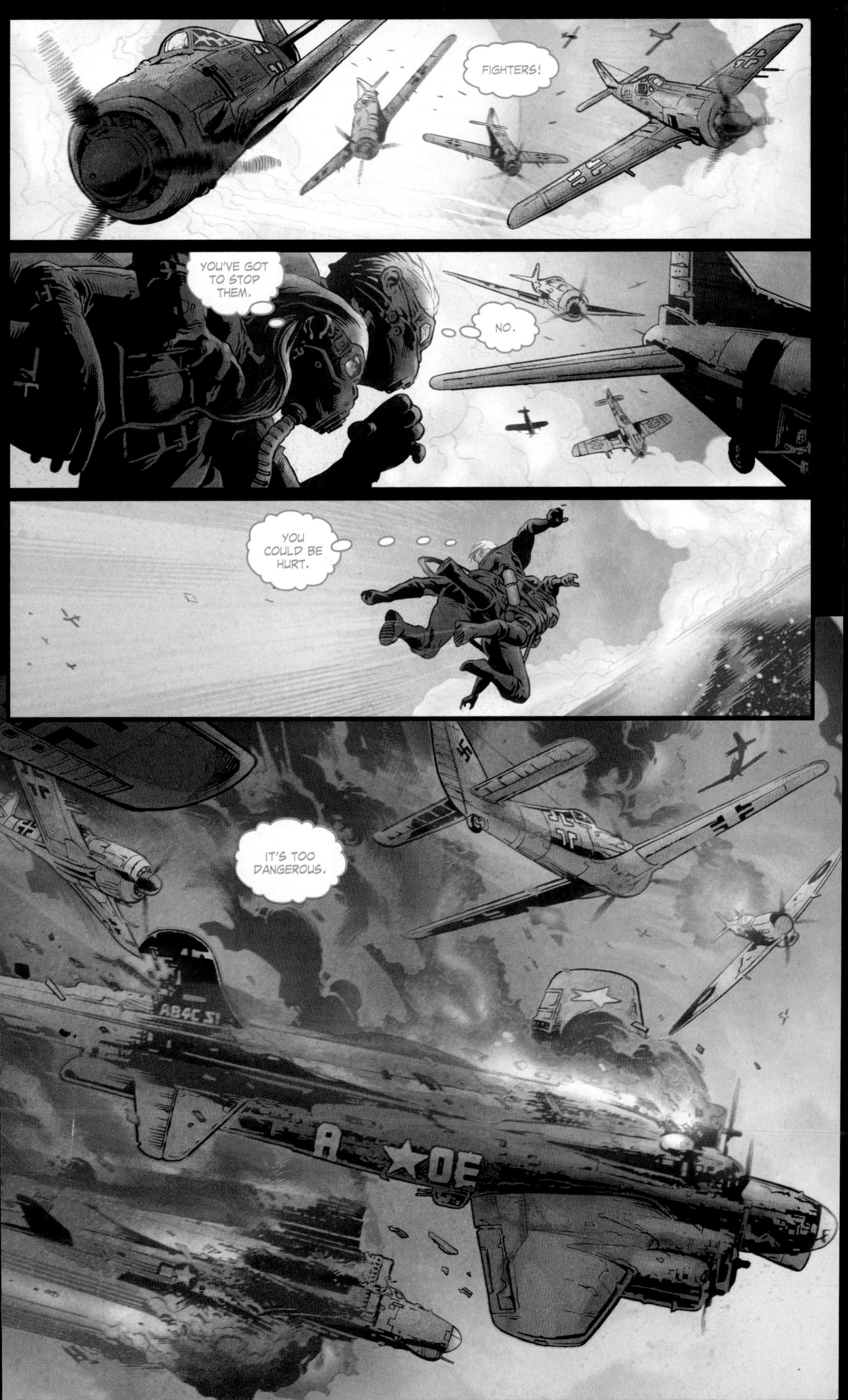
FIGHTERS!
YOU'VE GOT TO STOP THEM.
NO.
YOU COULD BE HURT.
IT'S TOO DANGEROUS.

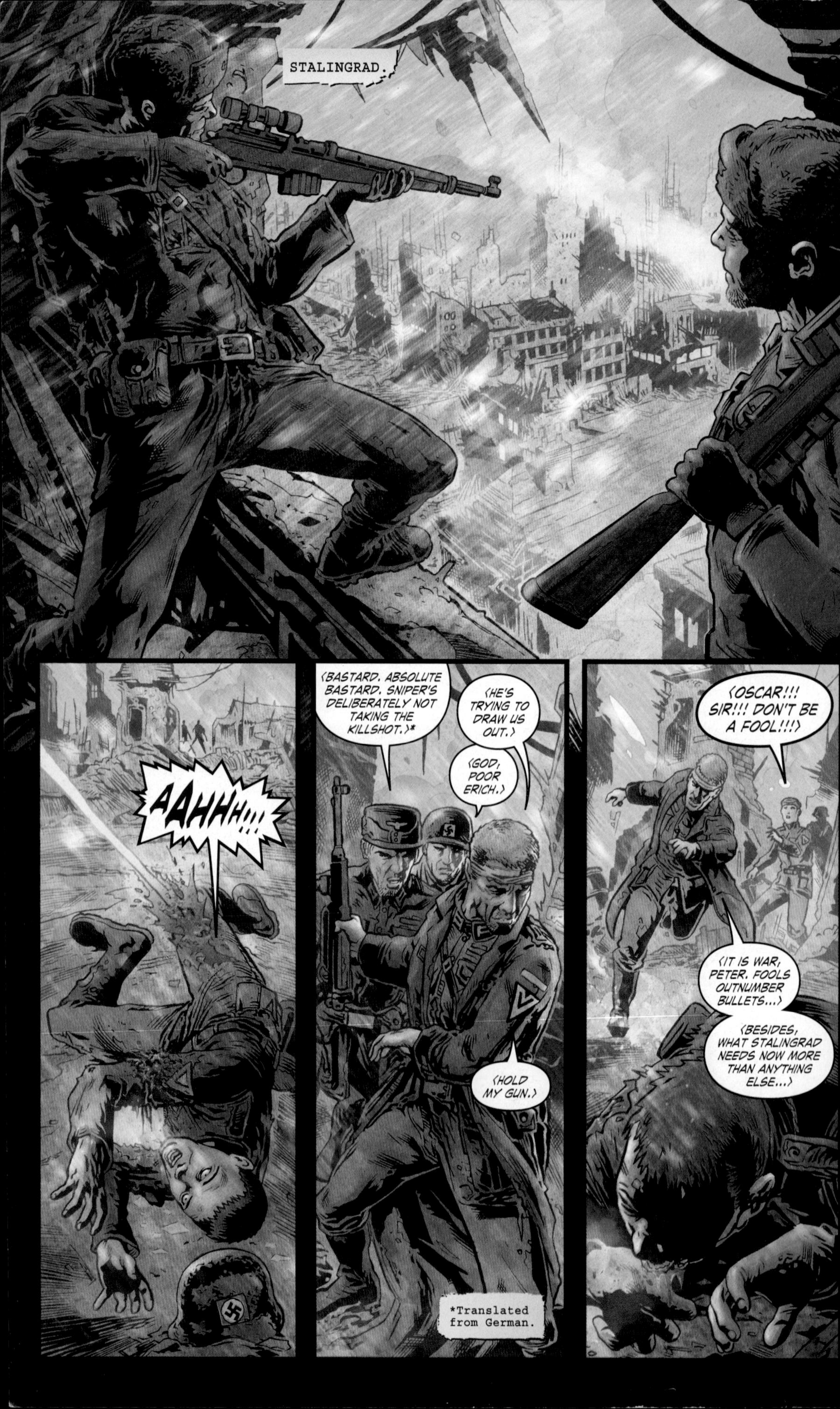
STALINGRAD.
AAHHH!!!
⟨BASTARD. ABSOLUTE BASTARD. SNIPER'S DELIBERATELY NOT TAKING THE KILLSHOT.⟩*
⟨HE'S TRYING TO DRAW US OUT.⟩
⟨GOD, POOR ERICH.⟩
⟨HOLD MY GUN.⟩
*Translated from German.
⟨OSCAR!!! SIR!!! DON'T BE A FOOL!!!⟩
⟨IT IS WAR, PETER. FOOLS OUTNUMBER BULLETS...⟩
⟨BESIDES, WHAT STALINGRAD NEEDS NOW MORE THAN ANYTHING ELSE...⟩

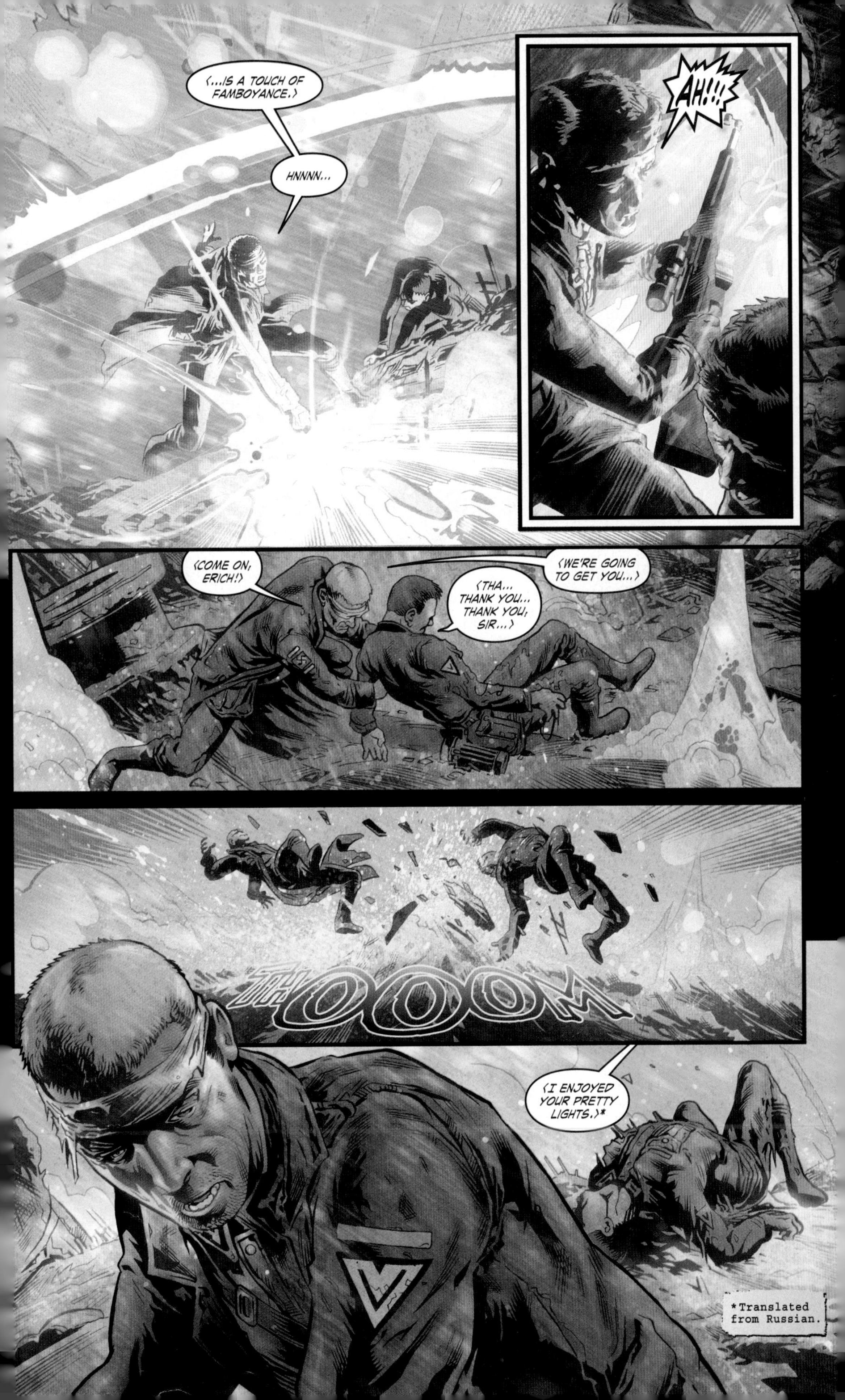

‹...IS A TOUCH OF FAMBOYANCE.›
HNNNN...
AH!!!
‹COME ON, ERICH!›
‹WE'RE GOING TO GET YOU...›
‹THA... THANK YOU... THANK YOU, SIR...›
THOOOM
‹I ENJOYED YOUR PRETTY LIGHTS.›*
*Translated from Russian.

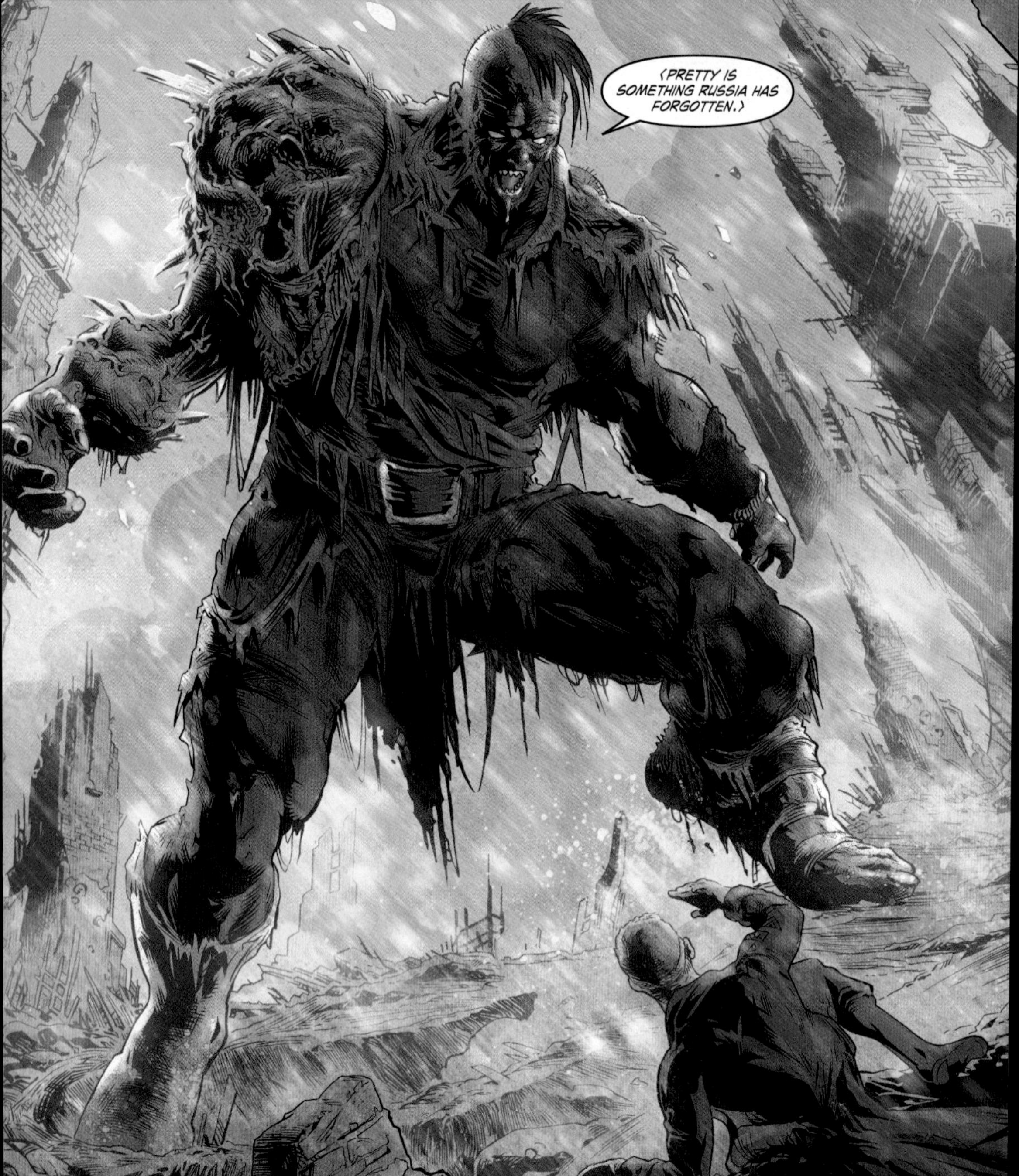
⟨PRETTY IS SOMETHING RUSSIA HAS FORGOTTEN.⟩

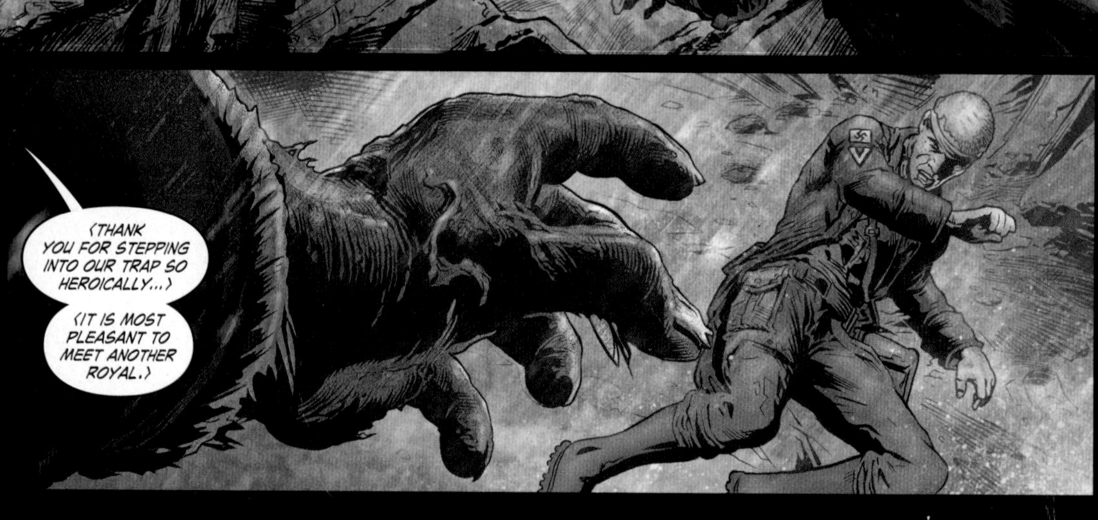
⟨THANK YOU FOR STEPPING INTO OUR TRAP SO HEROICALLY...⟩
⟨IT IS MOST PLEASANT TO MEET ANOTHER ROYAL.⟩

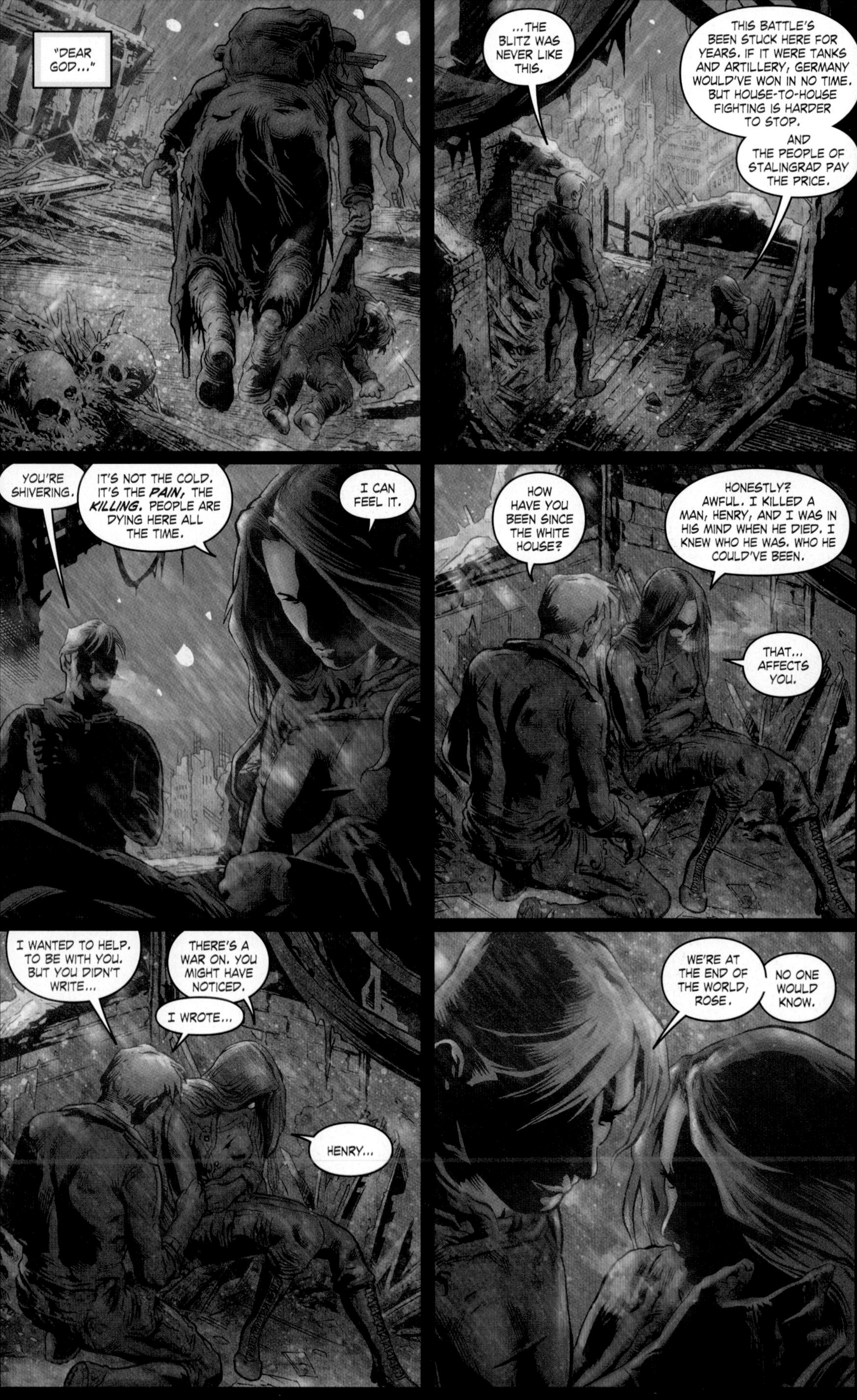
"DEAR GOD..."
...THE BLITZ WAS NEVER LIKE THIS.
THIS BATTLE'S BEEN STUCK HERE FOR YEARS. IF IT WERE TANKS AND ARTILLERY, GERMANY WOULD'VE WON IN NO TIME. BUT HOUSE-TO-HOUSE FIGHTING IS HARDER TO STOP.
AND THE PEOPLE OF STALINGRAD PAY THE PRICE.
YOU'RE SHIVERING.
IT'S NOT THE COLD. IT'S THE PAIN, THE KILLING. PEOPLE ARE DYING HERE ALL THE TIME.
I CAN FEEL IT.
HOW HAVE YOU BEEN SINCE THE WHITE HOUSE?
HONESTLY? AWFUL. I KILLED A MAN, HENRY, AND I WAS IN HIS MIND WHEN HE DIED. I KNEW WHO HE WAS. WHO HE COULD'VE BEEN.
THAT... AFFECTS YOU.
I WANTED TO HELP. TO BE WITH YOU. BUT YOU DIDN'T WRITE...
THERE'S A WAR ON. YOU MIGHT HAVE NOTICED.
I WROTE...
HENRY...
WE'RE AT THE END OF THE WORLD, ROSE.
NO ONE WOULD KNOW.

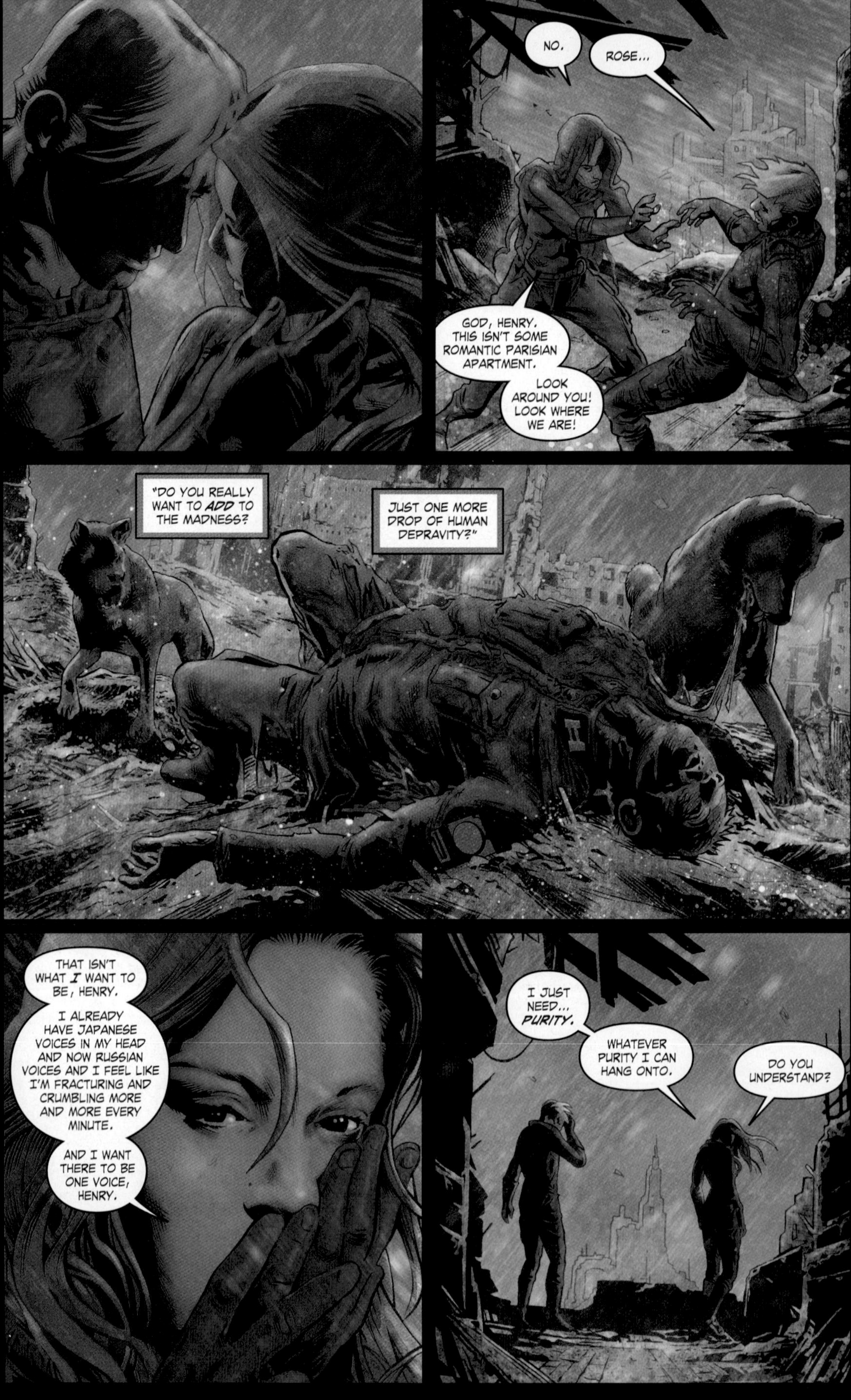
NO.
ROSE...
GOD, HENRY. THIS ISN'T SOME ROMANTIC PARISIAN APARTMENT.
LOOK AROUND YOU! LOOK WHERE WE ARE!
"DO YOU REALLY WANT TO ADD TO THE MADNESS?
JUST ONE MORE DROP OF HUMAN DEPRAVITY?"
THAT ISN'T WHAT I WANT TO BE, HENRY.
I ALREADY HAVE JAPANESE VOICES IN MY HEAD AND NOW RUSSIAN VOICES AND I FEEL LIKE I'M FRACTURING AND CRUMBLING MORE AND MORE EVERY MINUTE.
AND I WANT THERE TO BE ONE VOICE, HENRY.
I JUST NEED... PURITY.
WHATEVER PURITY I CAN HANG ONTO.
DO YOU UNDERSTAND?

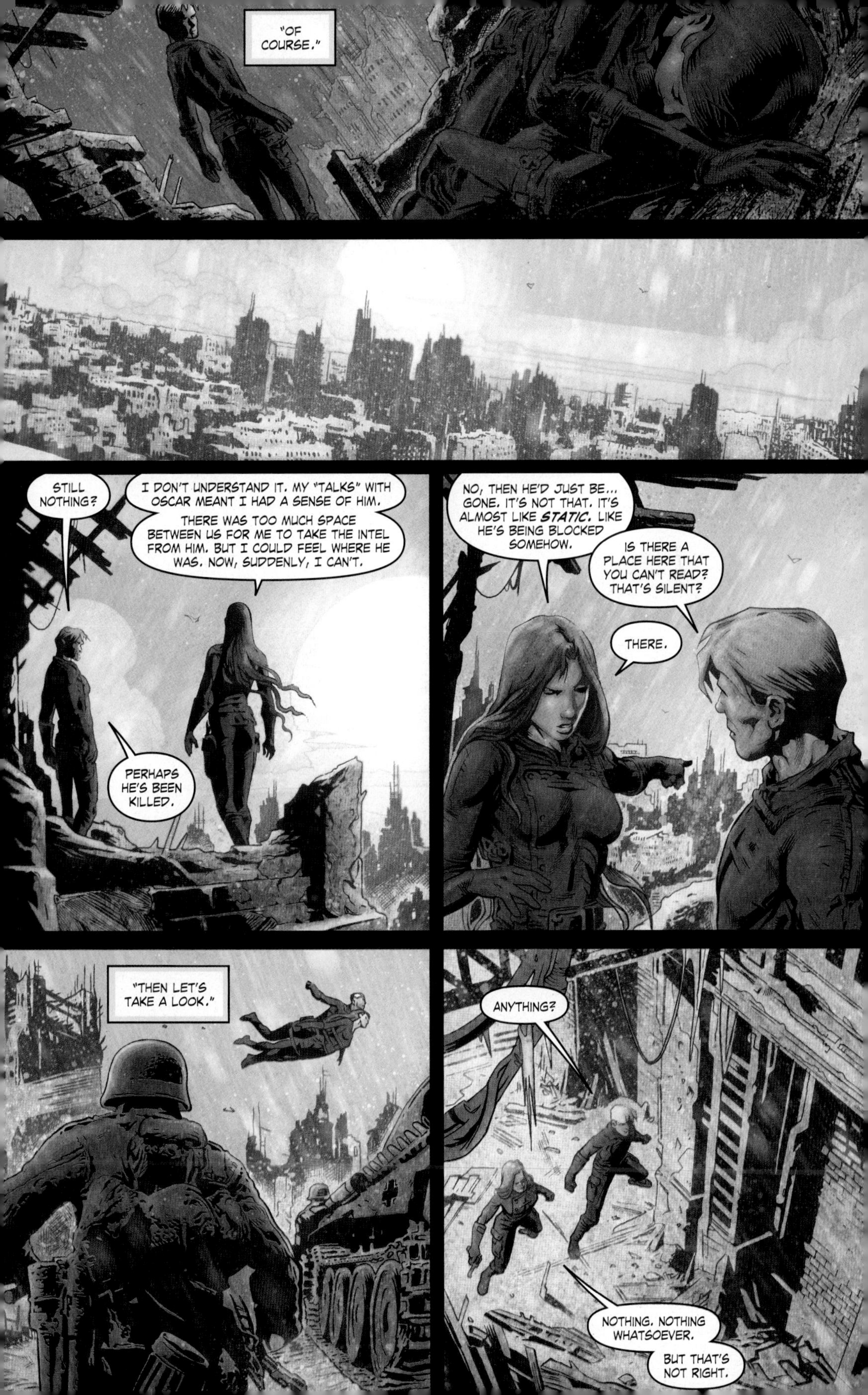
"OF COURSE."
STILL NOTHING?
I DON'T UNDERSTAND IT. MY "TALKS" WITH OSCAR MEANT I HAD A SENSE OF HIM.
THERE WAS TOO MUCH SPACE BETWEEN US FOR ME TO TAKE THE INTEL FROM HIM. BUT I COULD FEEL WHERE HE WAS. NOW, SUDDENLY, I CAN'T.
PERHAPS HE'S BEEN KILLED.
NO, THEN HE'D JUST BE... GONE. IT'S NOT THAT. IT'S ALMOST LIKE STATIC. LIKE HE'S BEING BLOCKED SOMEHOW.
IS THERE A PLACE HERE THAT YOU CAN'T READ? THAT'S SILENT?
THERE.
"THEN LET'S TAKE A LOOK."
ANYTHING?
NOTHING. NOTHING WHATSOEVER.
BUT THAT'S NOT RIGHT.

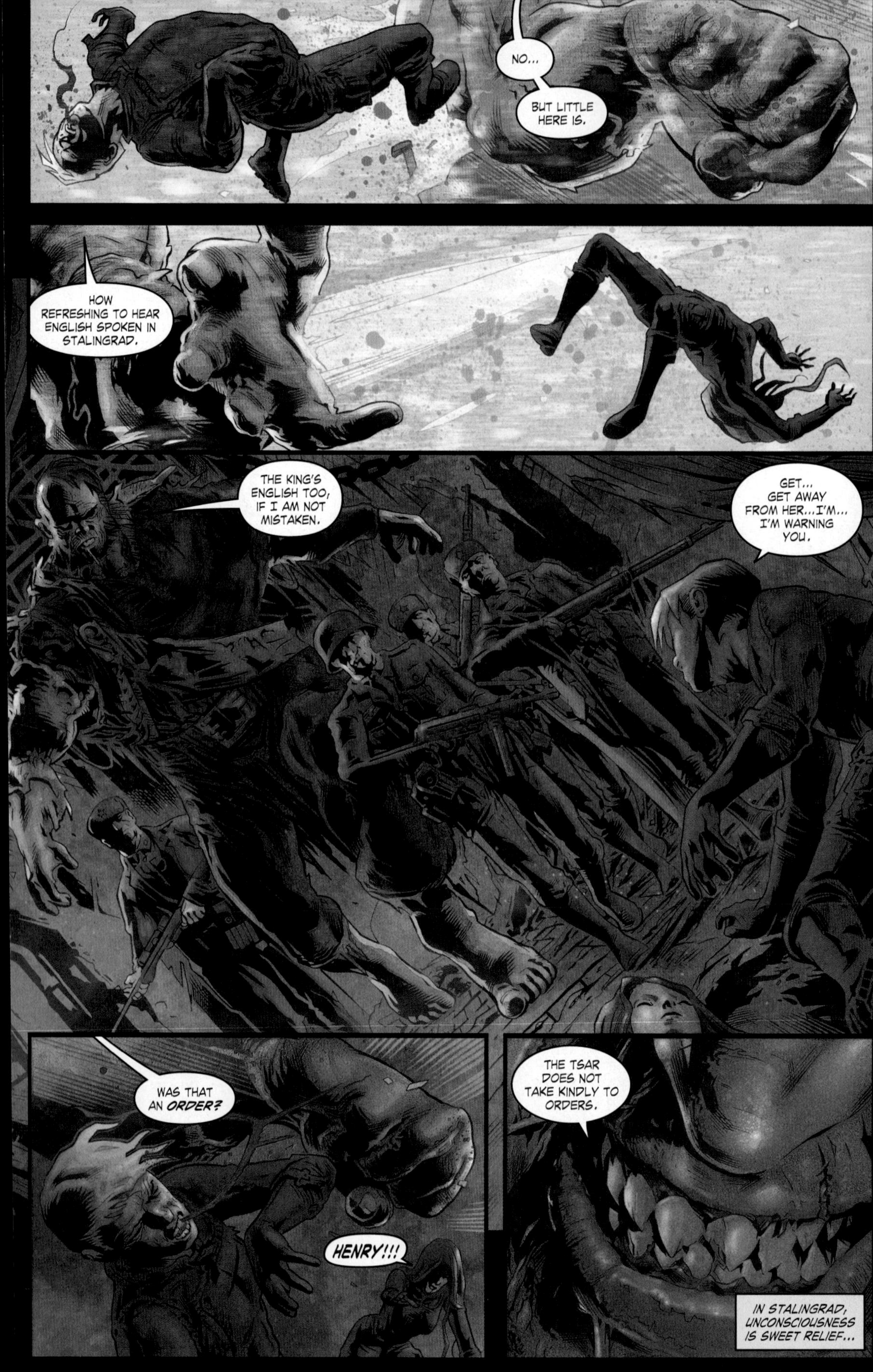
NO...
BUT LITTLE HERE IS.
HOW REFRESHING TO HEAR ENGLISH SPOKEN IN STALINGRAD.
THE KING'S ENGLISH TOO, IF I AM NOT MISTAKEN.
GET... GET AWAY FROM HER...I'M... I'M WARNING YOU.
WAS THAT AN *ORDER?*
HENRY!!!
THE TSAR DOES NOT TAKE KINDLY TO ORDERS.
IN STALINGRAD, UNCONSCIOUSNESS IS SWEET RELIEF...

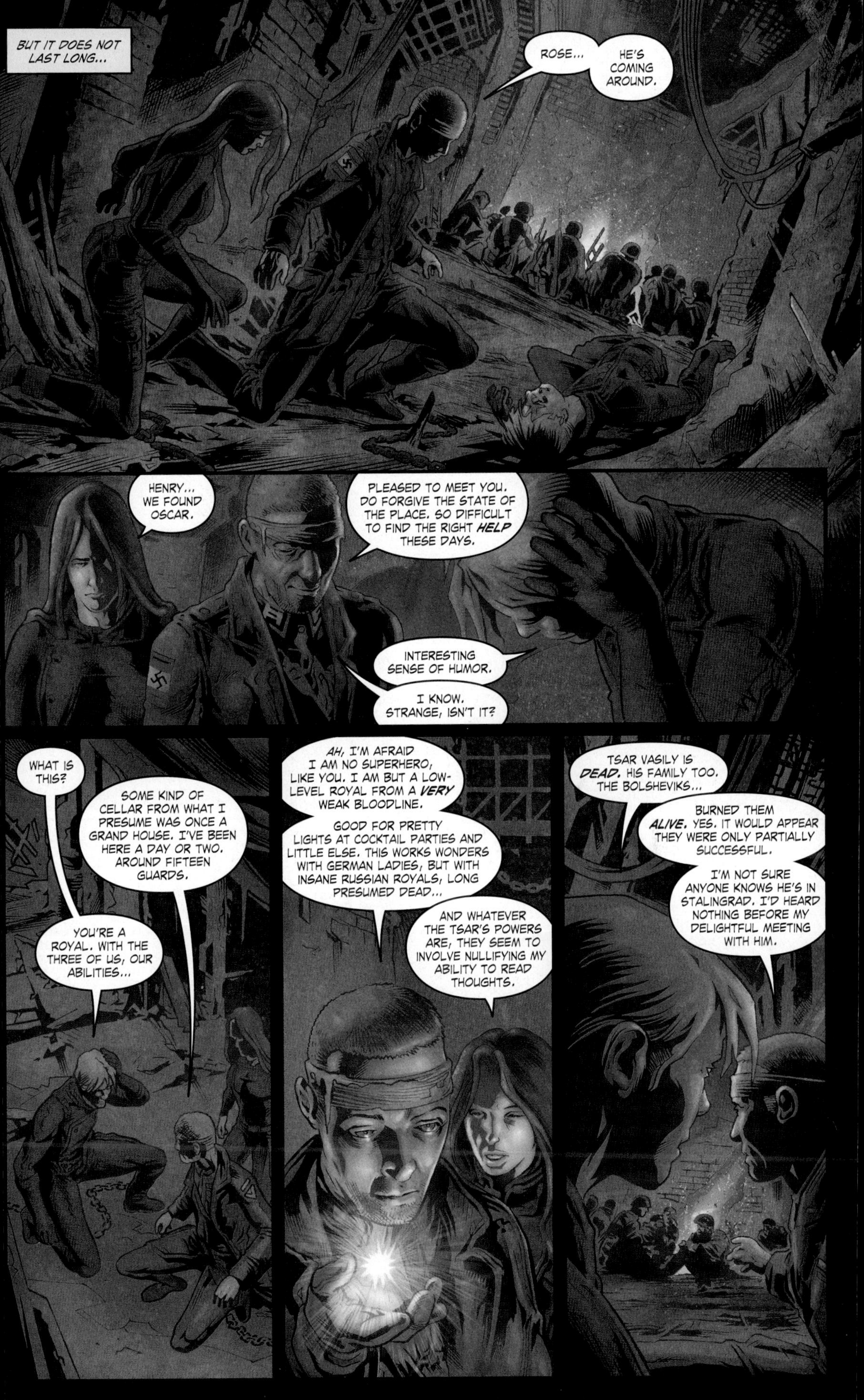
BUT IT DOES NOT LAST LONG...
ROSE...
HE'S COMING AROUND.
HENRY... WE FOUND OSCAR.
PLEASED TO MEET YOU. DO FORGIVE THE STATE OF THE PLACE. SO DIFFICULT TO FIND THE RIGHT HELP THESE DAYS.
INTERESTING SENSE OF HUMOR.
I KNOW. STRANGE, ISN'T IT?
WHAT IS THIS?
SOME KIND OF CELLAR FROM WHAT I PRESUME WAS ONCE A GRAND HOUSE. I'VE BEEN HERE A DAY OR TWO. AROUND FIFTEEN GUARDS.
YOU'RE A ROYAL. WITH THE THREE OF US, OUR ABILITIES...
AH, I'M AFRAID I AM NO SUPERHERO, LIKE YOU. I AM BUT A LOW-LEVEL ROYAL FROM A VERY WEAK BLOODLINE.
GOOD FOR PRETTY LIGHTS AT COCKTAIL PARTIES AND LITTLE ELSE. THIS WORKS WONDERS WITH GERMAN LADIES, BUT WITH INSANE RUSSIAN ROYALS, LONG PRESUMED DEAD...
AND WHATEVER THE TSAR'S POWERS ARE, THEY SEEM TO INVOLVE NULLIFYING MY ABILITY TO READ THOUGHTS.
TSAR VASILY IS DEAD. HIS FAMILY TOO. THE BOLSHEVIKS...
BURNED THEM ALIVE. YES. IT WOULD APPEAR THEY WERE ONLY PARTIALLY SUCCESSFUL.
I'M NOT SURE ANYONE KNOWS HE'S IN STALINGRAD. I'D HEARD NOTHING BEFORE MY DELIGHTFUL MEETING WITH HIM.

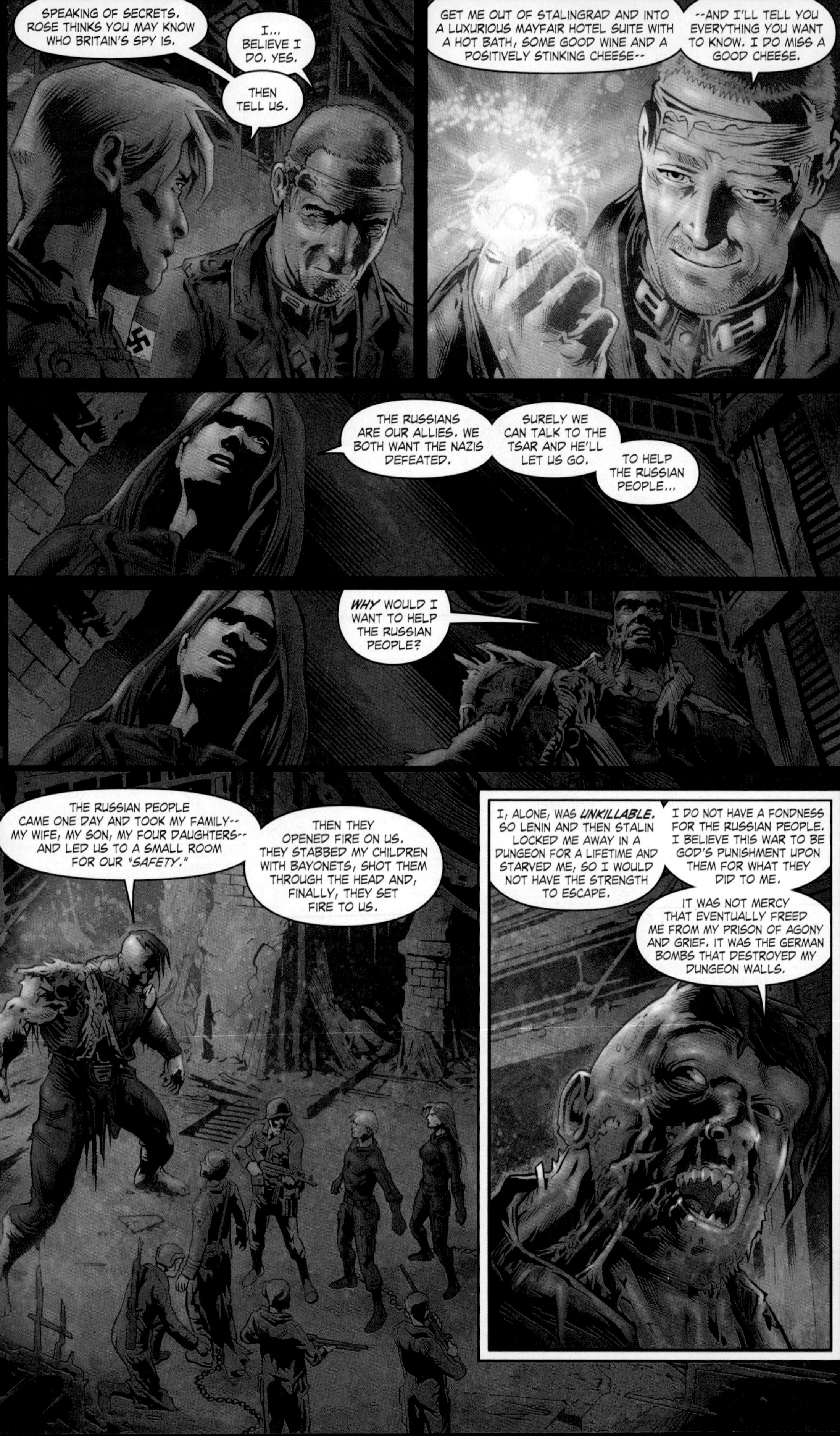
SPEAKING OF SECRETS. ROSE THINKS YOU MAY KNOW WHO BRITAIN'S SPY IS.
I... BELIEVE I DO. YES.
THEN TELL US.
GET ME OUT OF STALINGRAD AND INTO A LUXURIOUS MAYFAIR HOTEL SUITE WITH A HOT BATH, SOME GOOD WINE AND A POSITIVELY STINKING CHEESE--
--AND I'LL TELL YOU EVERYTHING YOU WANT TO KNOW. I DO MISS A GOOD CHEESE.
THE RUSSIANS ARE OUR ALLIES. WE BOTH WANT THE NAZIS DEFEATED.
SURELY WE CAN TALK TO THE TSAR AND HE'LL LET US GO.
TO HELP THE RUSSIAN PEOPLE...
WHY WOULD I WANT TO HELP THE RUSSIAN PEOPLE?
THE RUSSIAN PEOPLE CAME ONE DAY AND TOOK MY FAMILY-- MY WIFE, MY SON, MY FOUR DAUGHTERS-- AND LED US TO A SMALL ROOM FOR OUR "SAFETY."
THEN THEY OPENED FIRE ON US. THEY STABBED MY CHILDREN WITH BAYONETS, SHOT THEM THROUGH THE HEAD AND, FINALLY, THEY SET FIRE TO US.
I, ALONE, WAS UNKILLABLE. SO LENIN AND THEN STALIN LOCKED ME AWAY IN A DUNGEON FOR A LIFETIME AND STARVED ME, SO I WOULD NOT HAVE THE STRENGTH TO ESCAPE.
I DO NOT HAVE A FONDNESS FOR THE RUSSIAN PEOPLE. I BELIEVE THIS WAR TO BE GOD'S PUNISHMENT UPON THEM FOR WHAT THEY DID TO ME.
IT WAS NOT MERCY THAT EVENTUALLY FREED ME FROM MY PRISON OF AGONY AND GRIEF. IT WAS THE GERMAN BOMBS THAT DESTROYED MY DUNGEON WALLS.

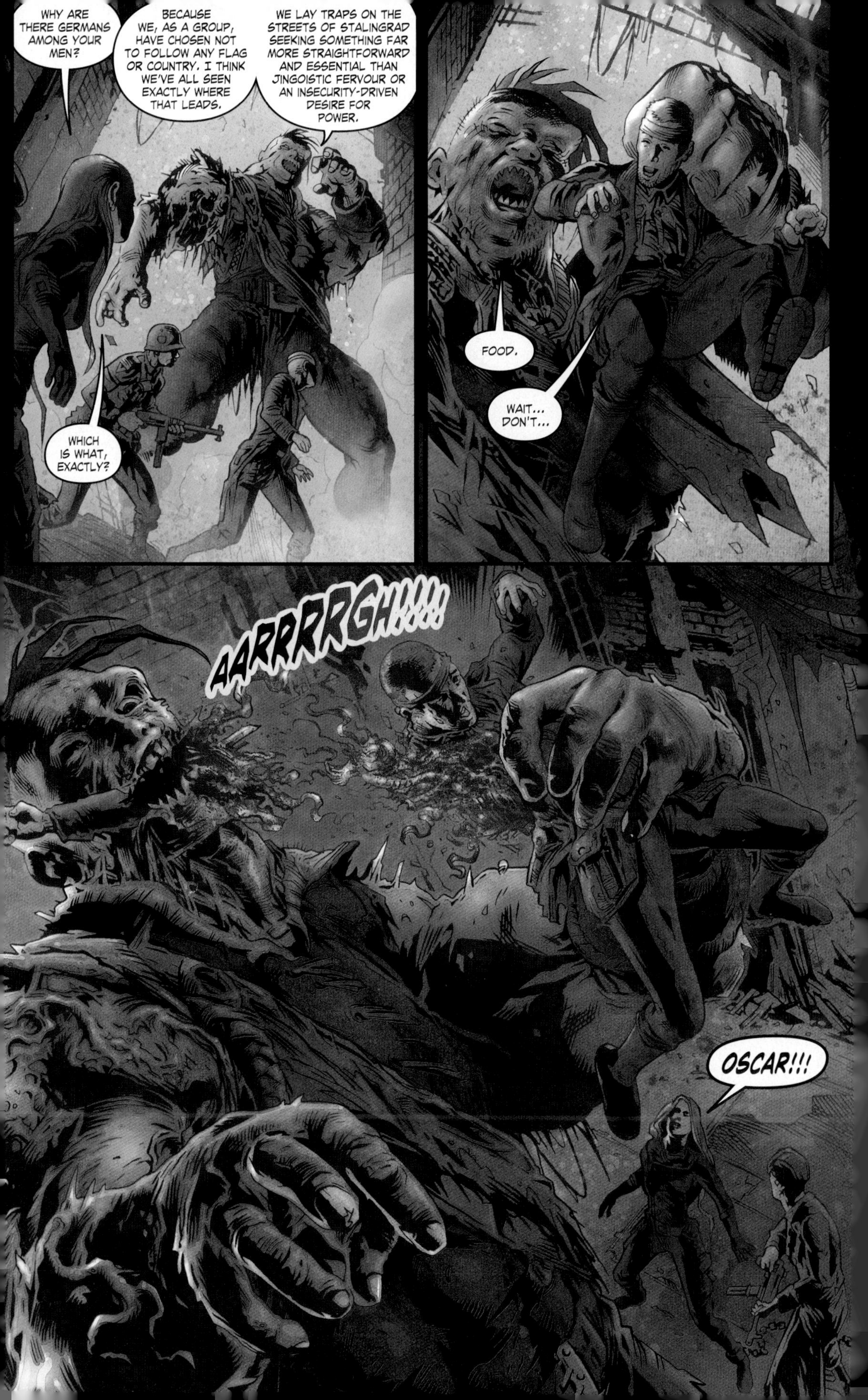
WHY ARE THERE GERMANS AMONG YOUR MEN?
BECAUSE WE, AS A GROUP, HAVE CHOSEN NOT TO FOLLOW ANY FLAG OR COUNTRY. I THINK WE'VE ALL SEEN EXACTLY WHERE THAT LEADS.
WHICH IS WHAT, EXACTLY?
WE LAY TRAPS ON THE STREETS OF STALINGRAD SEEKING SOMETHING FAR MORE STRAIGHTFORWARD AND ESSENTIAL THAN JINGOISTIC FERVOUR OR AN INSECURITY-DRIVEN DESIRE FOR POWER.
FOOD.
WAIT... DON'T...
AARRRRGH!!!!
OSCAR!!!

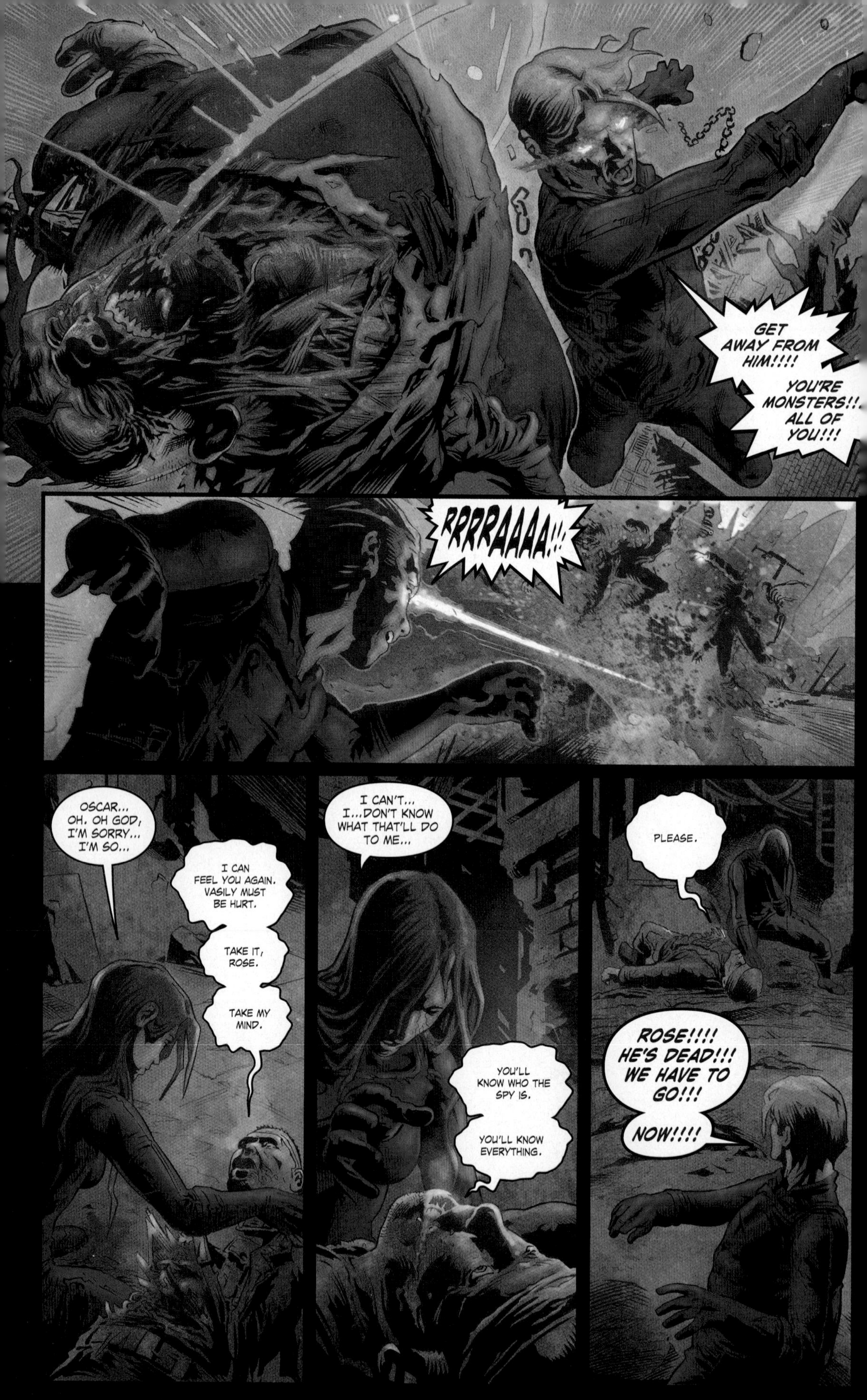
GET AWAY FROM HIM!!!!
YOU'RE MONSTERS!! ALL OF YOU!!!
RRRRAAAA!!!
OSCAR... OH. OH GOD, I'M SORRY... I'M SO...
I CAN FEEL YOU AGAIN. VASILY MUST BE HURT.
TAKE IT, ROSE.
TAKE MY MIND.
I CAN'T... I...DON'T KNOW WHAT THAT'LL DO TO ME...
YOU'LL KNOW WHO THE SPY IS.
YOU'LL KNOW EVERYTHING.
PLEASE.
ROSE!!!! HE'S DEAD!!! WE HAVE TO GO!!!
NOW!!!!

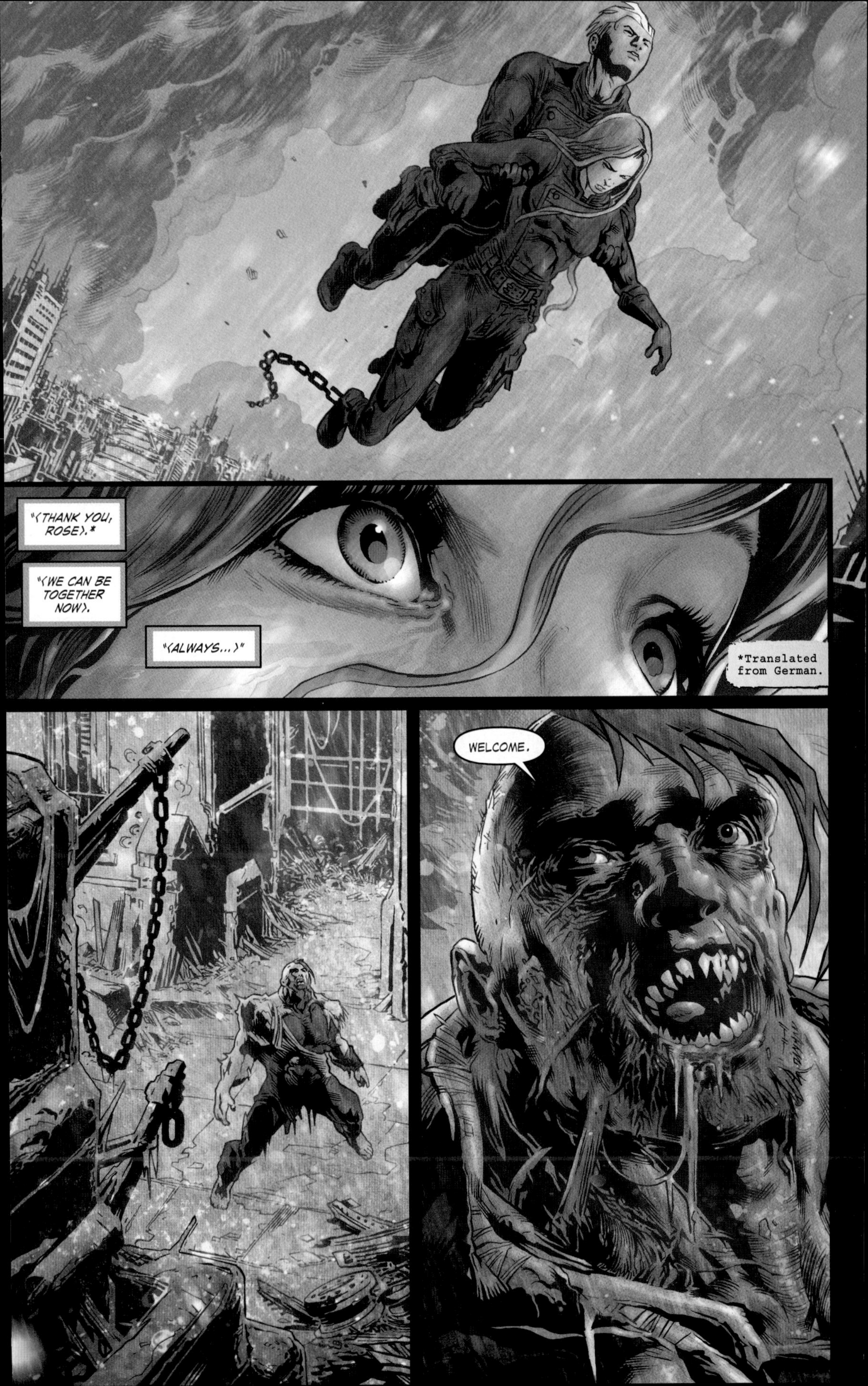
"⟨THANK YOU, ROSE⟩.*
"⟨WE CAN BE TOGETHER NOW⟩.
"⟨ALWAYS...⟩"
*Translated from German.
WELCOME.

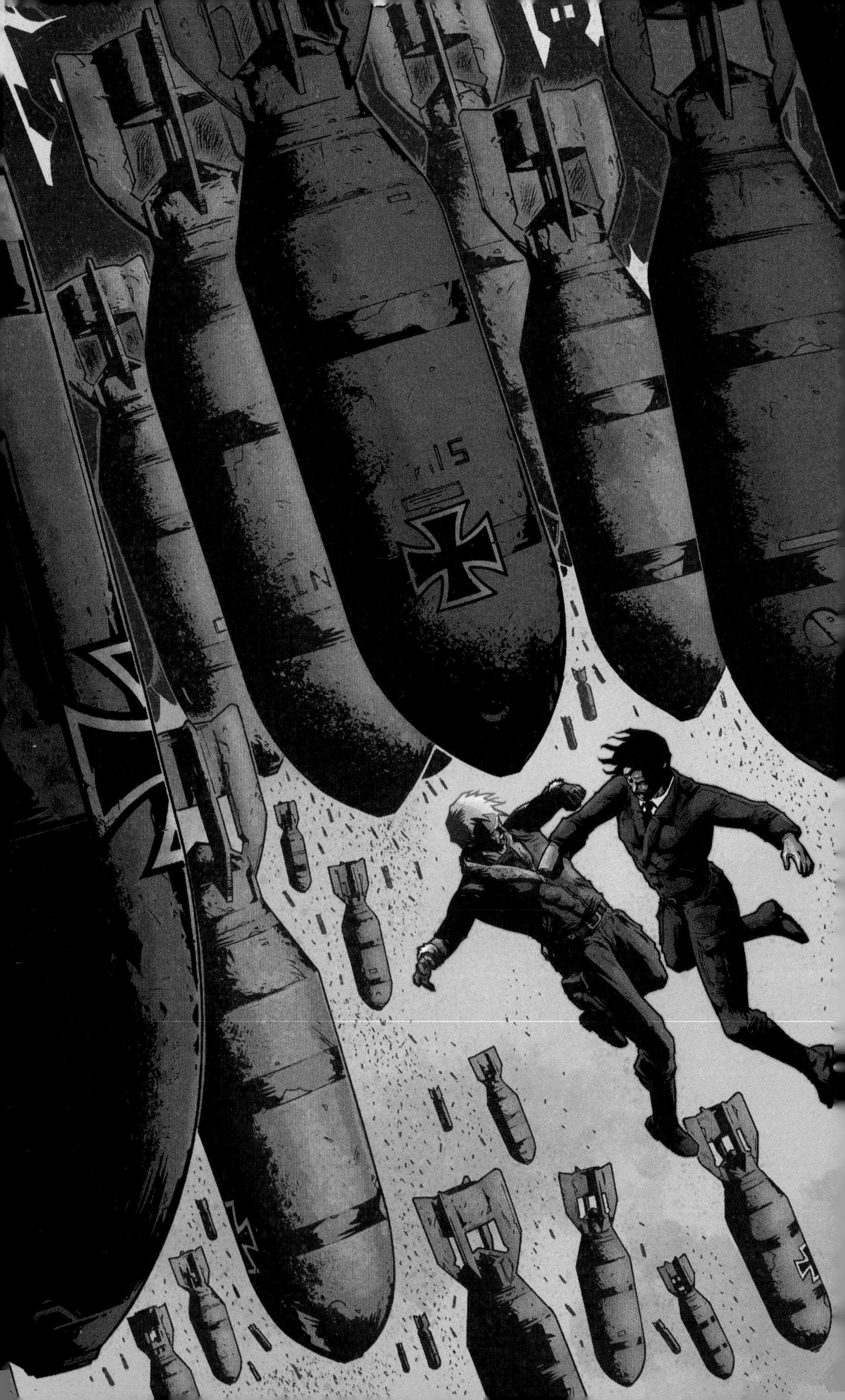
15

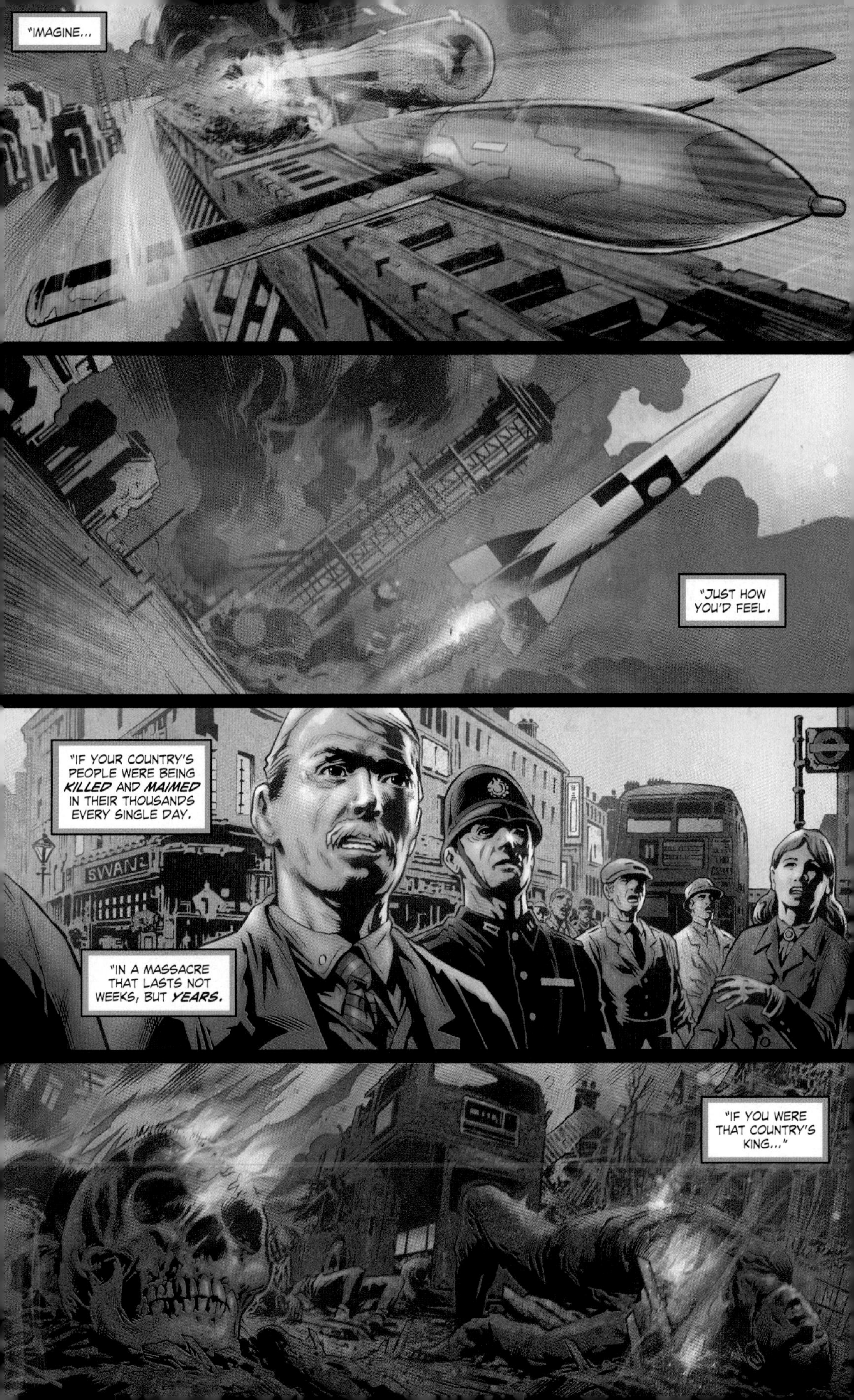
"IMAGINE...
"JUST HOW YOU'D FEEL.
"IF YOUR COUNTRY'S PEOPLE WERE BEING KILLED AND MAIMED IN THEIR THOUSANDS EVERY SINGLE DAY.
SWAN
"IN A MASSACRE THAT LASTS NOT WEEKS, BUT YEARS.
"IF YOU WERE THAT COUNTRY'S KING..."

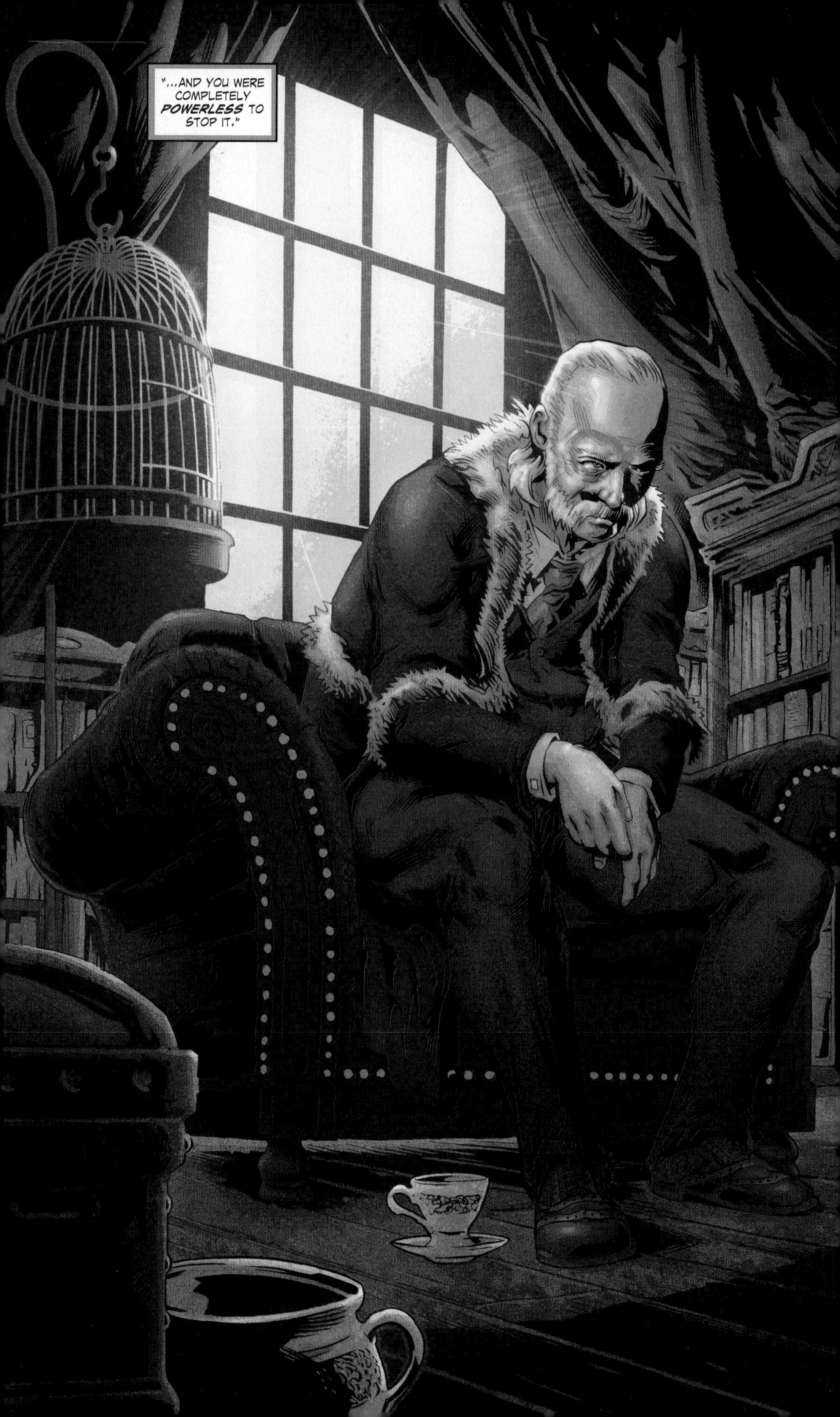
"...AND YOU WERE COMPLETELY POWERLESS TO STOP IT."

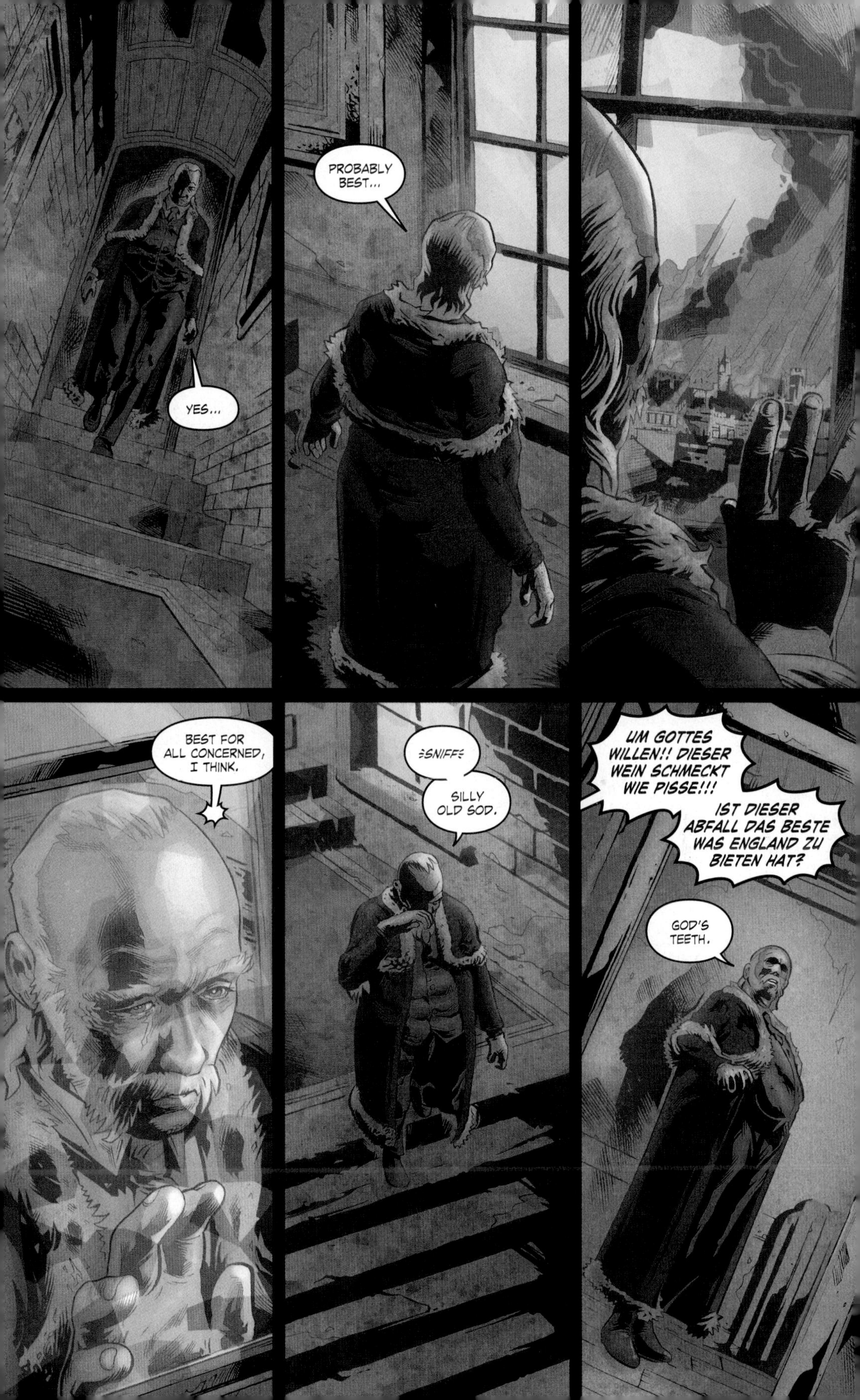
YES...
PROBABLY BEST...
BEST FOR ALL CONCERNED, I THINK.
=SNIFF=
SILLY OLD SOD.
UM GOTTES WILLEN!! DIESER WEIN SCHMECKT WIE PISSE!!!
IST DIESER ABFALL DAS BESTE WAS ENGLAND ZU BIETEN HAT?
GOD'S TEETH.

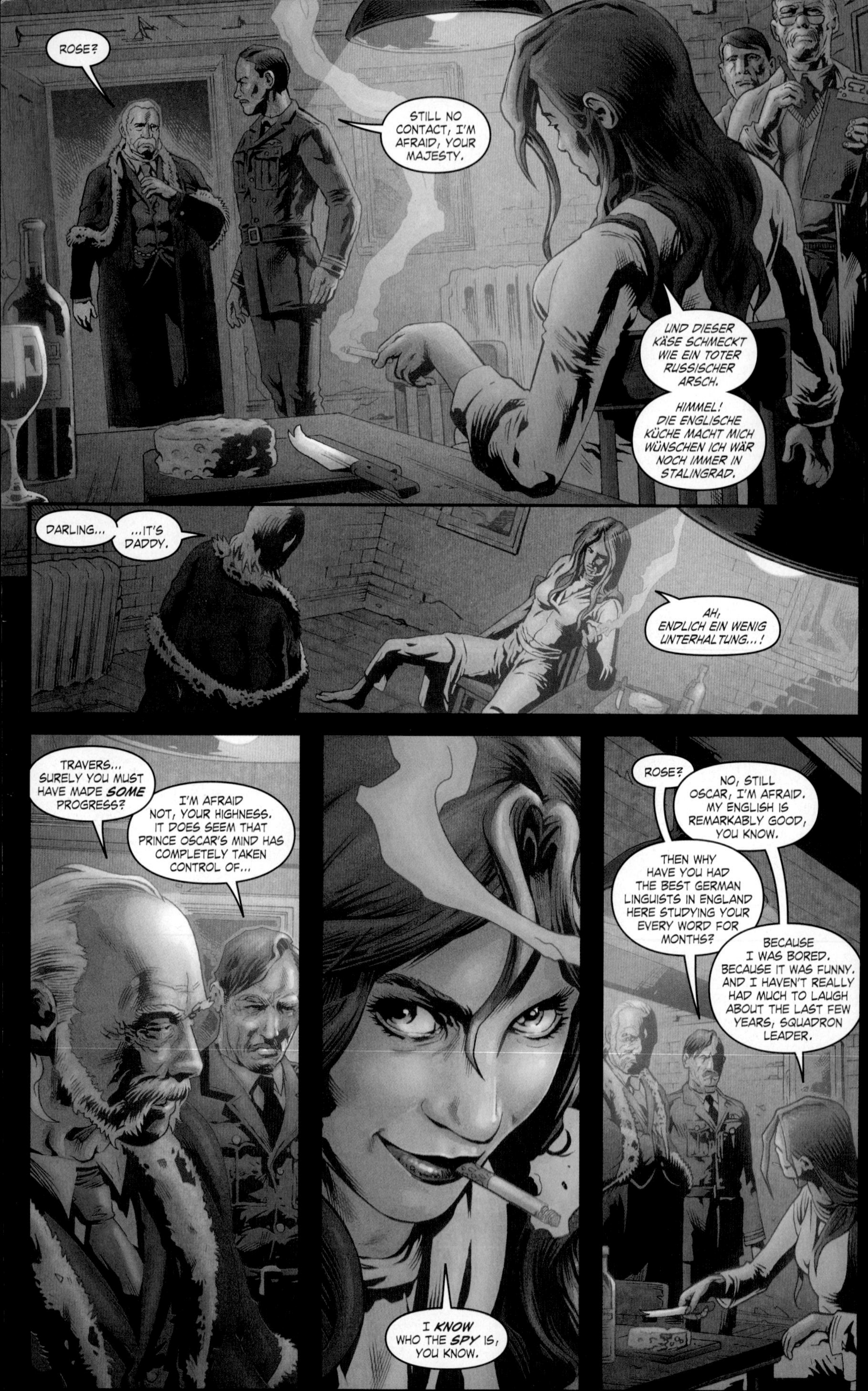
ROSE?
STILL NO CONTACT, I'M AFRAID, YOUR MAJESTY.
UND DIESER KÄSE SCHMECKT WIE EIN TOTER RUSSISCHER ARSCH.
HIMMEL! DIE ENGLISCHE KÜCHE MACHT MICH WÜNSCHEN ICH WÄR NOCH IMMER IN STALINGRAD.
DARLING...
...IT'S DADDY.
AH, ENDLICH EIN WENIG UNTERHALTUNG...!
TRAVERS... SURELY YOU MUST HAVE MADE SOME PROGRESS?
I'M AFRAID NOT, YOUR HIGHNESS. IT DOES SEEM THAT PRINCE OSCAR'S MIND HAS COMPLETELY TAKEN CONTROL OF...
I KNOW WHO THE SPY IS, YOU KNOW.
ROSE?
NO, STILL OSCAR, I'M AFRAID. MY ENGLISH IS REMARKABLY GOOD, YOU KNOW.
THEN WHY HAVE YOU HAD THE BEST GERMAN LINGUISTS IN ENGLAND HERE STUDYING YOUR EVERY WORD FOR MONTHS?
BECAUSE I WAS BORED. BECAUSE IT WAS FUNNY. AND I HAVEN'T REALLY HAD MUCH TO LAUGH ABOUT THE LAST FEW YEARS, SQUADRON LEADER.

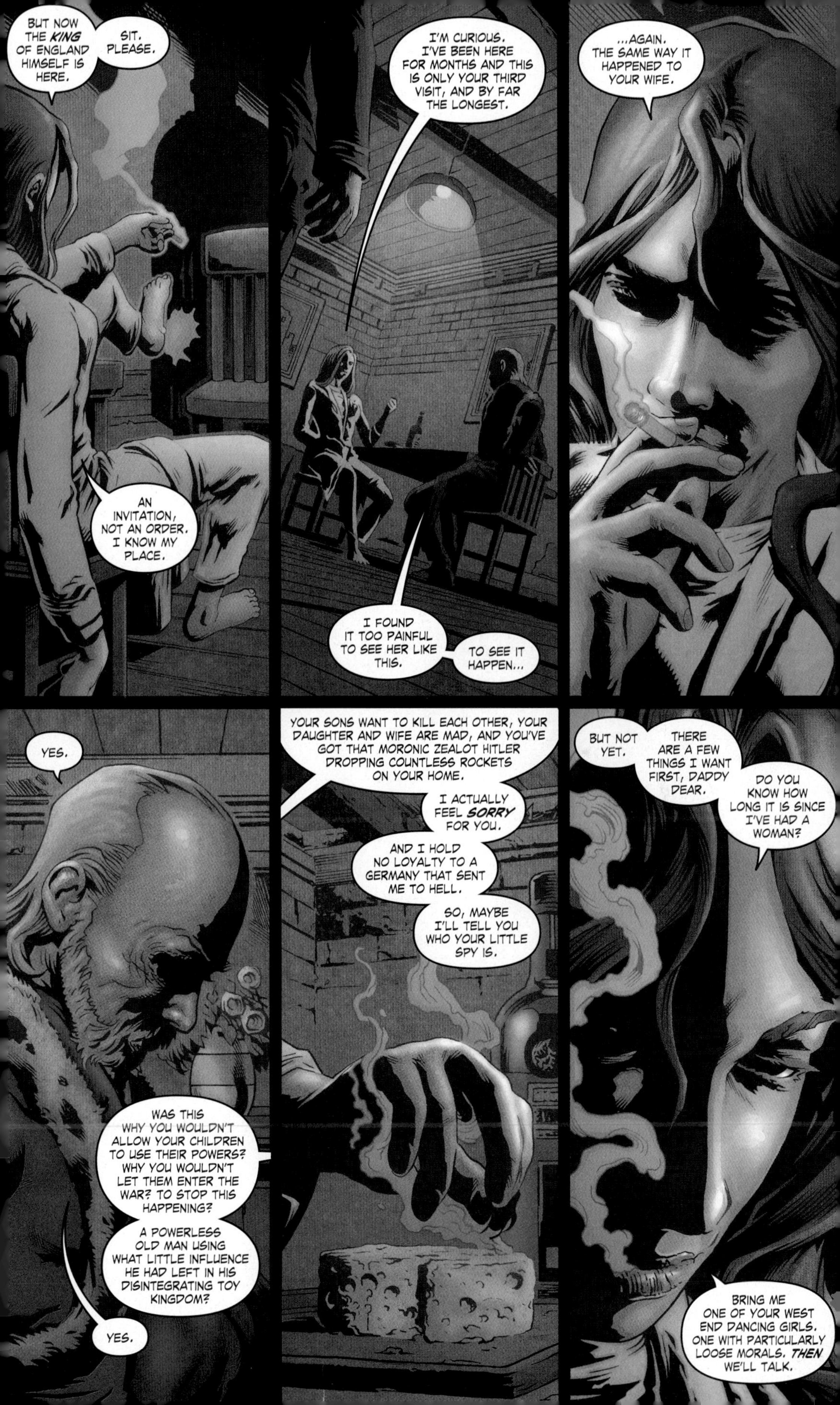

BUT NOW THE KING OF ENGLAND HIMSELF IS HERE.
SIT. PLEASE.
AN INVITATION, NOT AN ORDER. I KNOW MY PLACE.
I'M CURIOUS. I'VE BEEN HERE FOR MONTHS AND THIS IS ONLY YOUR THIRD VISIT, AND BY FAR THE LONGEST.
I FOUND IT TOO PAINFUL TO SEE HER LIKE THIS.
TO SEE IT HAPPEN...
...AGAIN. THE SAME WAY IT HAPPENED TO YOUR WIFE.
YES.
WAS THIS WHY YOU WOULDN'T ALLOW YOUR CHILDREN TO USE THEIR POWERS? WHY YOU WOULDN'T LET THEM ENTER THE WAR? TO STOP THIS HAPPENING?
A POWERLESS OLD MAN USING WHAT LITTLE INFLUENCE HE HAD LEFT IN HIS DISINTEGRATING TOY KINGDOM?
YES.
YOUR SONS WANT TO KILL EACH OTHER, YOUR DAUGHTER AND WIFE ARE MAD, AND YOU'VE GOT THAT MORONIC ZEALOT HITLER DROPPING COUNTLESS ROCKETS ON YOUR HOME.
I ACTUALLY FEEL SORRY FOR YOU.
AND I HOLD NO LOYALTY TO A GERMANY THAT SENT ME TO HELL.
SO, MAYBE I'LL TELL YOU WHO YOUR LITTLE SPY IS.
BUT NOT YET.
THERE ARE A FEW THINGS I WANT FIRST, DADDY DEAR.
DO YOU KNOW HOW LONG IT IS SINCE I'VE HAD A WOMAN?
BRING ME ONE OF YOUR WEST END DANCING GIRLS. ONE WITH PARTICULARLY LOOSE MORALS. THEN WE'LL TALK.

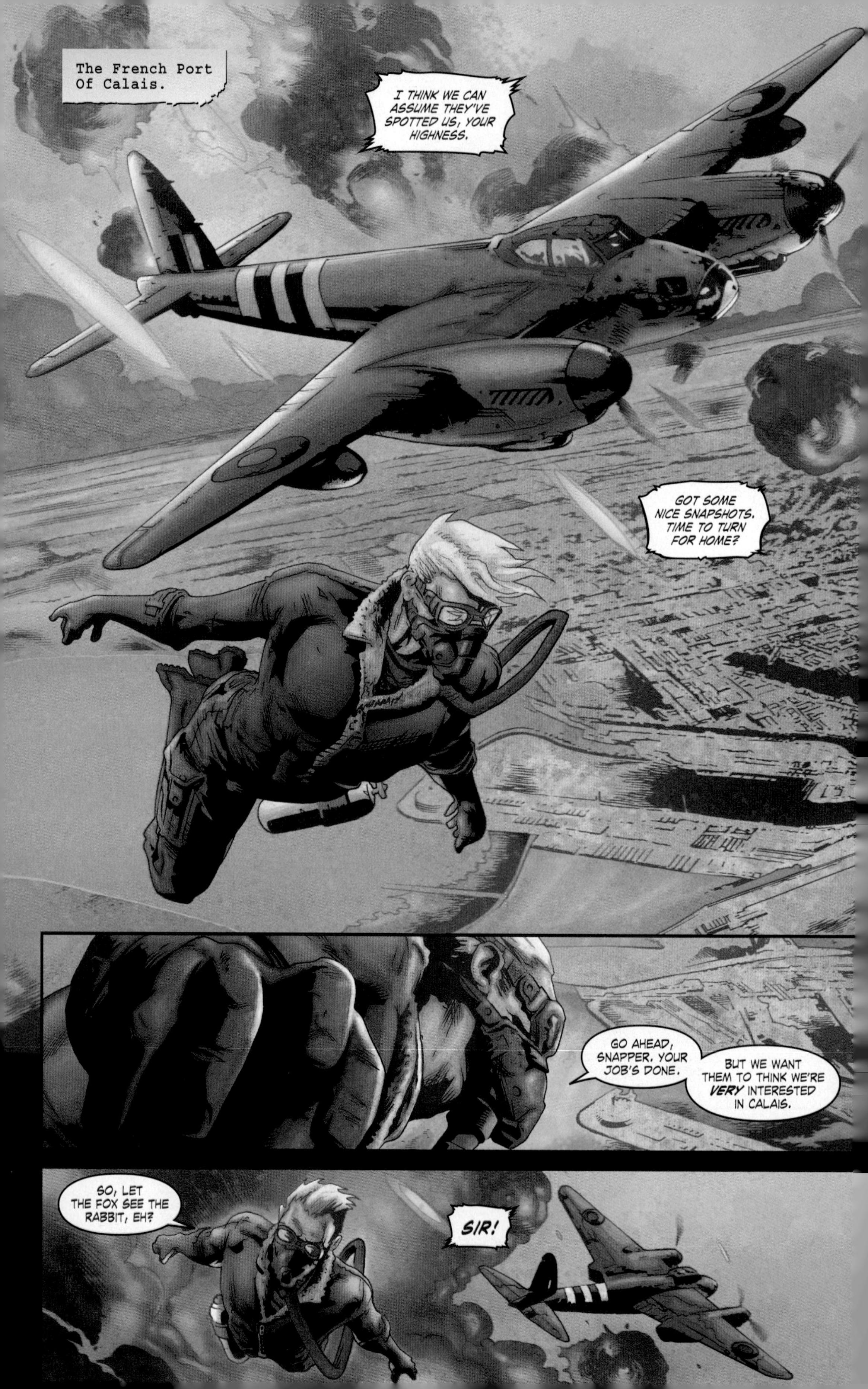
The French Port Of Calais.
I THINK WE CAN ASSUME THEY'VE SPOTTED US, YOUR HIGHNESS.
GOT SOME NICE SNAPSHOTS. TIME TO TURN FOR HOME?
GO AHEAD, SNAPPER. YOUR JOB'S DONE.
BUT WE WANT THEM TO THINK WE'RE VERY INTERESTED IN CALAIS.
SO, LET THE FOX SEE THE RABBIT, EH?
SIR!

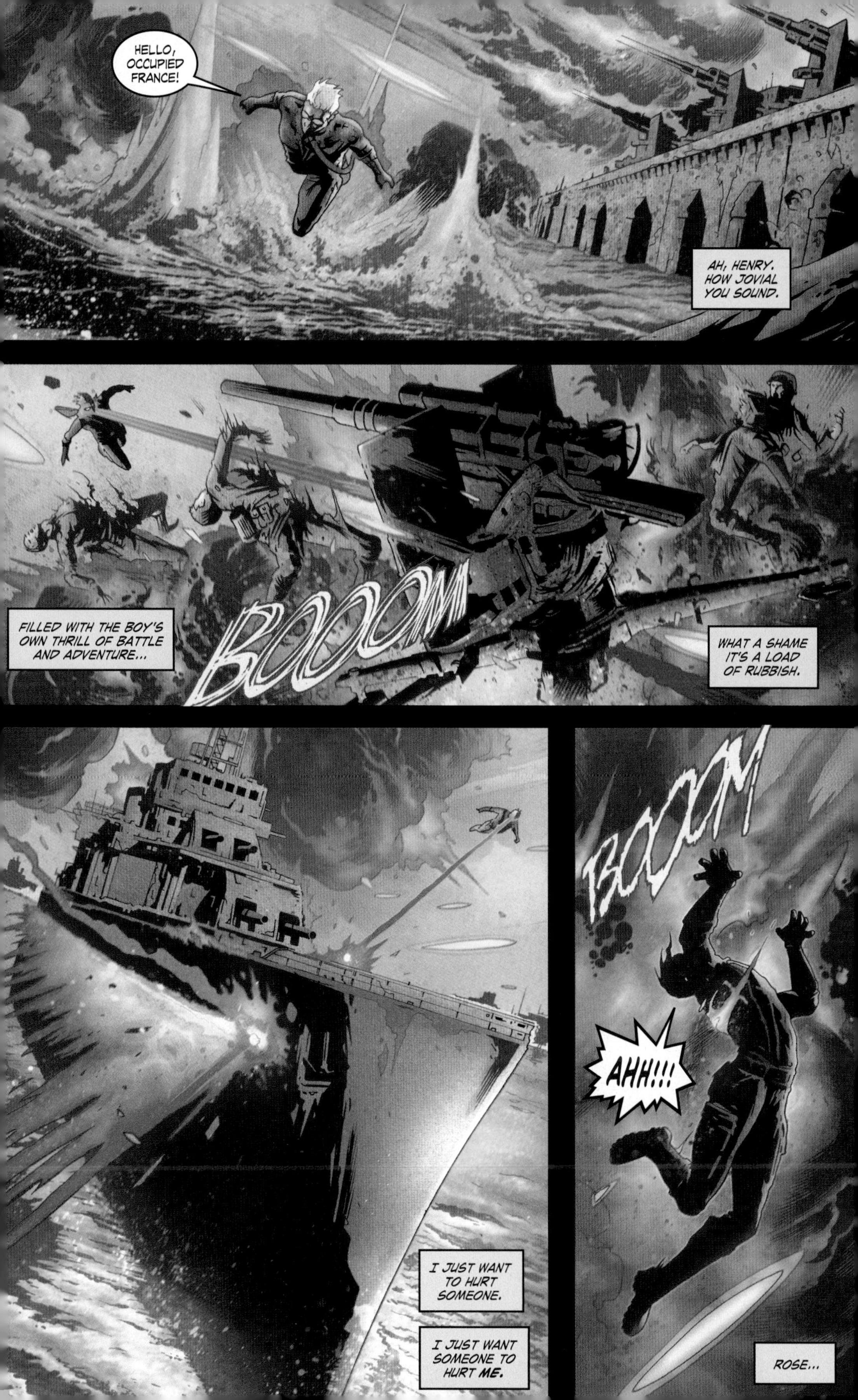
HELLO, OCCUPIED FRANCE!
AH, HENRY. HOW JOVIAL YOU SOUND.
FILLED WITH THE BOY'S OWN THRILL OF BATTLE AND ADVENTURE...
BOOOOM
WHAT A SHAME IT'S A LOAD OF RUBBISH.
I JUST WANT TO HURT SOMEONE.
I JUST WANT SOMEONE TO HURT **ME**.
BOOOM
AHH!!!
ROSE...

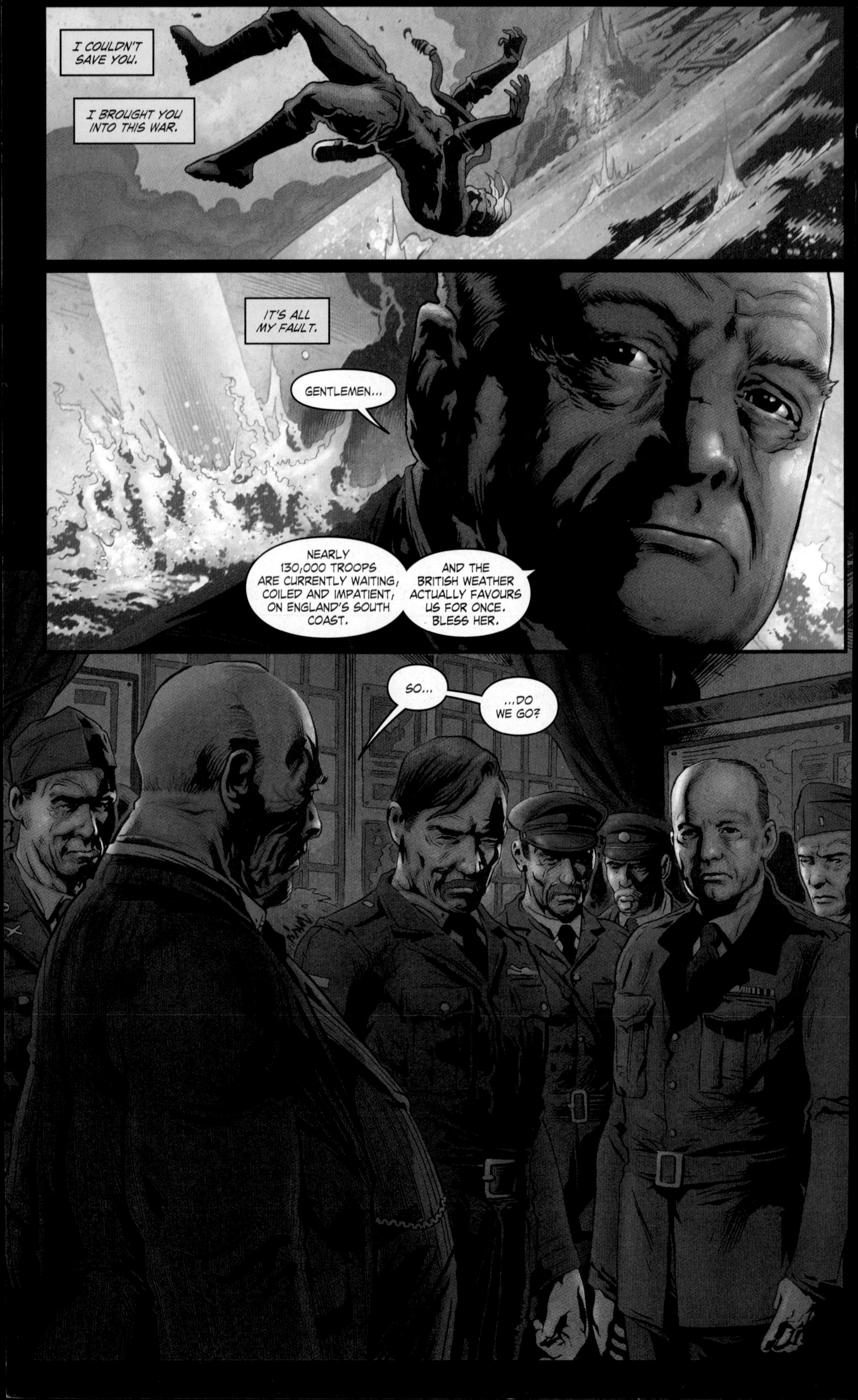

I COULDN'T SAVE YOU.
I BROUGHT YOU INTO THIS WAR.
IT'S ALL MY FAULT.
GENTLEMEN...
NEARLY 130,000 TROOPS ARE CURRENTLY WAITING, COILED AND IMPATIENT, ON ENGLAND'S SOUTH COAST.
AND THE BRITISH WEATHER ACTUALLY FAVOURS US FOR ONCE. BLESS HER.
SO...
...DO WE GO?

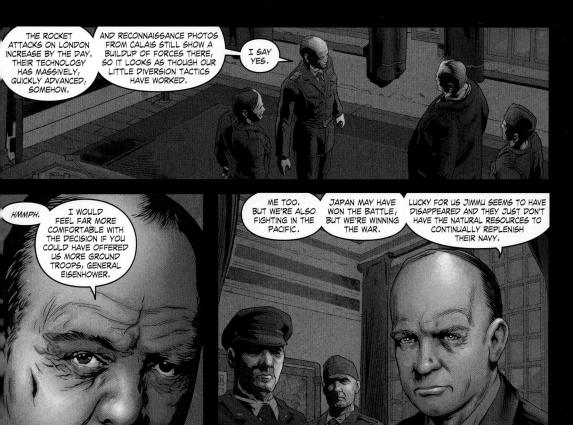

THE ROCKET ATTACKS ON LONDON INCREASE BY THE DAY. THEIR TECHNOLOGY HAS MASSIVELY, QUICKLY ADVANCED, SOMEHOW.

AND RECONNAISSANCE PHOTOS FROM CALAIS STILL SHOW A BUILDUP OF FORCES THERE, SO IT LOOKS AS THOUGH OUR LITTLE DIVERSION TACTICS HAVE WORKED.

I SAY YES.

HMMPH. I WOULD FEEL FAR MORE COMFORTABLE WITH THE DECISION IF YOU COULD HAVE OFFERED US MORE GROUND TROOPS, GENERAL EISENHOWER.

ME TOO. BUT WE'RE ALSO FIGHTING IN THE PACIFIC.

JAPAN MAY HAVE WON THE BATTLE, BUT WE'RE WINNING THE WAR.

LUCKY FOR US JIMMU SEEMS TO HAVE DISAPPEARED AND THEY JUST DON'T HAVE THE NATURAL RESOURCES TO CONTINUALLY REPLENISH THEIR NAVY.

WE DO. BUT THAT TAKES FOCUS, TIME AND MANPOWER.

BESIDES, NUMBERS AIN'T THE MAIN QUESTION AT THIS POINT. I THINK WE BOTH KNOW THAT.

INDEED.

SURPRISE IS ALL. WHICH BRINGS US TO THE QUESTION OF OUR TROUBLESOME SPY, SQUADRON LEADER TRAVERS.

STILL NOTHING; I'M AFRAID. PRINCE OSCAR CONTINUES TO TEASE.

AND IT'S DIFFICULT TO...CONVINCE HIM OTHERWISE WHEN IT WOULD MEAN DOING HARM TO PRINCESS ROSE IN THE PROCESS.

DAMMIT.

WELL, IT'D HELP IF WE HAD A COUPLE OF ROYALS WITH US WHEN WE HIT THOSE BEACHES.

YOU'LL HAVE THEM.

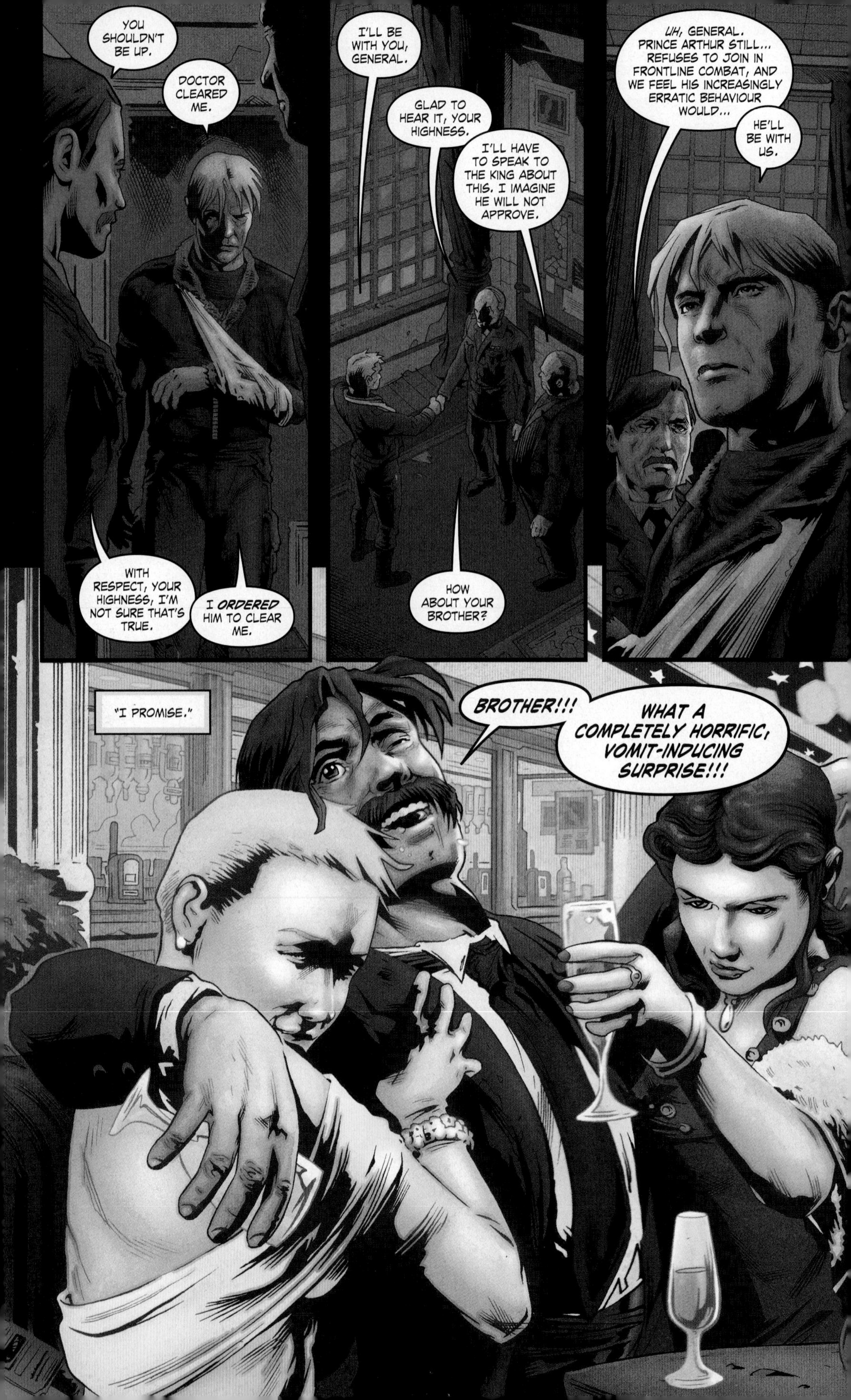
YOU SHOULDN'T BE UP.
DOCTOR CLEARED ME.
WITH RESPECT, YOUR HIGHNESS, I'M NOT SURE THAT'S TRUE.
I *ORDERED* HIM TO CLEAR ME.
I'LL BE WITH YOU, GENERAL.
GLAD TO HEAR IT, YOUR HIGHNESS.
I'LL HAVE TO SPEAK TO THE KING ABOUT THIS. I IMAGINE HE WILL NOT APPROVE.
HOW ABOUT YOUR BROTHER?
UH, GENERAL. PRINCE ARTHUR STILL... REFUSES TO JOIN IN FRONTLINE COMBAT, AND WE FEEL HIS INCREASINGLY ERRATIC BEHAVIOUR WOULD...
HE'LL BE WITH US.
"I PROMISE."
BROTHER!!!
WHAT A COMPLETELY HORRIFIC, VOMIT-INDUCING SURPRISE!!!

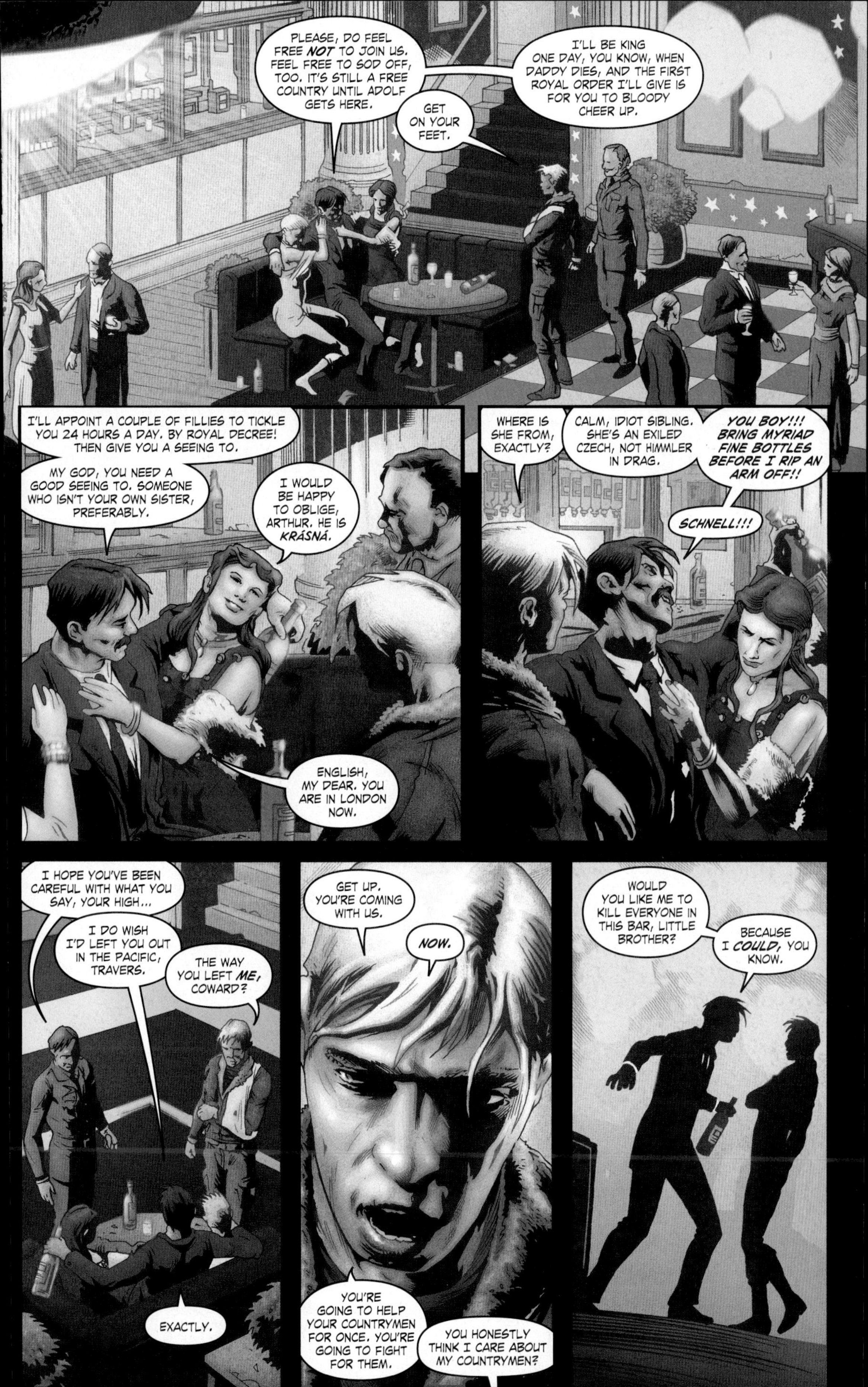
PLEASE, DO FEEL FREE **NOT** TO JOIN US. FEEL FREE TO SOD OFF, TOO. IT'S STILL A FREE COUNTRY UNTIL ADOLF GETS HERE.
GET ON YOUR FEET.
I'LL BE KING ONE DAY, YOU KNOW, WHEN DADDY DIES, AND THE FIRST ROYAL ORDER I'LL GIVE IS FOR YOU TO BLOODY CHEER UP.
I'LL APPOINT A COUPLE OF FILLIES TO TICKLE YOU 24 HOURS A DAY. BY ROYAL DECREE! THEN GIVE YOU A SEEING TO.
MY GOD, YOU NEED A GOOD SEEING TO. SOMEONE WHO ISN'T YOUR OWN SISTER, PREFERABLY.
I WOULD BE HAPPY TO OBLIGE, ARTHUR. HE IS **KRÁSNÁ**.
ENGLISH, MY DEAR. YOU ARE IN LONDON NOW.
WHERE IS SHE FROM, EXACTLY?
CALM, IDIOT SIBLING. SHE'S AN EXILED CZECH, NOT HIMMLER IN DRAG.
YOU BOY!!! BRING MYRIAD FINE BOTTLES BEFORE I RIP AN ARM OFF!!
SCHNELL!!!
I HOPE YOU'VE BEEN CAREFUL WITH WHAT YOU SAY, YOUR HIGH...
I DO WISH I'D LEFT YOU OUT IN THE PACIFIC, TRAVERS.
THE WAY YOU LEFT **ME,** COWARD?
EXACTLY.
GET UP. YOU'RE COMING WITH US.
NOW.
YOU'RE GOING TO HELP YOUR COUNTRYMEN FOR ONCE. YOU'RE GOING TO FIGHT FOR THEM.
YOU HONESTLY THINK I CARE ABOUT MY COUNTRYMEN?
WOULD YOU LIKE ME TO KILL EVERYONE IN THIS BAR, LITTLE BROTHER?
BECAUSE I ***COULD,*** YOU KNOW.

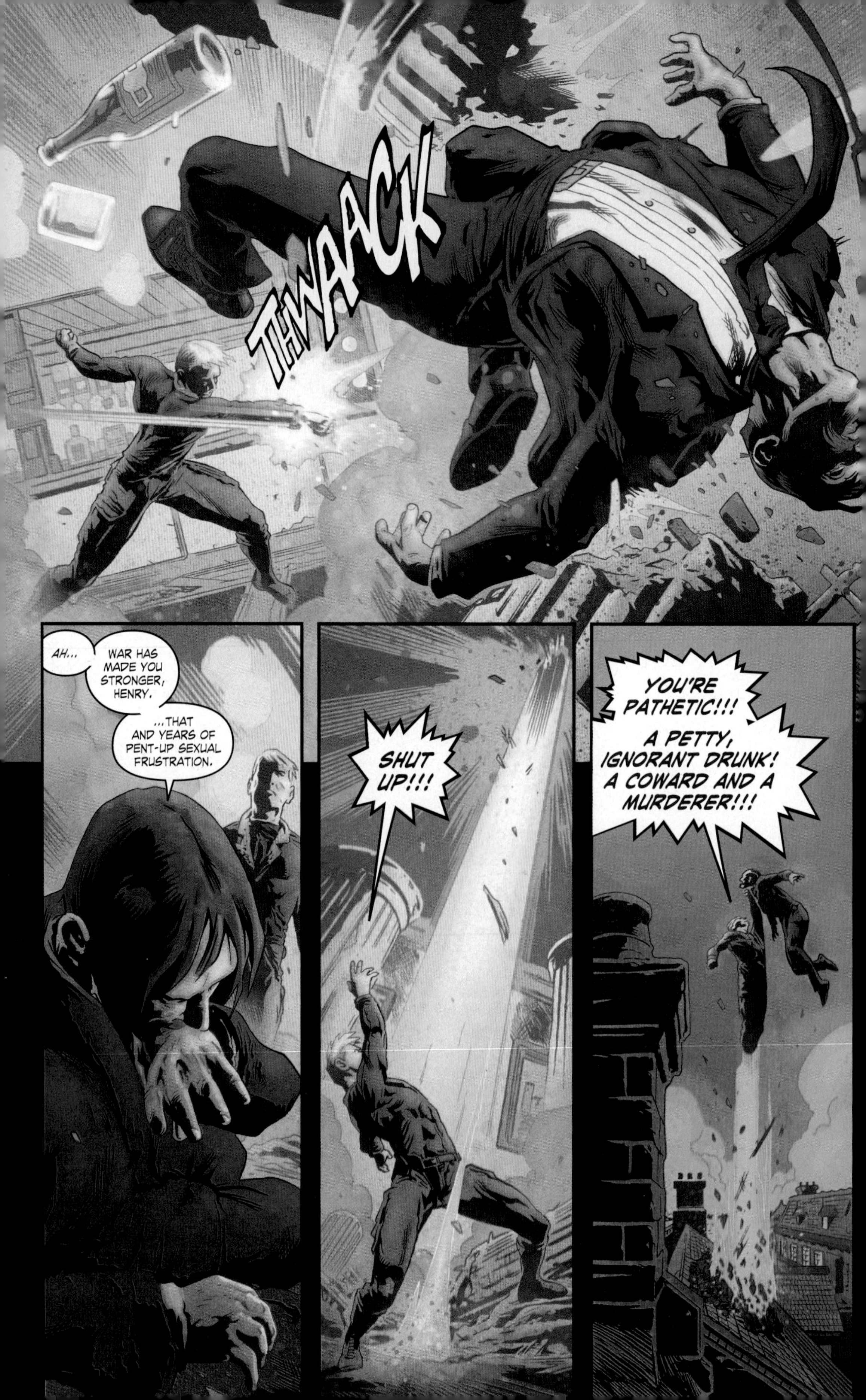
THWAACK
AH...
WAR HAS MADE YOU STRONGER, HENRY.
...THAT AND YEARS OF PENT-UP SEXUAL FRUSTRATION.
SHUT UP!!!
YOU'RE PATHETIC!!!
A PETTY, IGNORANT DRUNK! A COWARD AND A MURDERER!!!

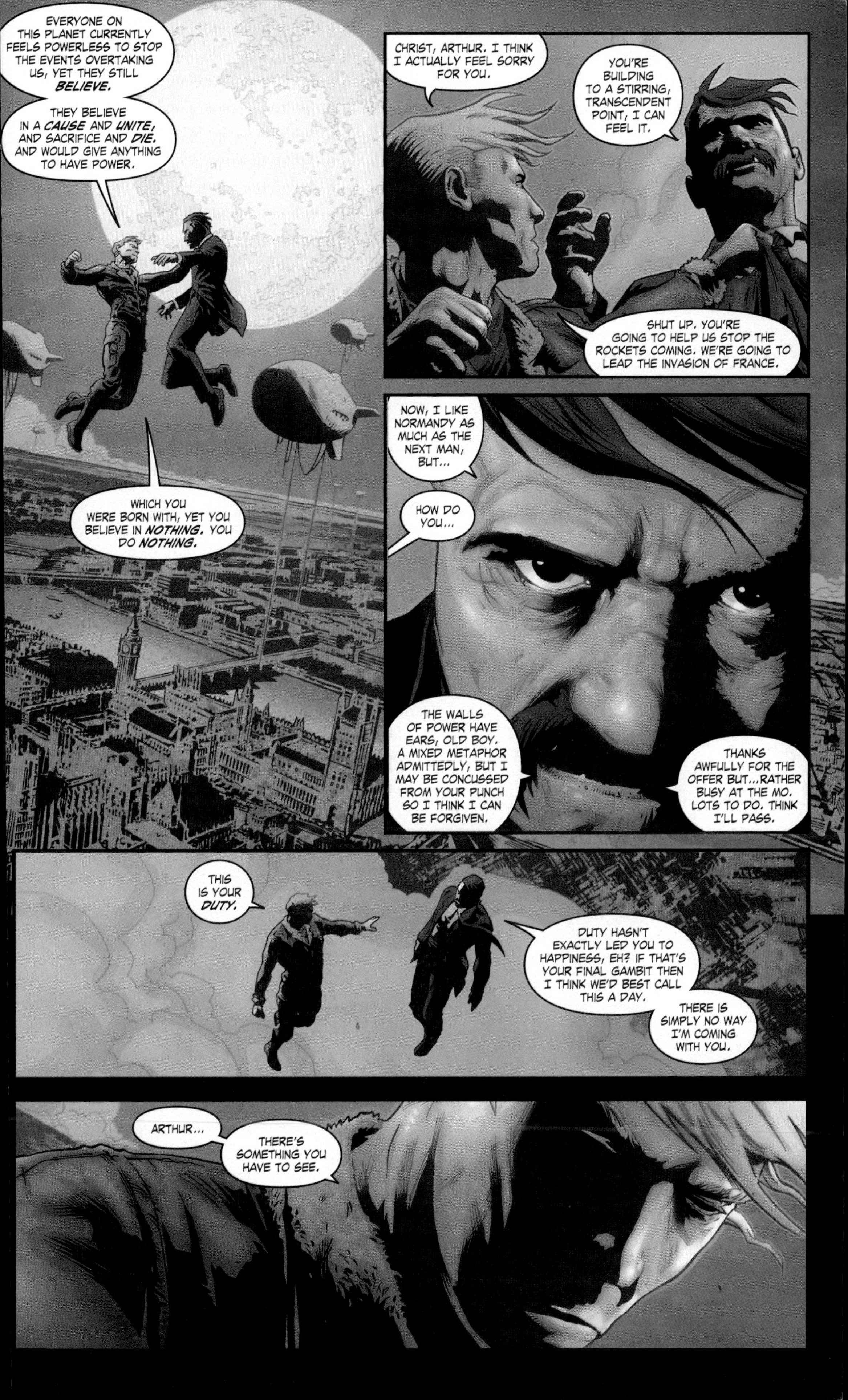
EVERYONE ON THIS PLANET CURRENTLY FEELS POWERLESS TO STOP THE EVENTS OVERTAKING US, YET THEY STILL *BELIEVE.*
THEY BELIEVE IN A *CAUSE* AND *UNITE*, AND SACRIFICE AND *DIE.* AND WOULD GIVE ANYTHING TO HAVE POWER.
WHICH YOU WERE BORN WITH, YET YOU BELIEVE IN *NOTHING.* YOU DO *NOTHING.*
CHRIST, ARTHUR. I THINK I ACTUALLY FEEL SORRY FOR YOU.
YOU'RE BUILDING TO A STIRRING, TRANSCENDENT POINT, I CAN FEEL IT.
SHUT UP. YOU'RE GOING TO HELP US STOP THE ROCKETS COMING. WE'RE GOING TO LEAD THE INVASION OF FRANCE.
NOW, I LIKE NORMANDY AS MUCH AS THE NEXT MAN, BUT...
HOW DO YOU...
THE WALLS OF POWER HAVE EARS, OLD BOY. A MIXED METAPHOR ADMITTEDLY, BUT I MAY BE CONCUSSED FROM YOUR PUNCH SO I THINK I CAN BE FORGIVEN.
THANKS AWFULLY FOR THE OFFER BUT...RATHER BUSY AT THE MO. LOTS TO DO. THINK I'LL PASS.
THIS IS YOUR *DUTY.*
DUTY HASN'T EXACTLY LED YOU TO HAPPINESS, EH? IF THAT'S YOUR FINAL GAMBIT THEN I THINK WE'D BEST CALL THIS A DAY.
THERE IS SIMPLY NO WAY I'M COMING WITH YOU.
ARTHUR...
THERE'S SOMETHING YOU HAVE TO SEE.

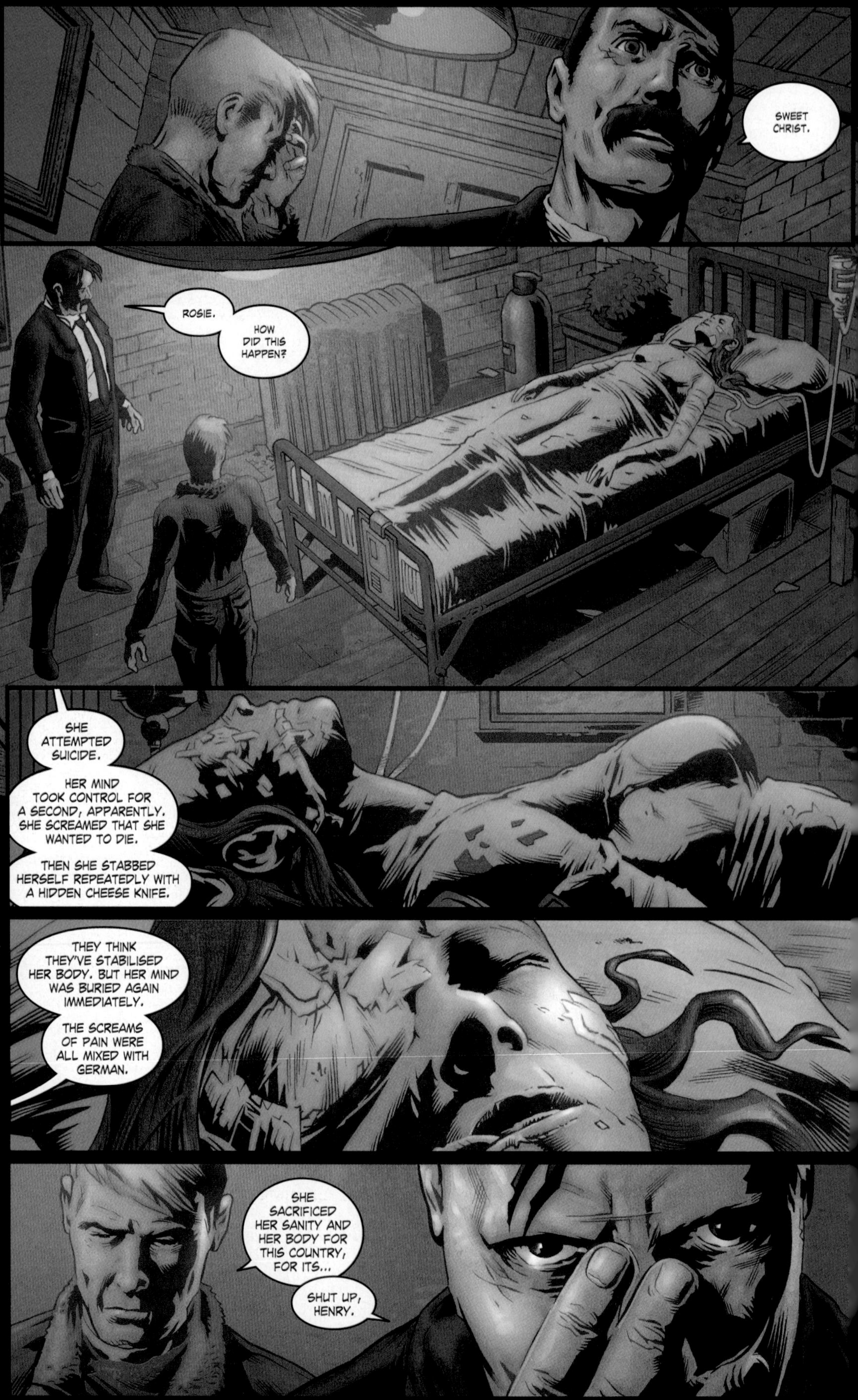
SWEET CHRIST.
ROSIE.
HOW DID THIS HAPPEN?
SHE ATTEMPTED SUICIDE.
HER MIND TOOK CONTROL FOR A SECOND, APPARENTLY. SHE SCREAMED THAT SHE WANTED TO DIE.
THEN SHE STABBED HERSELF REPEATEDLY WITH A HIDDEN CHEESE KNIFE.
THEY THINK THEY'VE STABILISED HER BODY. BUT HER MIND WAS BURIED AGAIN IMMEDIATELY.
THE SCREAMS OF PAIN WERE ALL MIXED WITH GERMAN.
SHE SACRIFICED HER SANITY AND HER BODY FOR THIS COUNTRY, FOR ITS...
SHUT UP, HENRY.

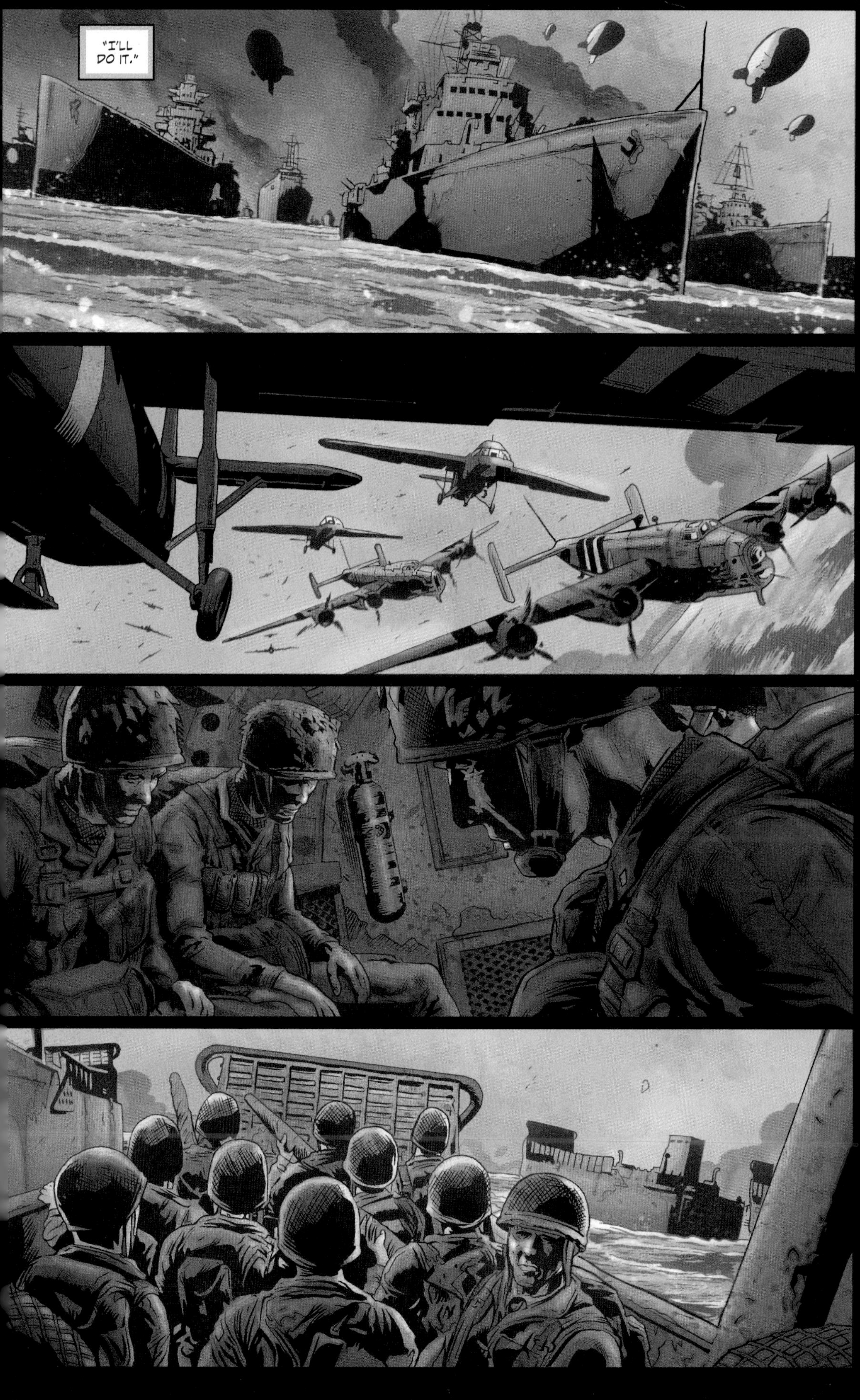
"I'LL DO IT."

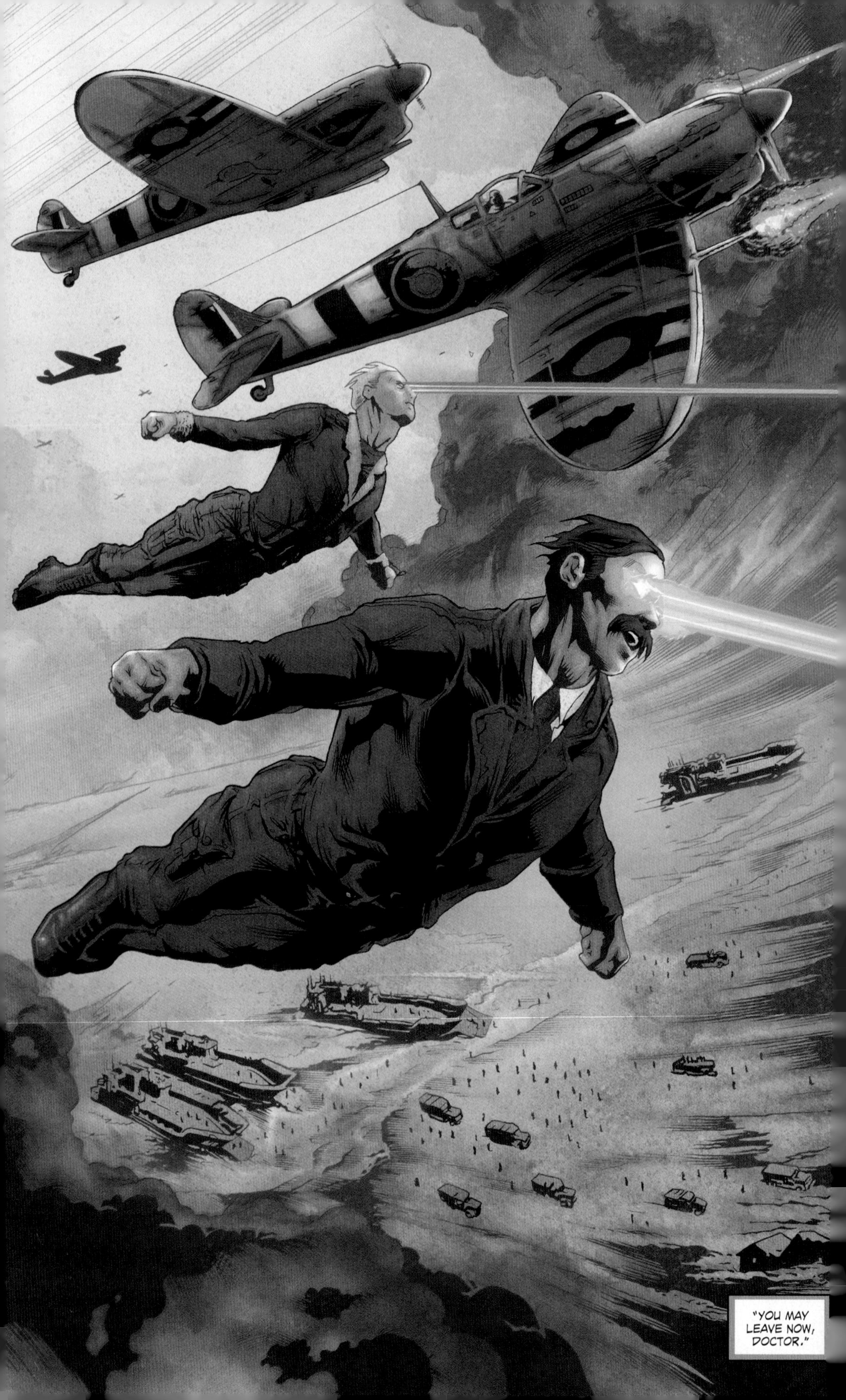
"YOU MAY
LEAVE NOW,
DOCTOR."

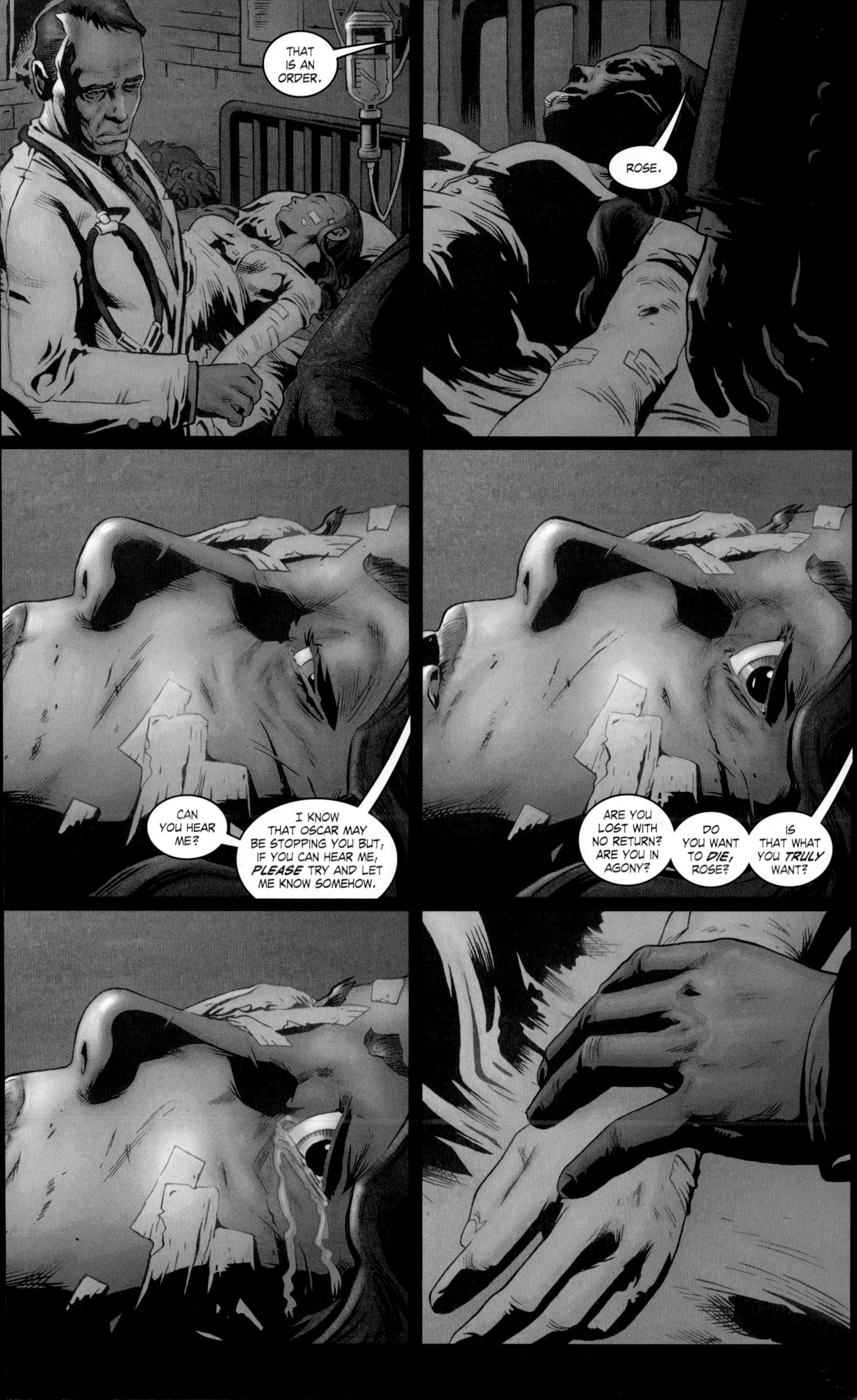
THAT IS AN ORDER.
ROSE.
CAN YOU HEAR ME?
I KNOW THAT OSCAR MAY BE STOPPING YOU BUT, IF YOU CAN HEAR ME, PLEASE TRY AND LET ME KNOW SOMEHOW.
ARE YOU LOST WITH NO RETURN? ARE YOU IN AGONY?
DO YOU WANT TO DIE, ROSE?
IS THAT WHAT YOU TRULY WANT?

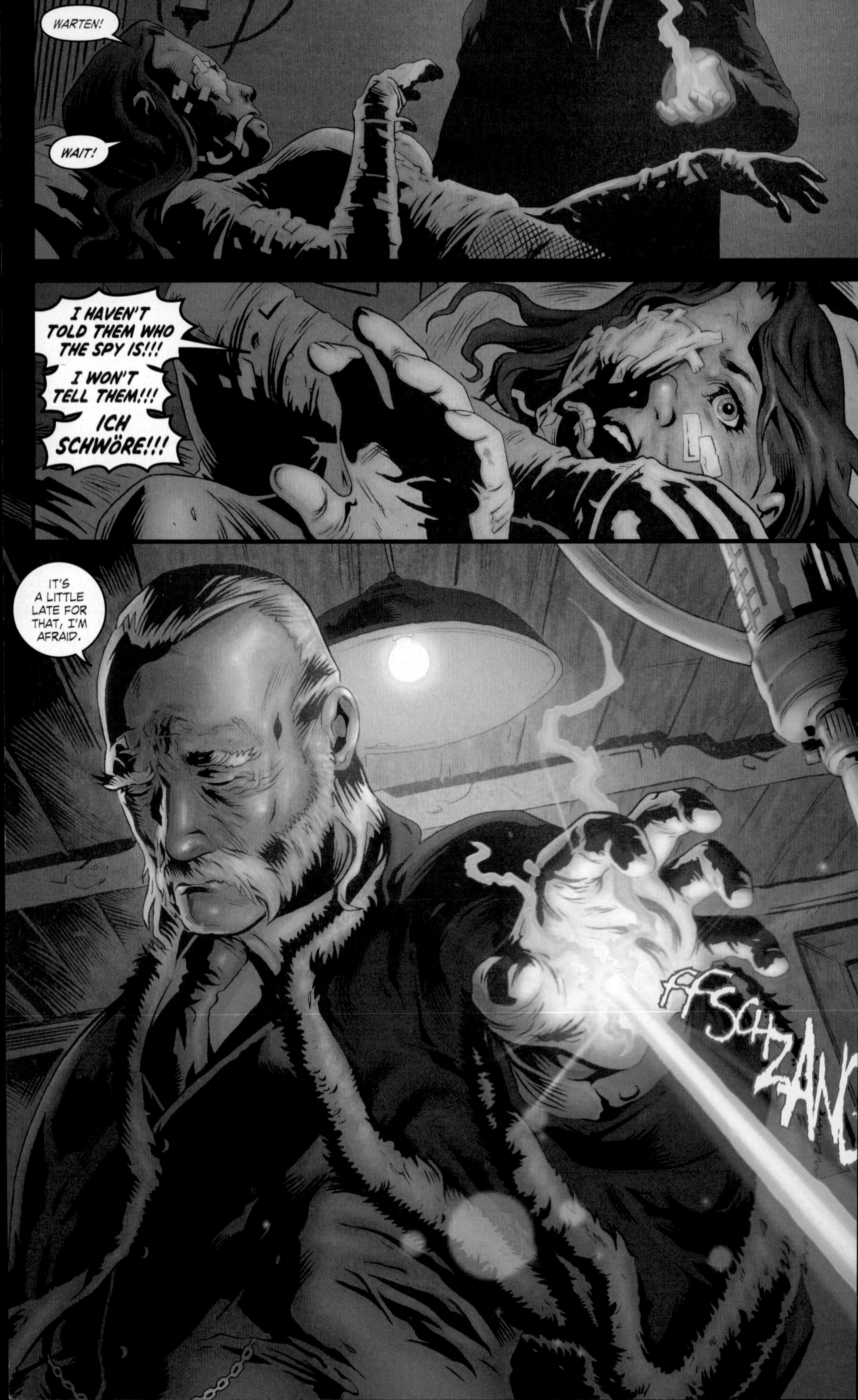
WARTEN!
WAIT!
I HAVEN'T TOLD THEM WHO THE SPY IS!!!
I WON'T TELL THEM!!!
ICH SCHWÖRE!!!
IT'S A LITTLE LATE FOR THAT, I'M AFRAID.
FFSCHZANG

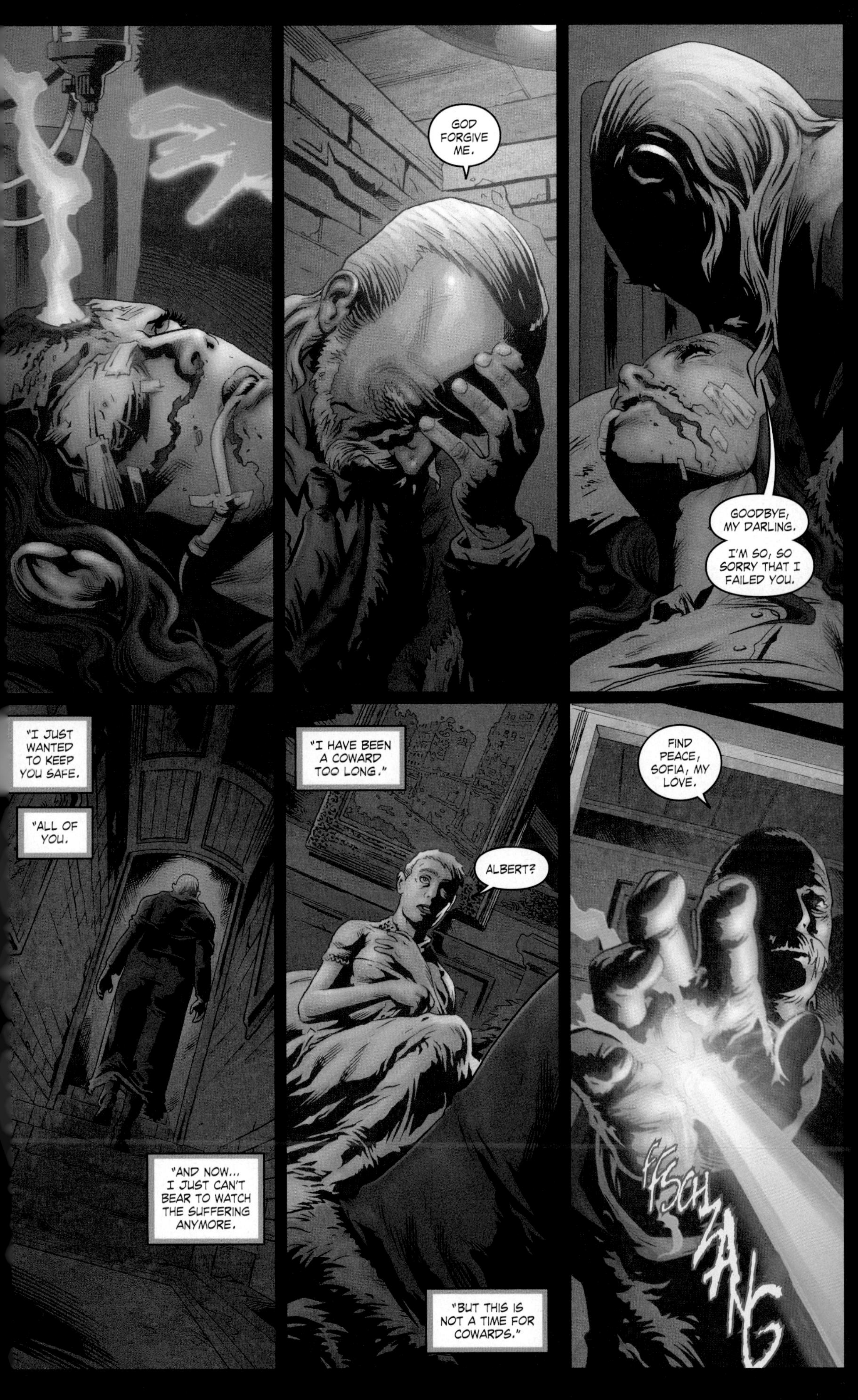
GOD FORGIVE ME.
GOODBYE, MY DARLING.
I'M SO, SO SORRY THAT I FAILED YOU.
"I JUST WANTED TO KEEP YOU SAFE.
"ALL OF YOU.
"AND NOW... I JUST CAN'T BEAR TO WATCH THE SUFFERING ANYMORE.
"I HAVE BEEN A COWARD TOO LONG."
ALBERT?
"BUT THIS IS NOT A TIME FOR COWARDS."
FIND PEACE, SOFIA, MY LOVE.
FFSCHZANG

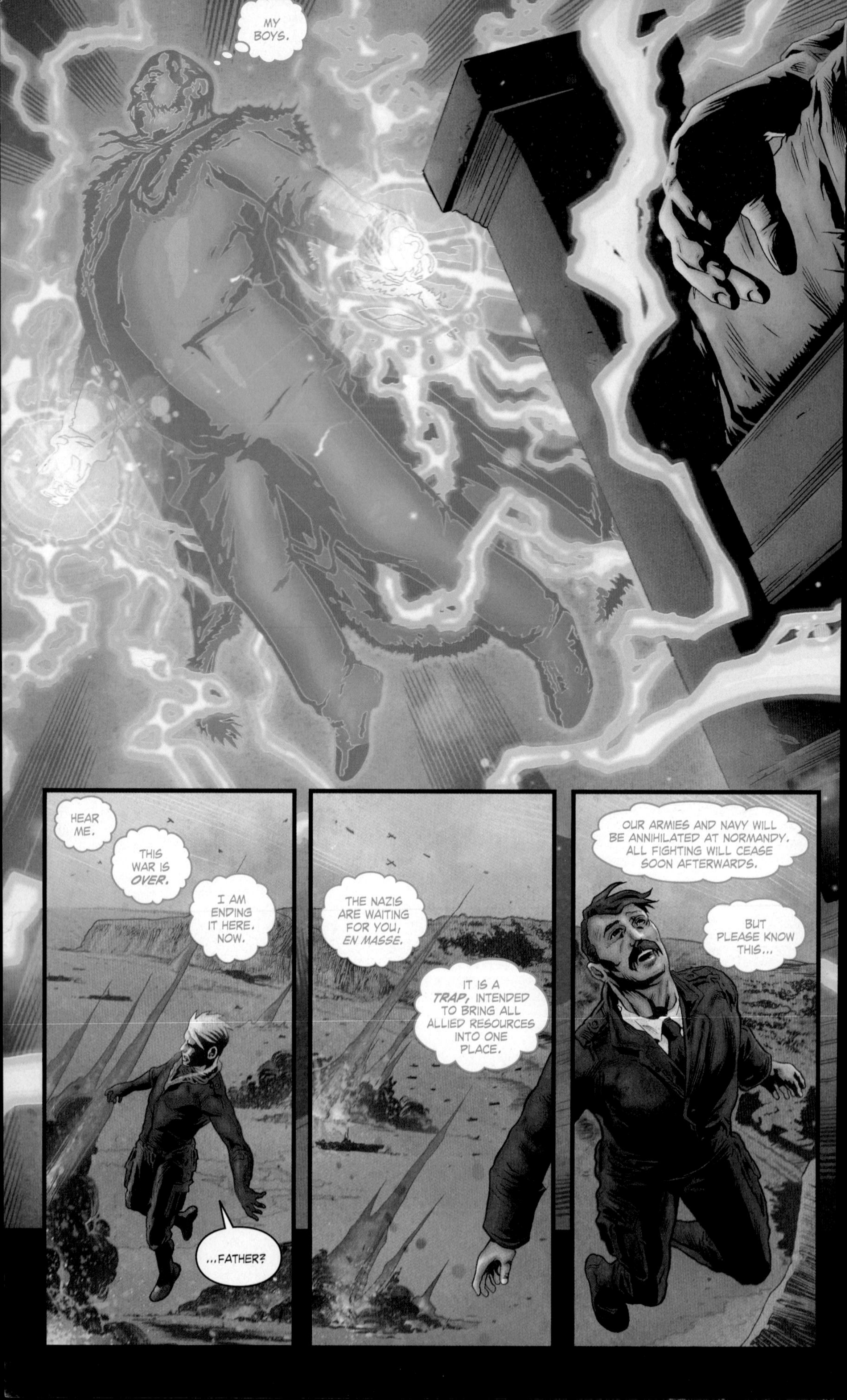
MY BOYS.
HEAR ME.
THIS WAR IS *OVER.*
I AM ENDING IT HERE. NOW.
...FATHER?
THE NAZIS ARE WAITING FOR YOU, *EN MASSE.*
IT IS A *TRAP,* INTENDED TO BRING ALL ALLIED RESOURCES INTO ONE PLACE.
OUR ARMIES AND NAVY WILL BE ANNIHILATED AT NORMANDY. ALL FIGHTING WILL CEASE SOON AFTERWARDS.
BUT PLEASE KNOW THIS...

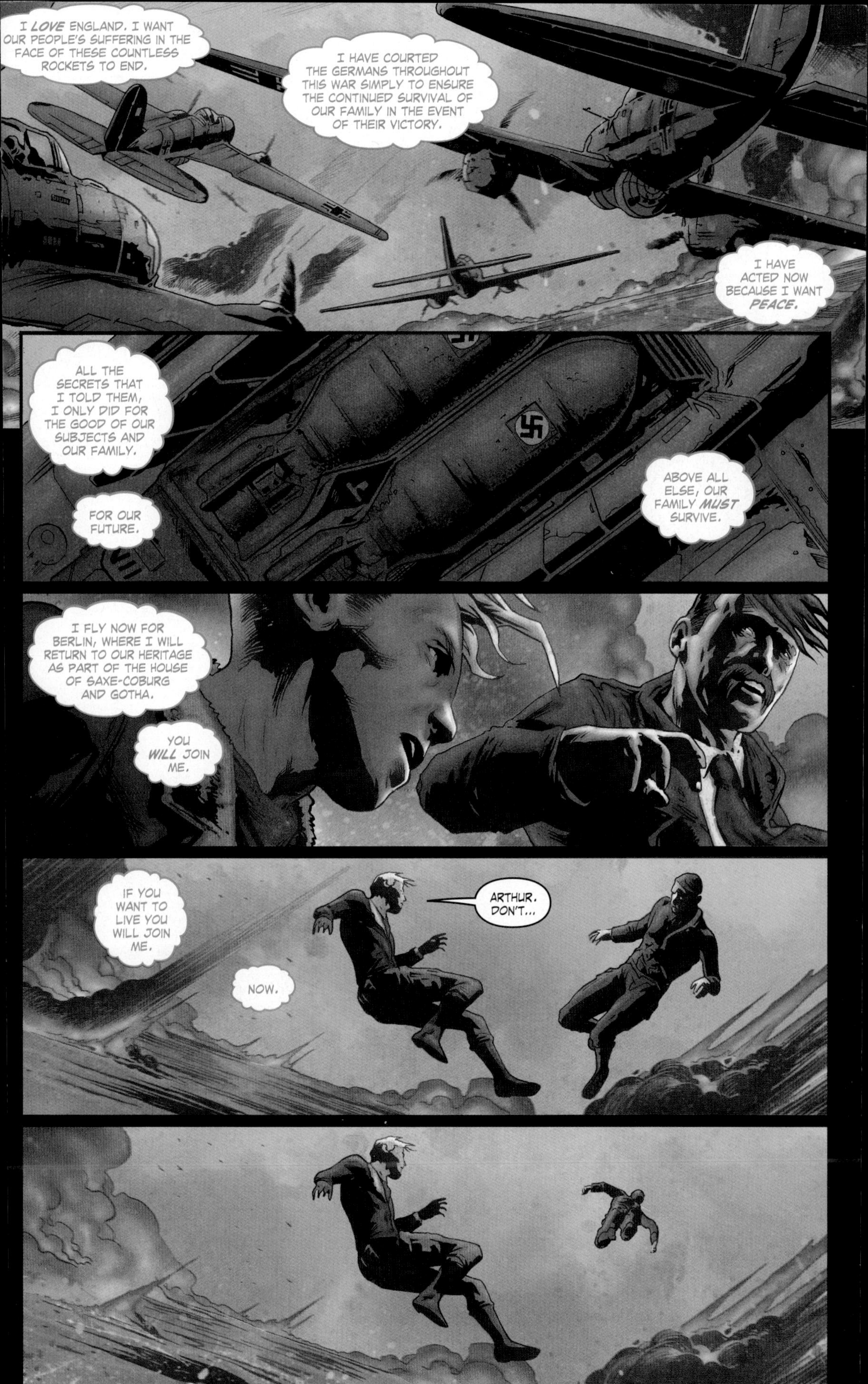
I LOVE ENGLAND. I WANT OUR PEOPLE'S SUFFERING IN THE FACE OF THESE COUNTLESS ROCKETS TO END.
I HAVE COURTED THE GERMANS THROUGHOUT THIS WAR SIMPLY TO ENSURE THE CONTINUED SURVIVAL OF OUR FAMILY IN THE EVENT OF THEIR VICTORY.
I HAVE ACTED NOW BECAUSE I WANT PEACE.
ALL THE SECRETS THAT I TOLD THEM, I ONLY DID FOR THE GOOD OF OUR SUBJECTS AND OUR FAMILY.
FOR OUR FUTURE.
ABOVE ALL ELSE, OUR FAMILY MUST SURVIVE.
I FLY NOW FOR BERLIN, WHERE I WILL RETURN TO OUR HERITAGE AS PART OF THE HOUSE OF SAXE-COBURG AND GOTHA.
YOU WILL JOIN ME.
IF YOU WANT TO LIVE YOU WILL JOIN ME.
ARTHUR. DON'T...
NOW.

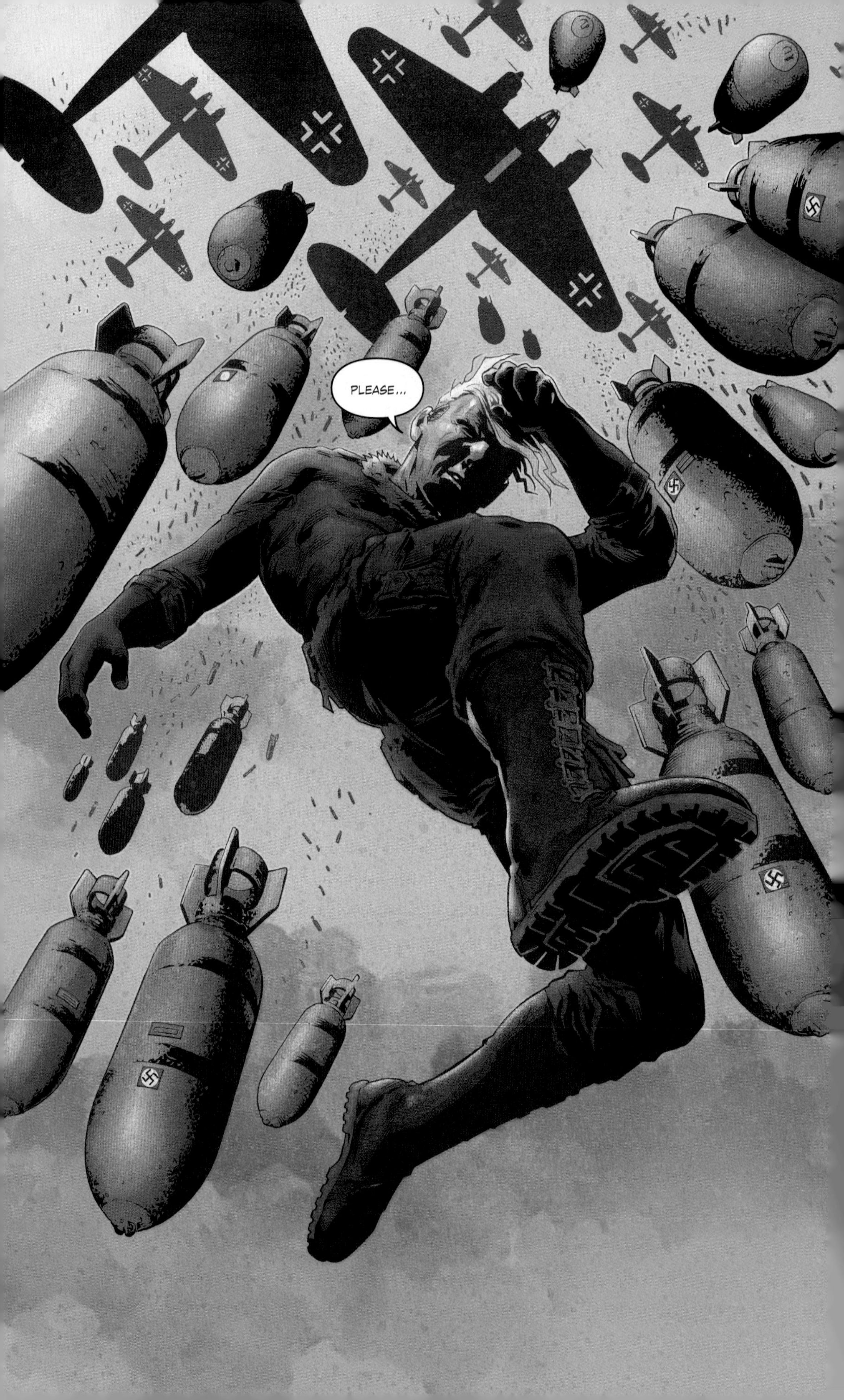
PLEASE...

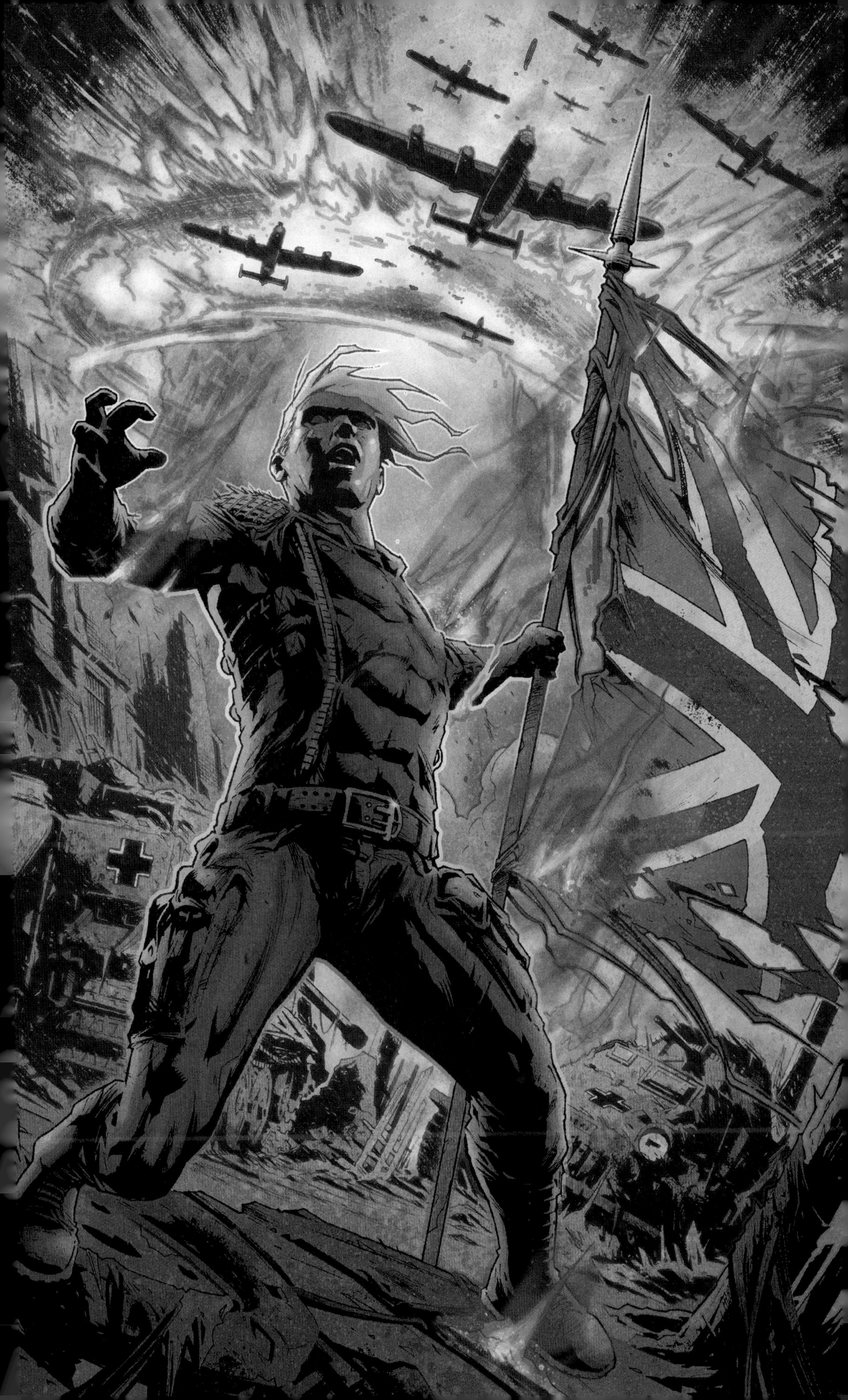

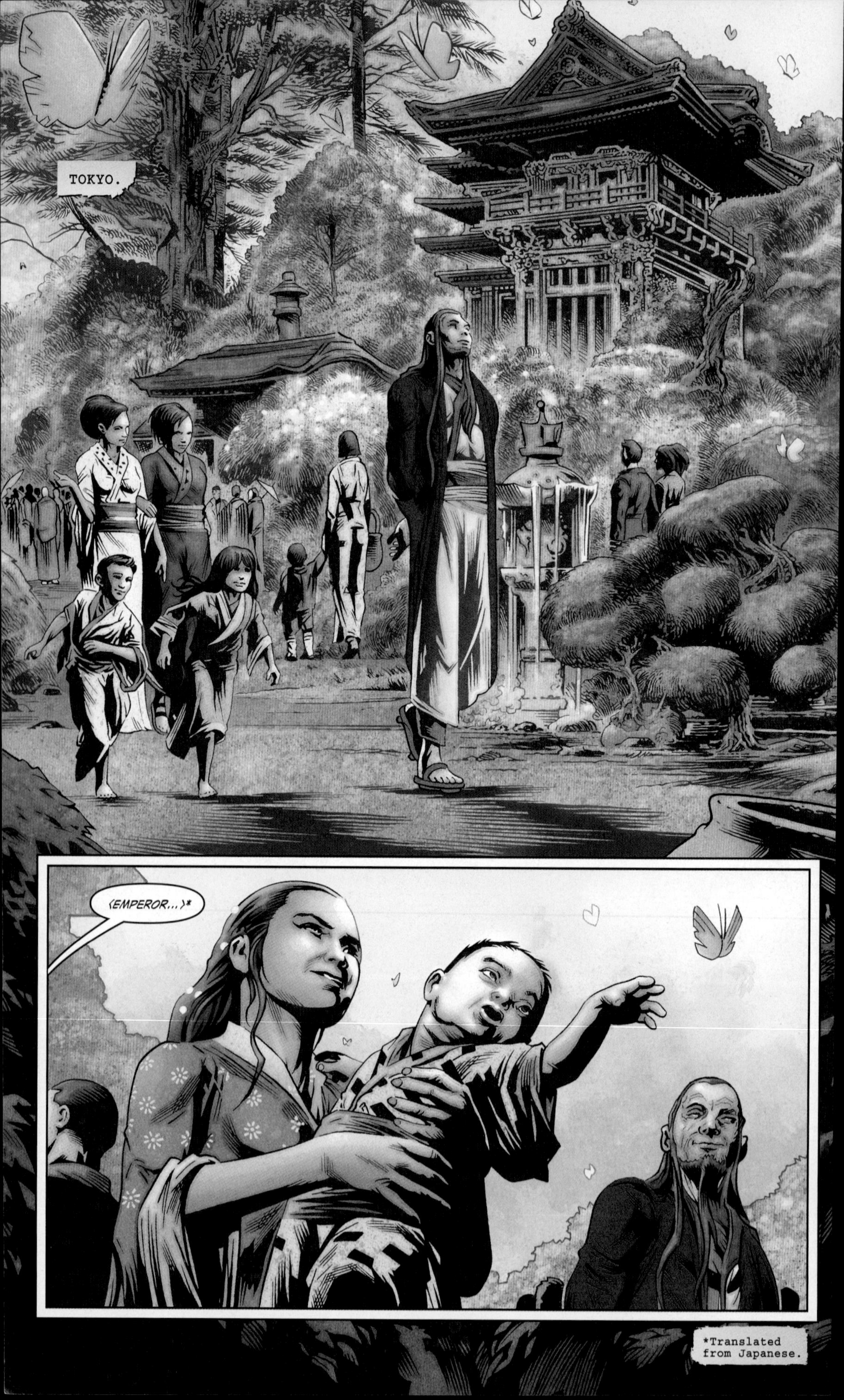
TOKYO.
‹EMPEROR...›*
*Translated from Japanese.

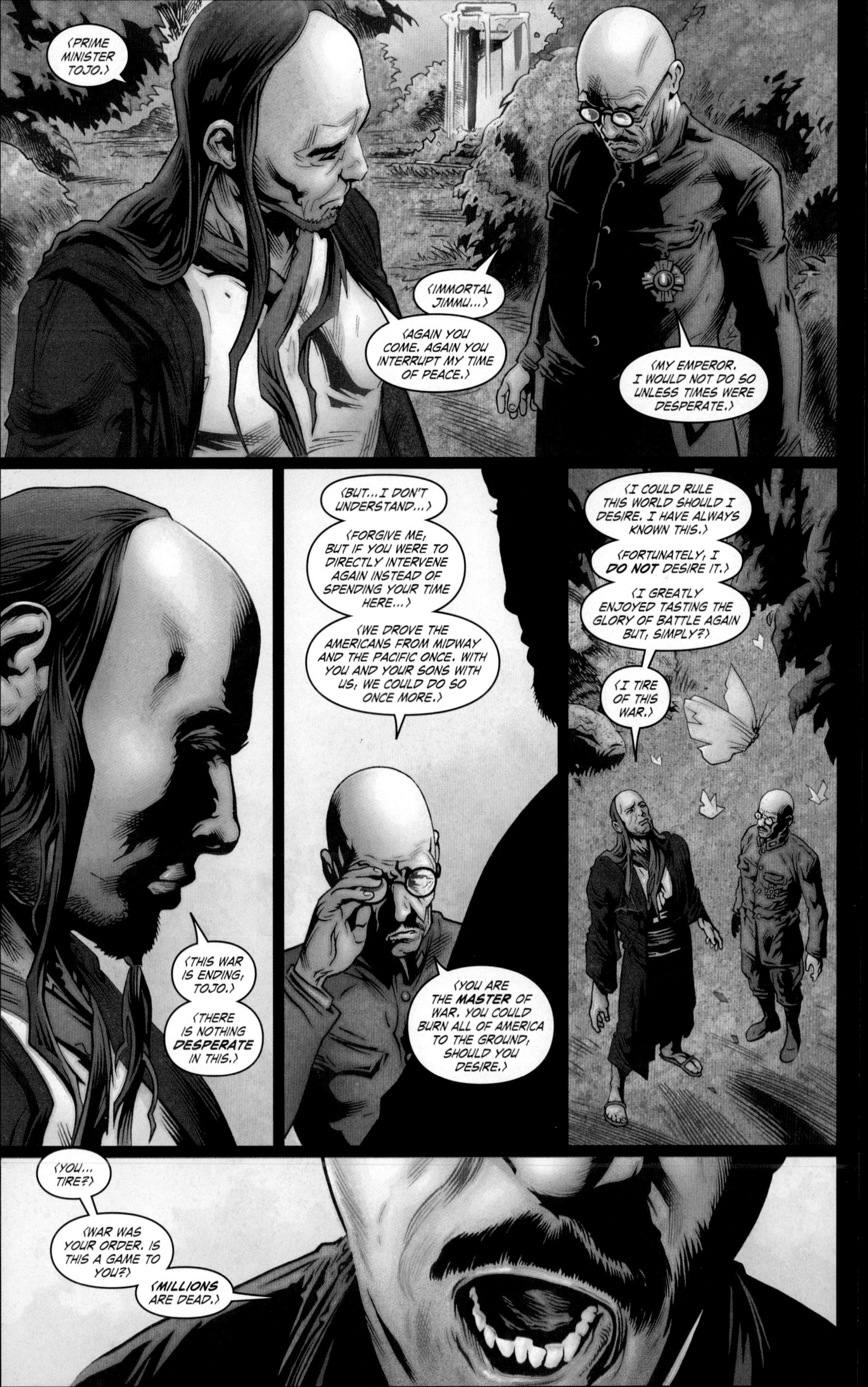

‹PRIME MINISTER TOJO.›
‹IMMORTAL JIMMU...›
‹AGAIN YOU COME. AGAIN YOU INTERRUPT MY TIME OF PEACE.›
‹MY EMPEROR. I WOULD NOT DO SO UNLESS TIMES WERE DESPERATE.›
‹THIS WAR IS ENDING, TOJO.›
‹THERE IS NOTHING **DESPERATE** IN THIS.›
‹BUT...I DON'T UNDERSTAND...›
‹FORGIVE ME, BUT IF YOU WERE TO DIRECTLY INTERVENE AGAIN INSTEAD OF SPENDING YOUR TIME HERE...›
‹WE DROVE THE AMERICANS FROM MIDWAY AND THE PACIFIC ONCE. WITH YOU AND YOUR SONS WITH US, WE COULD DO SO ONCE MORE.›
‹YOU ARE THE **MASTER** OF WAR. YOU COULD BURN ALL OF AMERICA TO THE GROUND, SHOULD YOU DESIRE.›
‹I COULD RULE THIS WORLD SHOULD I DESIRE. I HAVE ALWAYS KNOWN THIS.›
‹FORTUNATELY, I **DO NOT** DESIRE IT.›
‹I GREATLY ENJOYED TASTING THE GLORY OF BATTLE AGAIN BUT, SIMPLY?›
‹I TIRE OF THIS WAR.›
‹YOU... TIRE?›
‹WAR WAS YOUR ORDER. IS THIS A GAME TO YOU?›
‹**MILLIONS** ARE DEAD.›

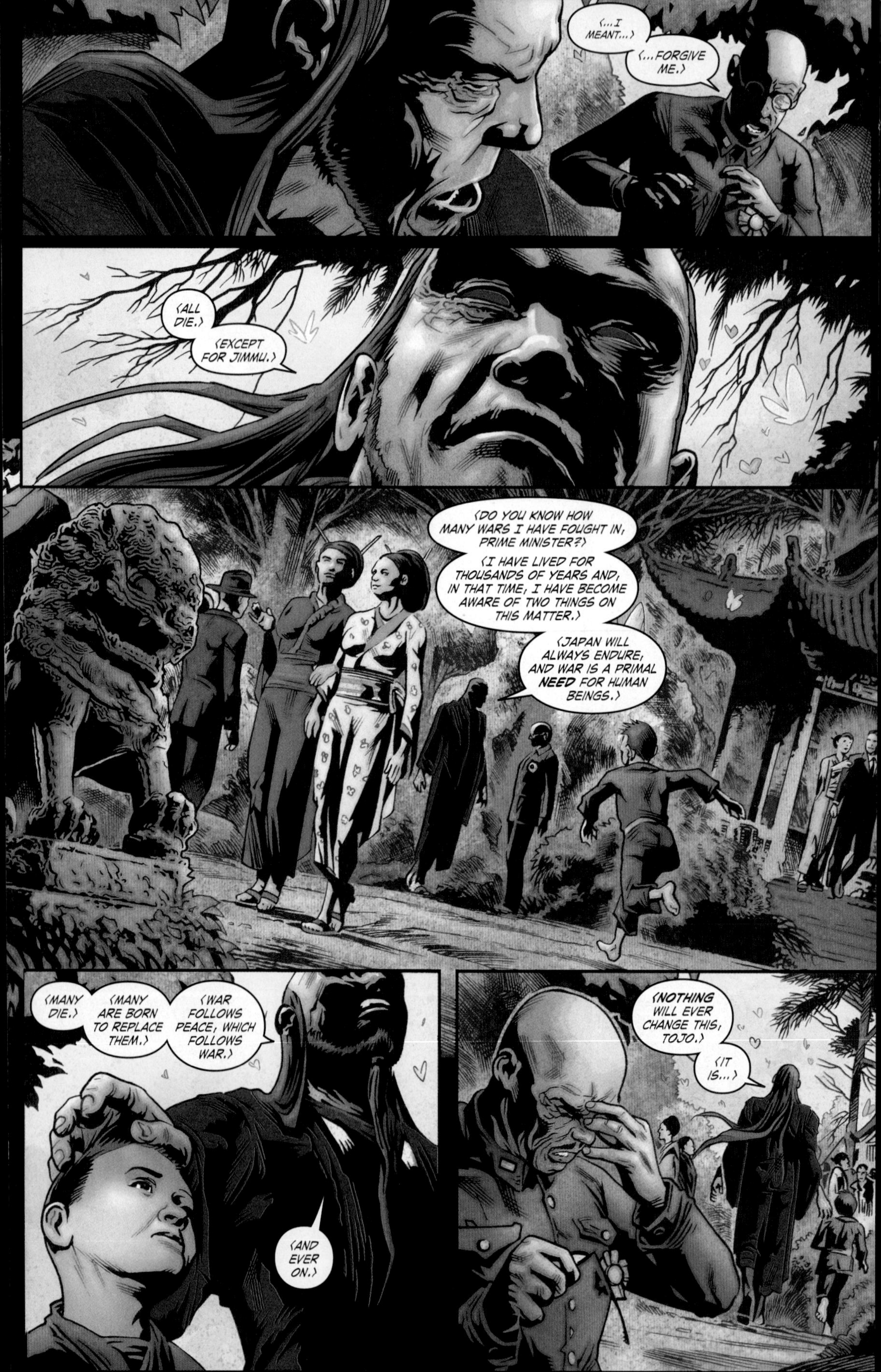
⟨...I MEANT...⟩
⟨...FORGIVE ME.⟩
⟨ALL DIE.⟩
⟨EXCEPT FOR JIMMU.⟩
⟨DO YOU KNOW HOW MANY WARS I HAVE FOUGHT IN, PRIME MINISTER?⟩
⟨I HAVE LIVED FOR THOUSANDS OF YEARS AND, IN THAT TIME, I HAVE BECOME AWARE OF TWO THINGS ON THIS MATTER.⟩
⟨JAPAN WILL ALWAYS ENDURE, AND WAR IS A PRIMAL **NEED** FOR HUMAN BEINGS.⟩
⟨MANY DIE.⟩
⟨MANY ARE BORN TO REPLACE THEM.⟩
⟨WAR FOLLOWS PEACE, WHICH FOLLOWS WAR.⟩
⟨AND EVER ON.⟩
⟨**NOTHING** WILL EVER CHANGE THIS, TOJO.⟩
⟨IT IS...⟩

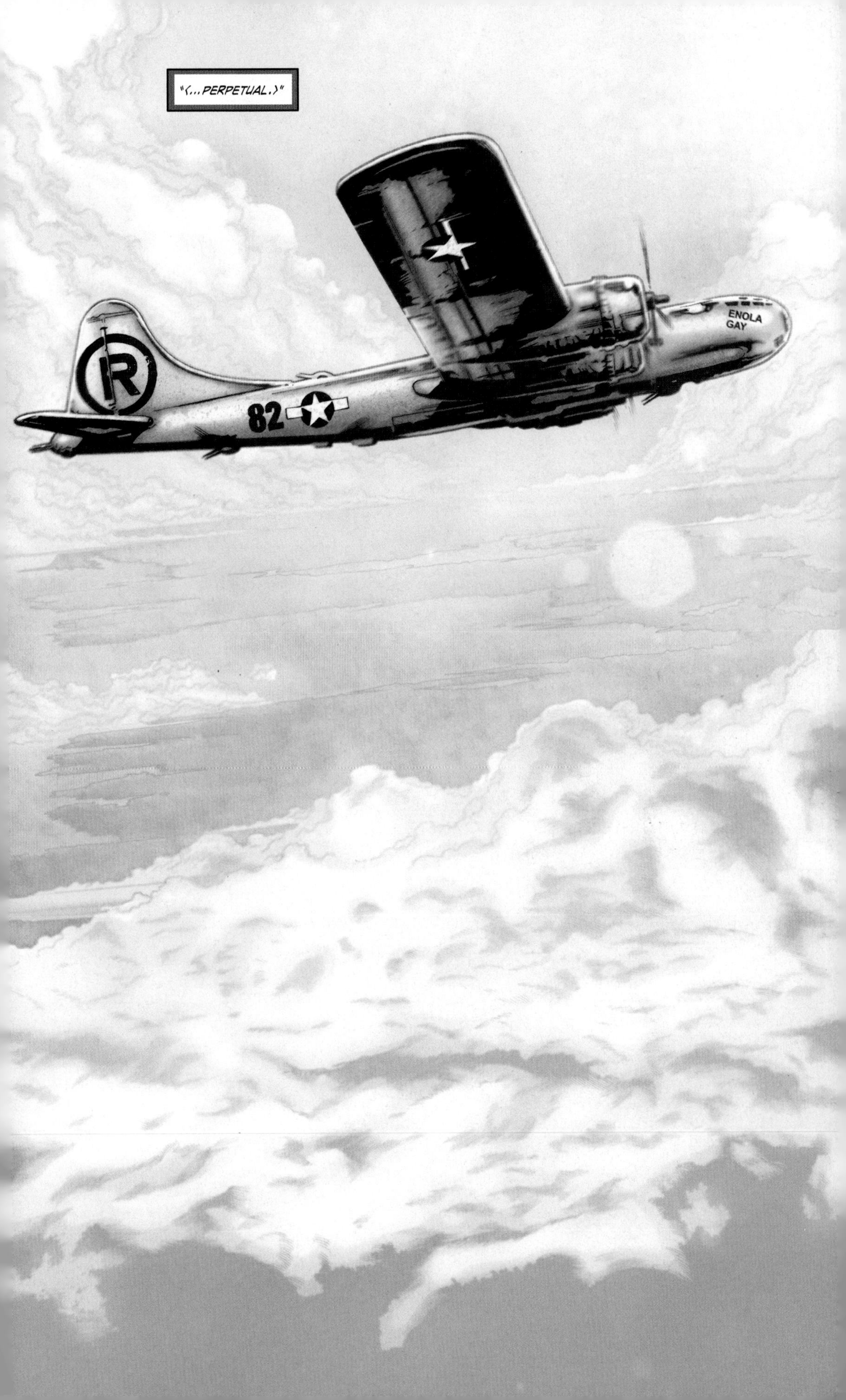
"<...PERPETUAL.>"
ENOLA
GAY
82
R

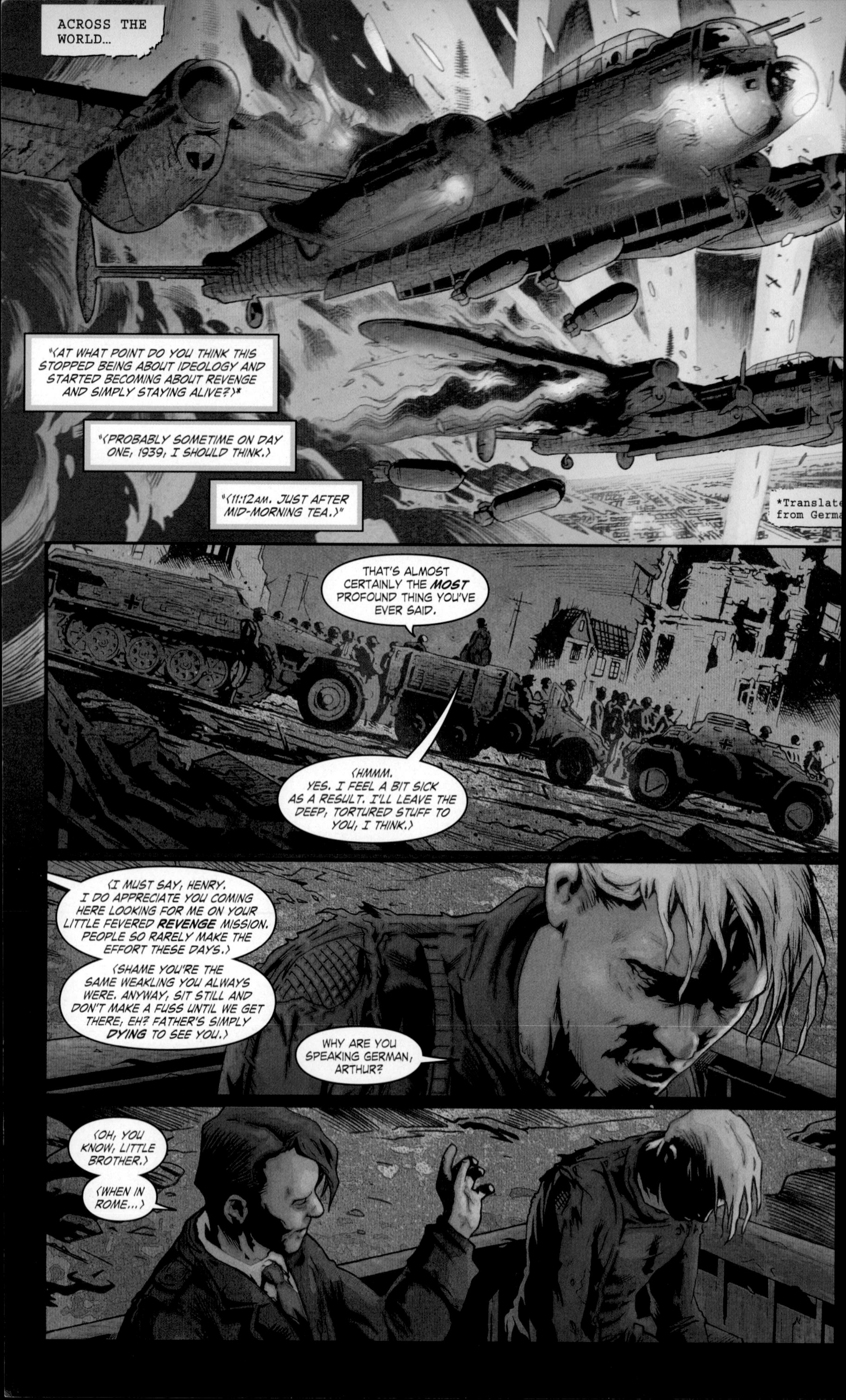
ACROSS THE WORLD...
"‹AT WHAT POINT DO YOU THINK THIS STOPPED BEING ABOUT IDEOLOGY AND STARTED BECOMING ABOUT REVENGE AND SIMPLY STAYING ALIVE?›*
"‹PROBABLY SOMETIME ON DAY ONE, 1939, I SHOULD THINK.›
"‹11:12AM. JUST AFTER MID-MORNING TEA.›"
*Translate from Germa
THAT'S ALMOST CERTAINLY THE **MOST** PROFOUND THING YOU'VE EVER SAID.
‹HMMM. YES. I FEEL A BIT SICK AS A RESULT. I'LL LEAVE THE DEEP, TORTURED STUFF TO YOU, I THINK.›
‹I MUST SAY, HENRY. I DO APPRECIATE YOU COMING HERE LOOKING FOR ME ON YOUR LITTLE FEVERED **REVENGE** MISSION. PEOPLE SO RARELY MAKE THE EFFORT THESE DAYS.›
‹SHAME YOU'RE THE SAME WEAKLING YOU ALWAYS WERE. ANYWAY, SIT STILL AND DON'T MAKE A FUSS UNTIL WE GET THERE, EH? FATHER'S SIMPLY **DYING** TO SEE YOU.›
WHY ARE YOU SPEAKING GERMAN, ARTHUR?
‹OH, YOU KNOW, LITTLE BROTHER.›
‹WHEN IN ROME...›

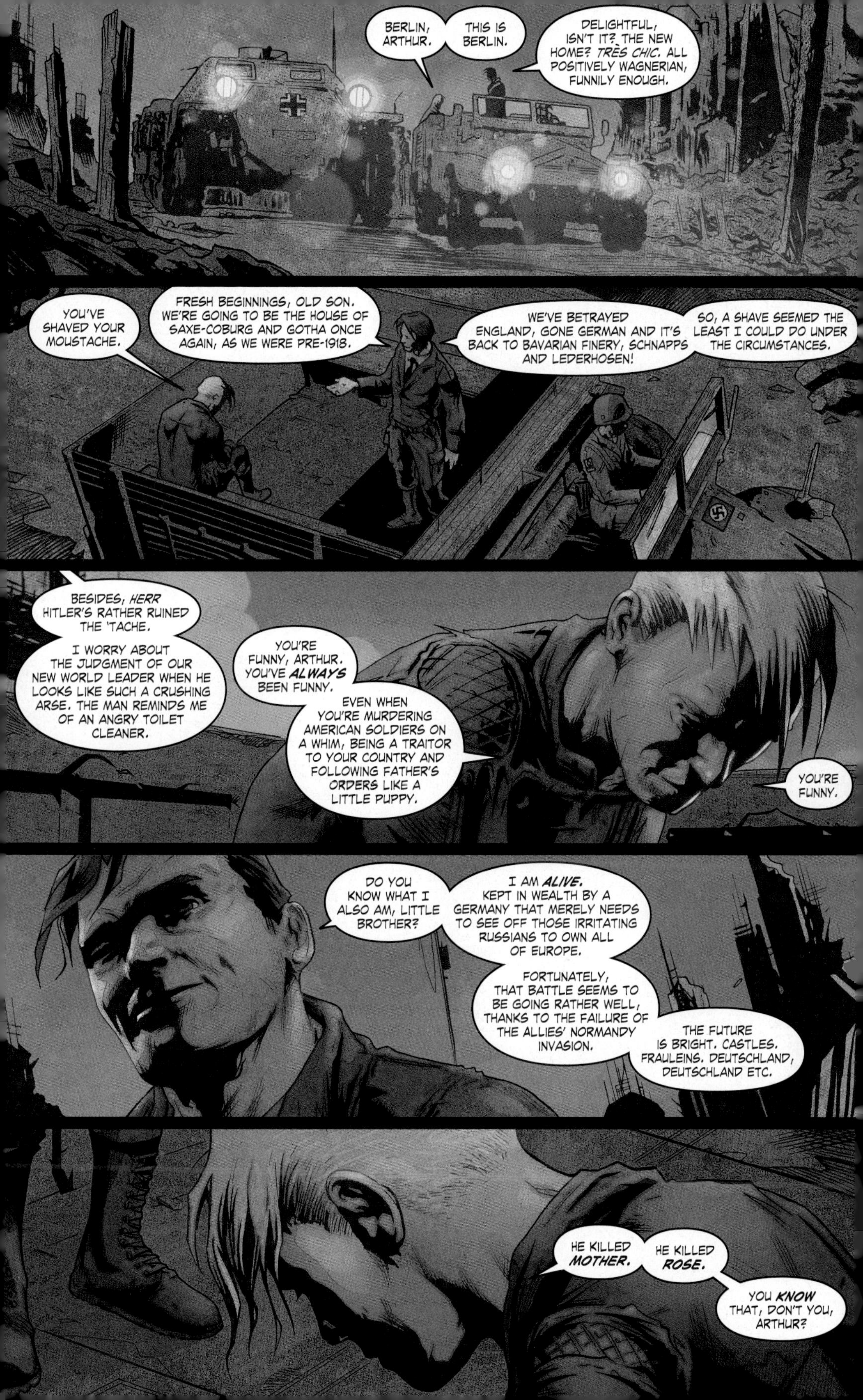
BERLIN, ARTHUR.
THIS IS BERLIN.
DELIGHTFUL, ISN'T IT? THE NEW HOME? TRÈS CHIC. ALL POSITIVELY WAGNERIAN, FUNNILY ENOUGH.
YOU'VE SHAVED YOUR MOUSTACHE.
FRESH BEGINNINGS, OLD SON. WE'RE GOING TO BE THE HOUSE OF SAXE-COBURG AND GOTHA ONCE AGAIN, AS WE WERE PRE-1918.
WE'VE BETRAYED ENGLAND, GONE GERMAN AND IT'S BACK TO BAVARIAN FINERY, SCHNAPPS AND LEDERHOSEN!
SO, A SHAVE SEEMED THE LEAST I COULD DO UNDER THE CIRCUMSTANCES.
BESIDES, HERR HITLER'S RATHER RUINED THE 'TACHE.
I WORRY ABOUT THE JUDGMENT OF OUR NEW WORLD LEADER WHEN HE LOOKS LIKE SUCH A CRUSHING ARSE. THE MAN REMINDS ME OF AN ANGRY TOILET CLEANER.
YOU'RE FUNNY, ARTHUR. YOU'VE ALWAYS BEEN FUNNY.
EVEN WHEN YOU'RE MURDERING AMERICAN SOLDIERS ON A WHIM, BEING A TRAITOR TO YOUR COUNTRY AND FOLLOWING FATHER'S ORDERS LIKE A LITTLE PUPPY.
YOU'RE FUNNY.
DO YOU KNOW WHAT I ALSO AM, LITTLE BROTHER?
I AM ALIVE. KEPT IN WEALTH BY A GERMANY THAT MERELY NEEDS TO SEE OFF THOSE IRRITATING RUSSIANS TO OWN ALL OF EUROPE.
FORTUNATELY, THAT BATTLE SEEMS TO BE GOING RATHER WELL, THANKS TO THE FAILURE OF THE ALLIES' NORMANDY INVASION.
THE FUTURE IS BRIGHT. CASTLES. FRAULEINS. DEUTSCHLAND, DEUTSCHLAND ETC.
HE KILLED MOTHER.
HE KILLED ROSE.
YOU KNOW THAT, DON'T YOU, ARTHUR?

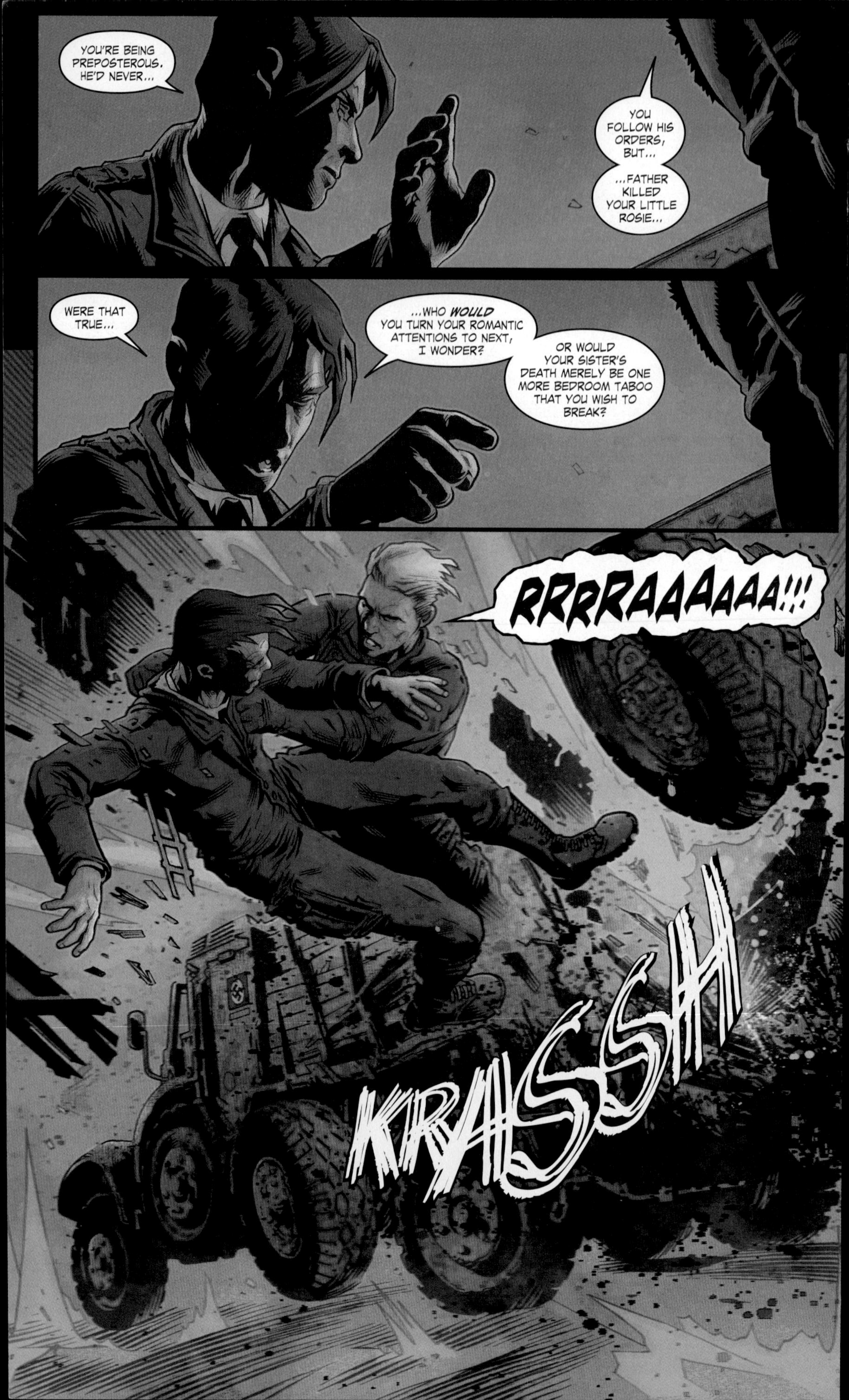

YOU'RE BEING PREPOSTEROUS. HE'D NEVER...
YOU FOLLOW HIS ORDERS, BUT...
...FATHER KILLED YOUR LITTLE ROSIE...
WERE THAT TRUE...
...WHO *WOULD* YOU TURN YOUR ROMANTIC ATTENTIONS TO NEXT, I WONDER?
OR WOULD YOUR SISTER'S DEATH MERELY BE ONE MORE BEDROOM TABOO THAT YOU WISH TO BREAK?
RRRRAAAAAA!!!
KRASSH

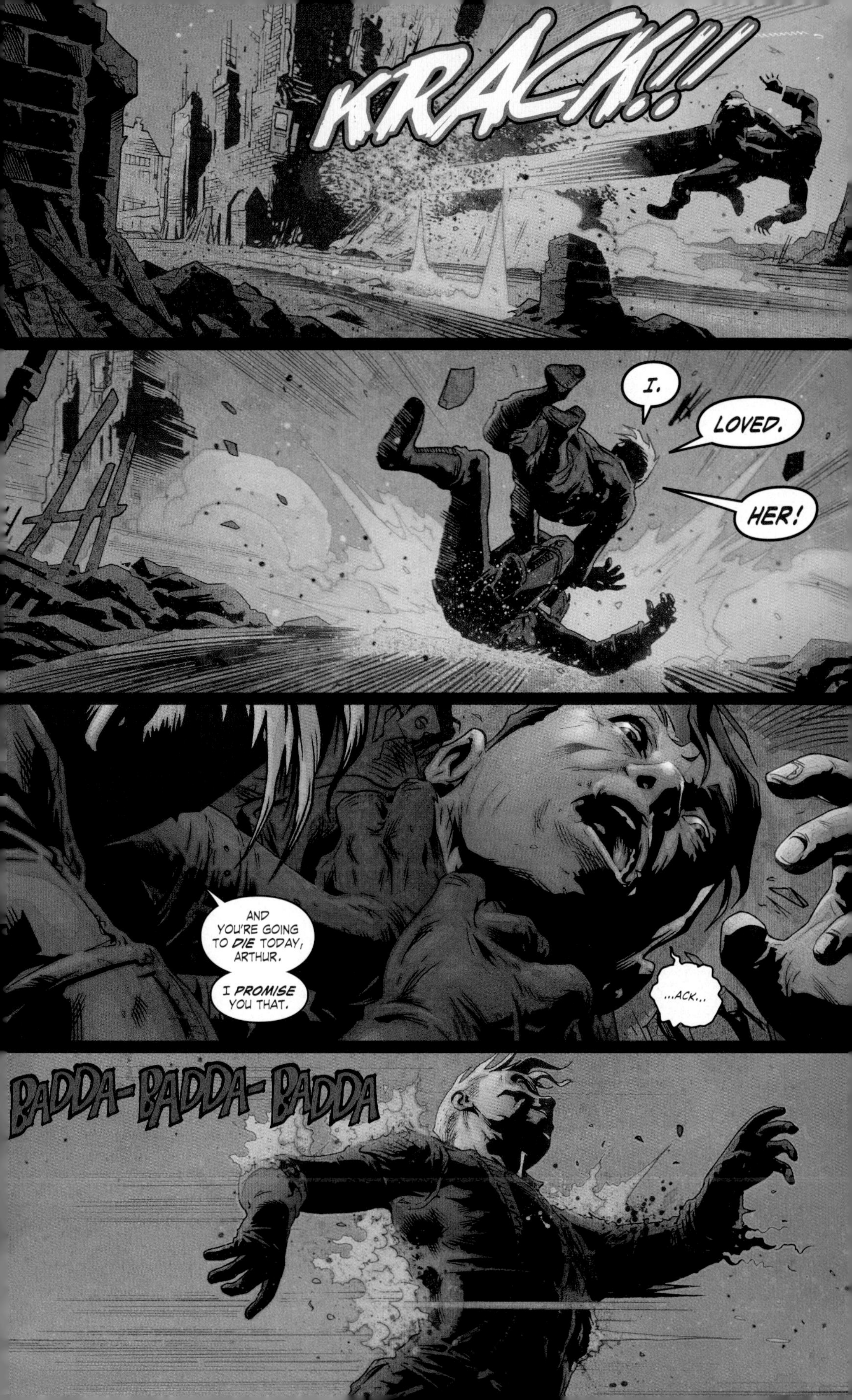
KRACK!!!
I.
LOVED.
HER!
AND YOU'RE GOING TO DIE TODAY, ARTHUR.
I PROMISE YOU THAT.
...ACK...
BADDA-BADDA-BADDA

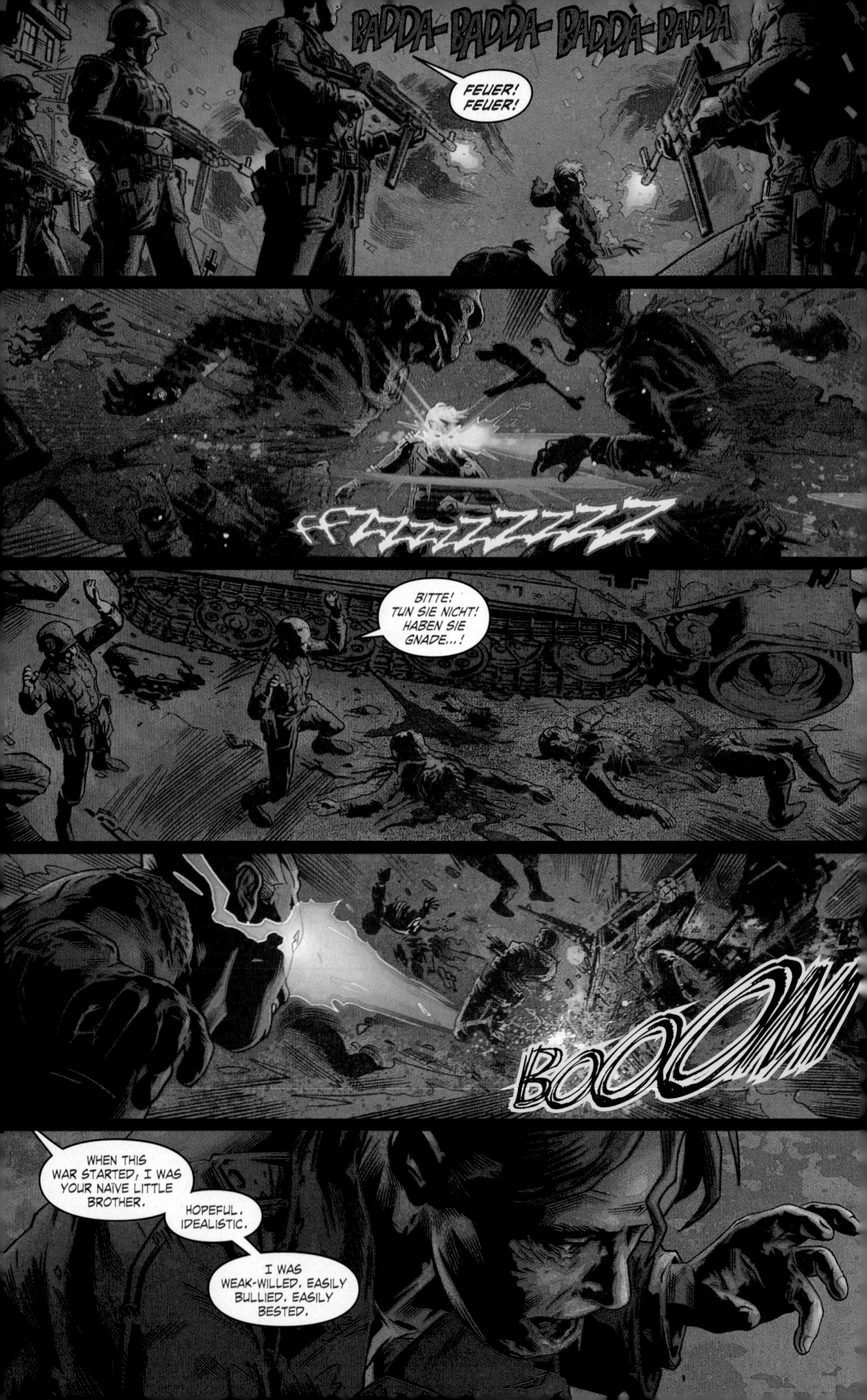
BADDA-BADDA-BADDA-BADDA
FEUER! FEUER!
ffZZZZZZZZZ
BITTE! TUN SIE NICHT! HABEN SIE GNADE...!
BOOOOM
WHEN THIS WAR STARTED, I WAS YOUR NAÏVE LITTLE BROTHER.
HOPEFUL. IDEALISTIC.
I WAS WEAK-WILLED. EASILY BULLIED. EASILY BESTED.

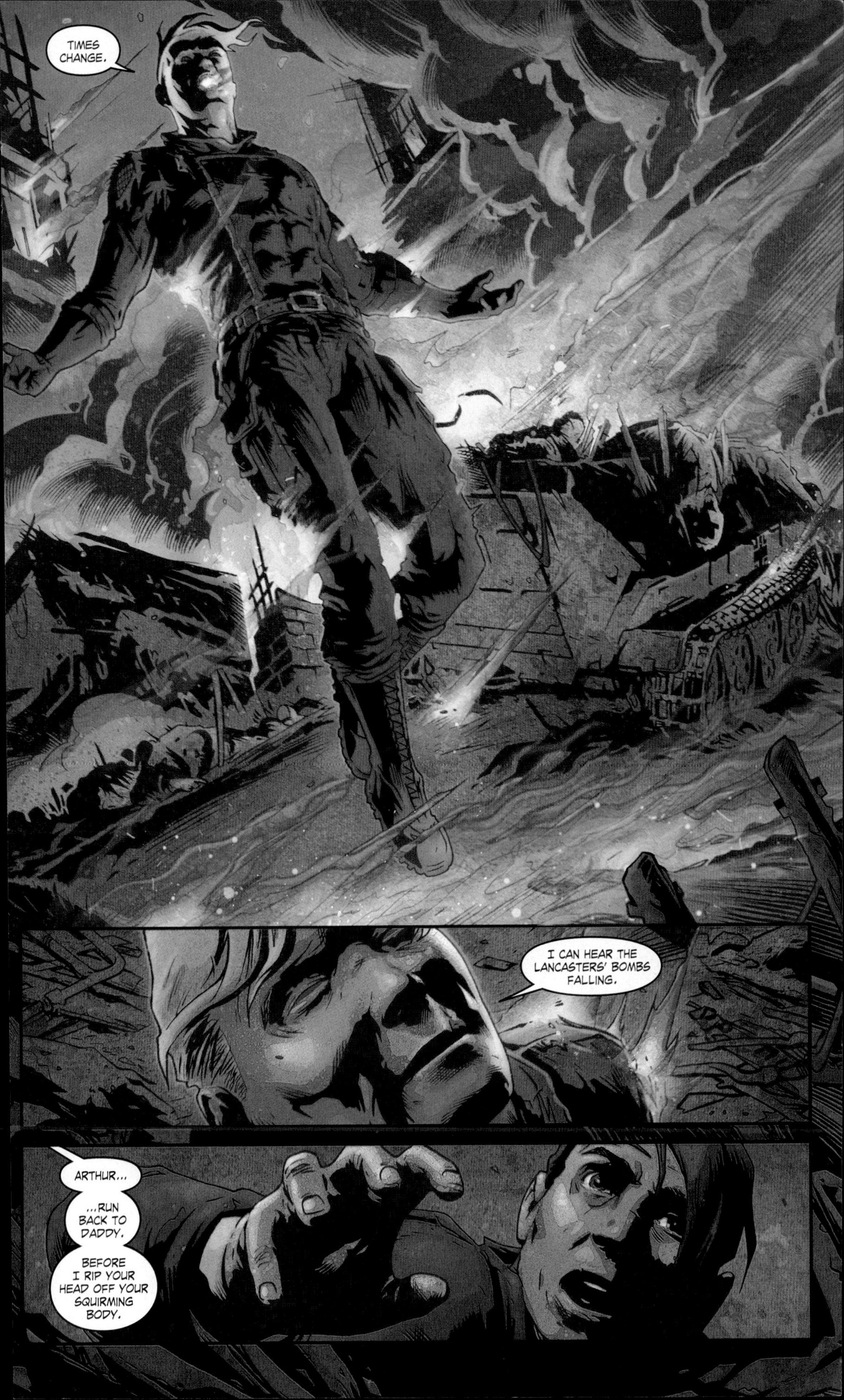
TIMES CHANGE.
I CAN HEAR THE LANCASTERS' BOMBS FALLING.
ARTHUR...
...RUN BACK TO DADDY.
BEFORE I RIP YOUR HEAD OFF YOUR SQUIRMING BODY.

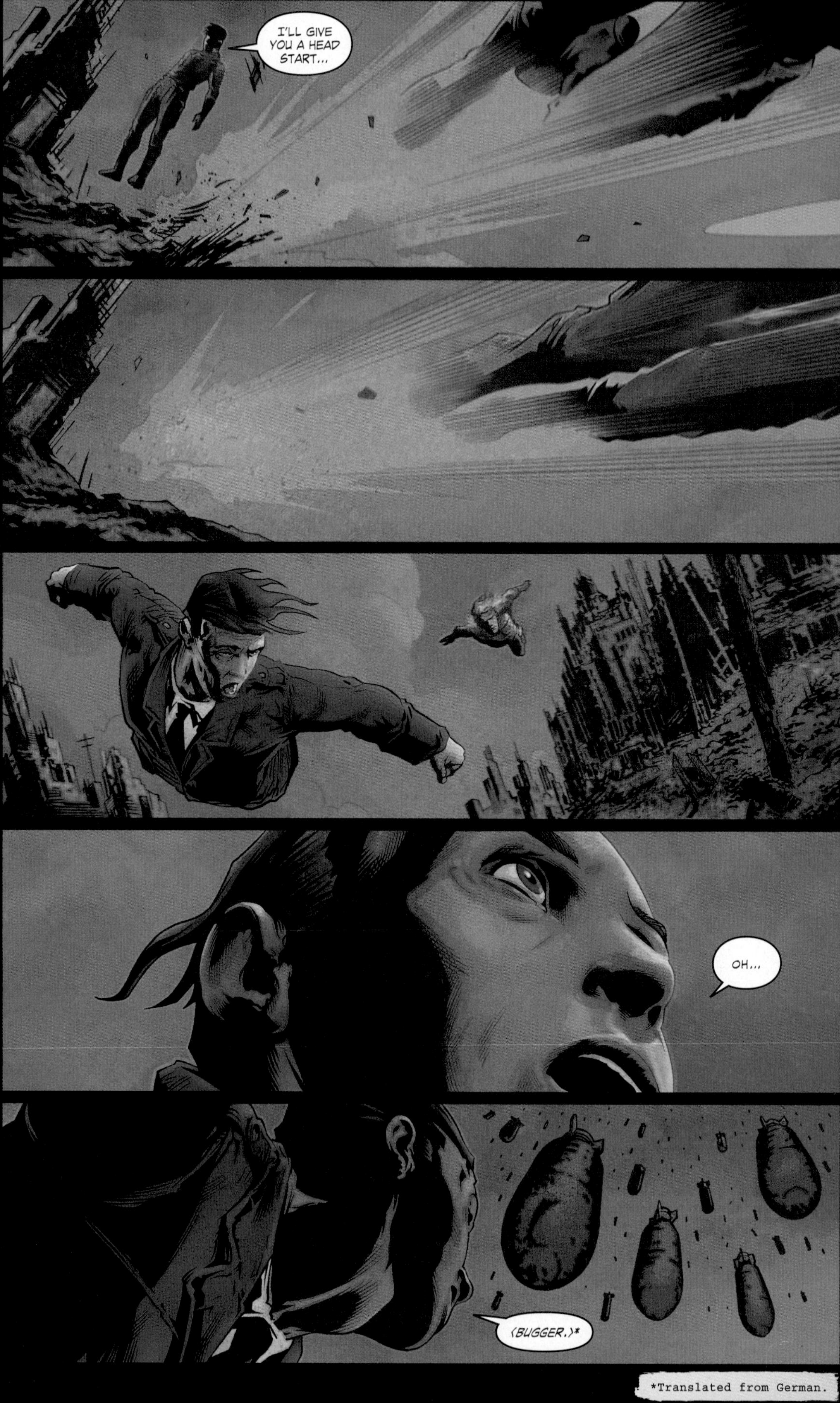
I'LL GIVE YOU A HEAD START...
OH...
‹BUGGER.›*
*Translated from German.

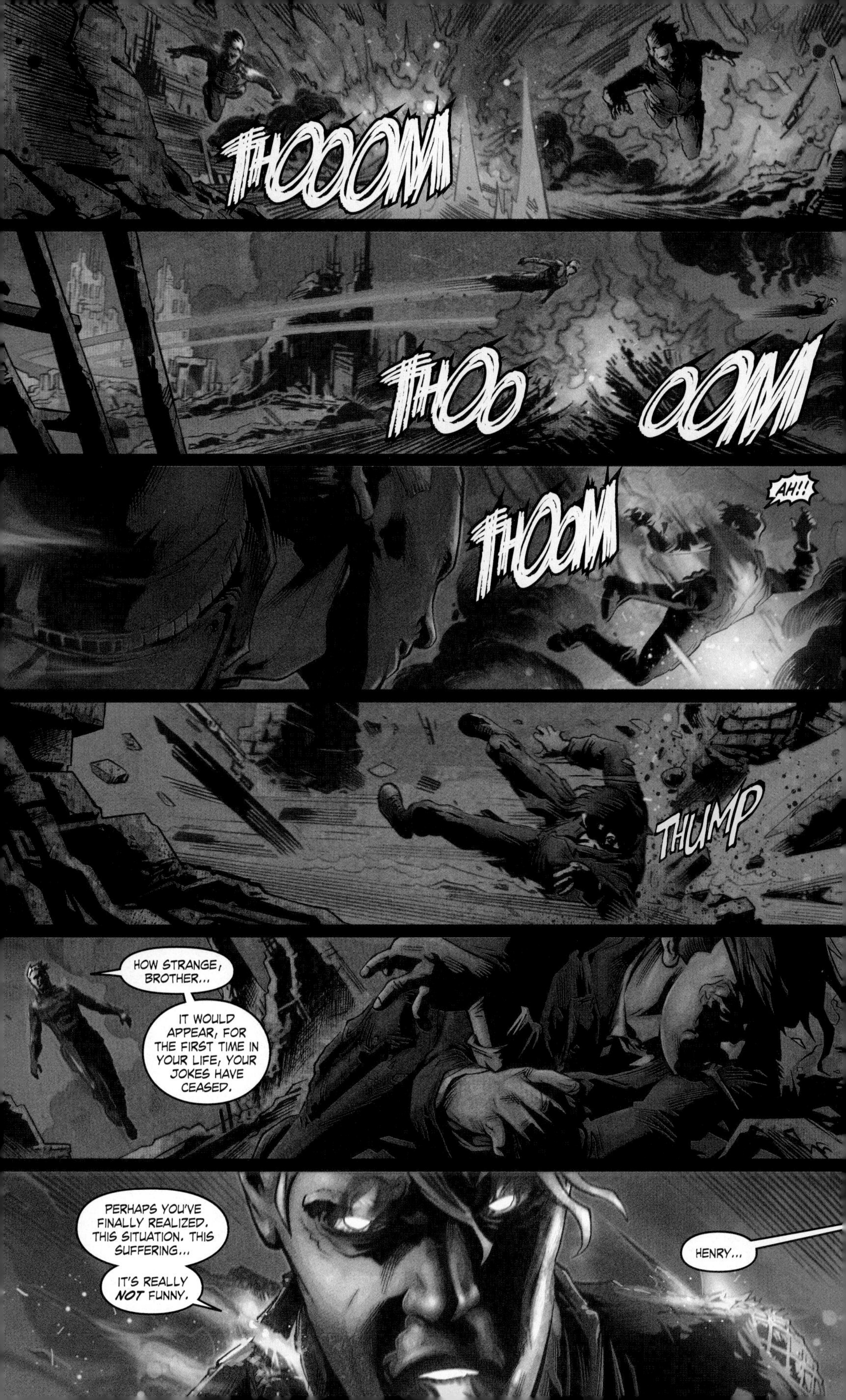
THOOOM
THOO OOM
THOOM
AH!!
THUMP
HOW STRANGE, BROTHER...
IT WOULD APPEAR, FOR THE FIRST TIME IN YOUR LIFE, YOUR JOKES HAVE CEASED.
PERHAPS YOU'VE FINALLY REALIZED. THIS SITUATION. THIS SUFFERING...
IT'S REALLY NOT FUNNY.
HENRY...

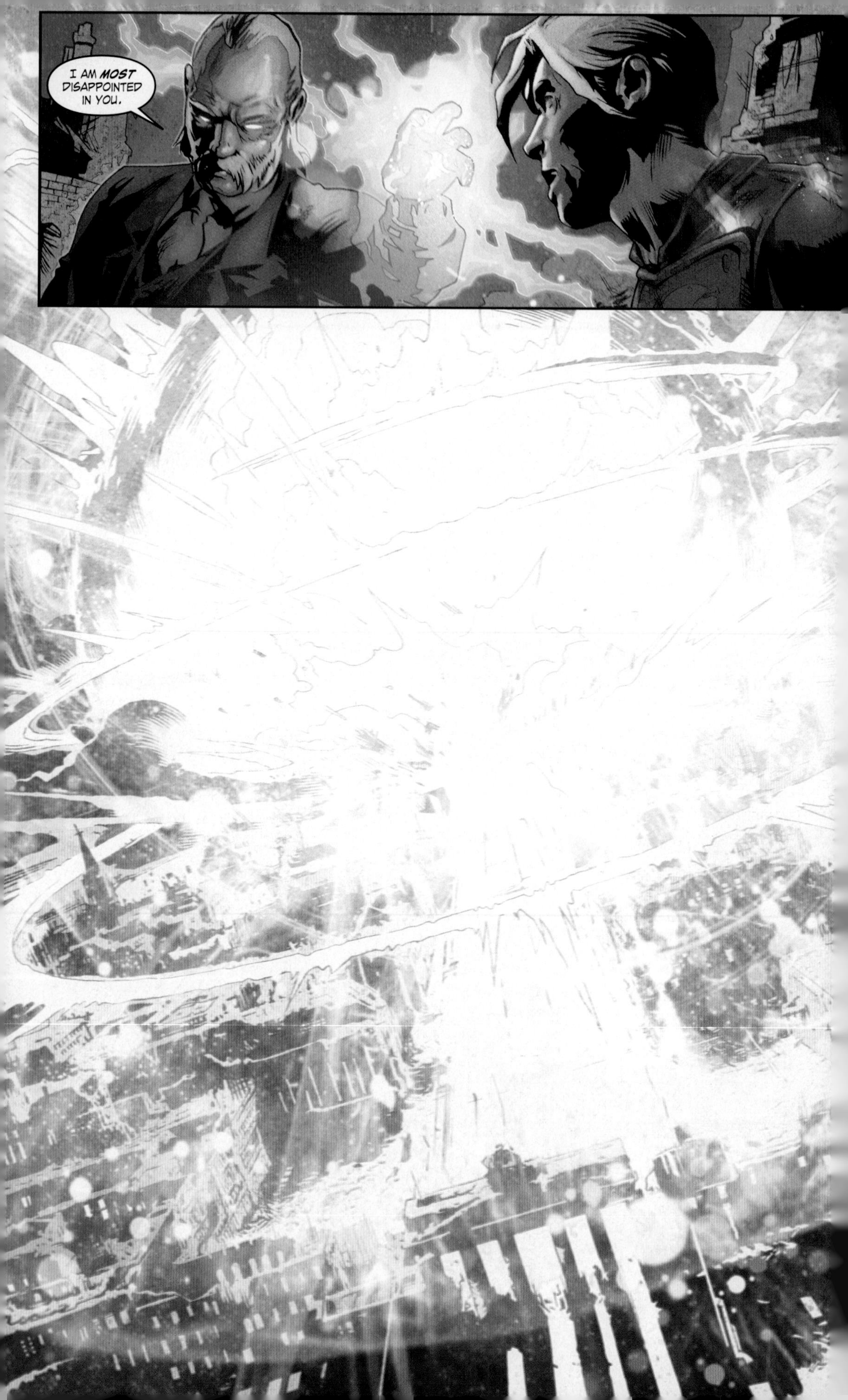
I AM MOST DISAPPOINTED IN YOU.

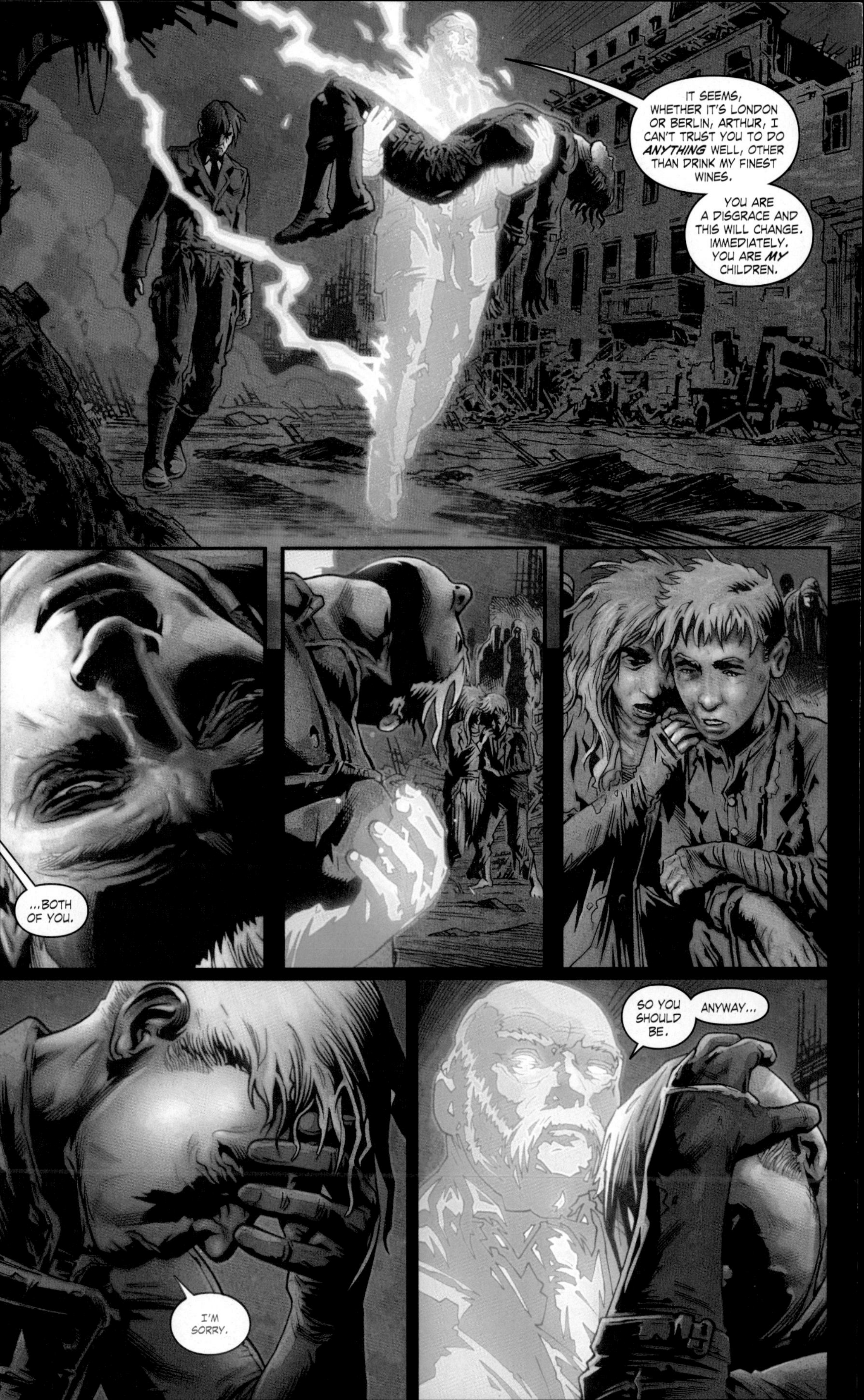
IT SEEMS, WHETHER IT'S LONDON OR BERLIN, ARTHUR, I CAN'T TRUST YOU TO DO ANYTHING WELL, OTHER THAN DRINK MY FINEST WINES.
YOU ARE A DISGRACE AND THIS WILL CHANGE. IMMEDIATELY. YOU ARE MY CHILDREN.
...BOTH OF YOU.
I'M SORRY.
SO YOU SHOULD BE.
ANYWAY...

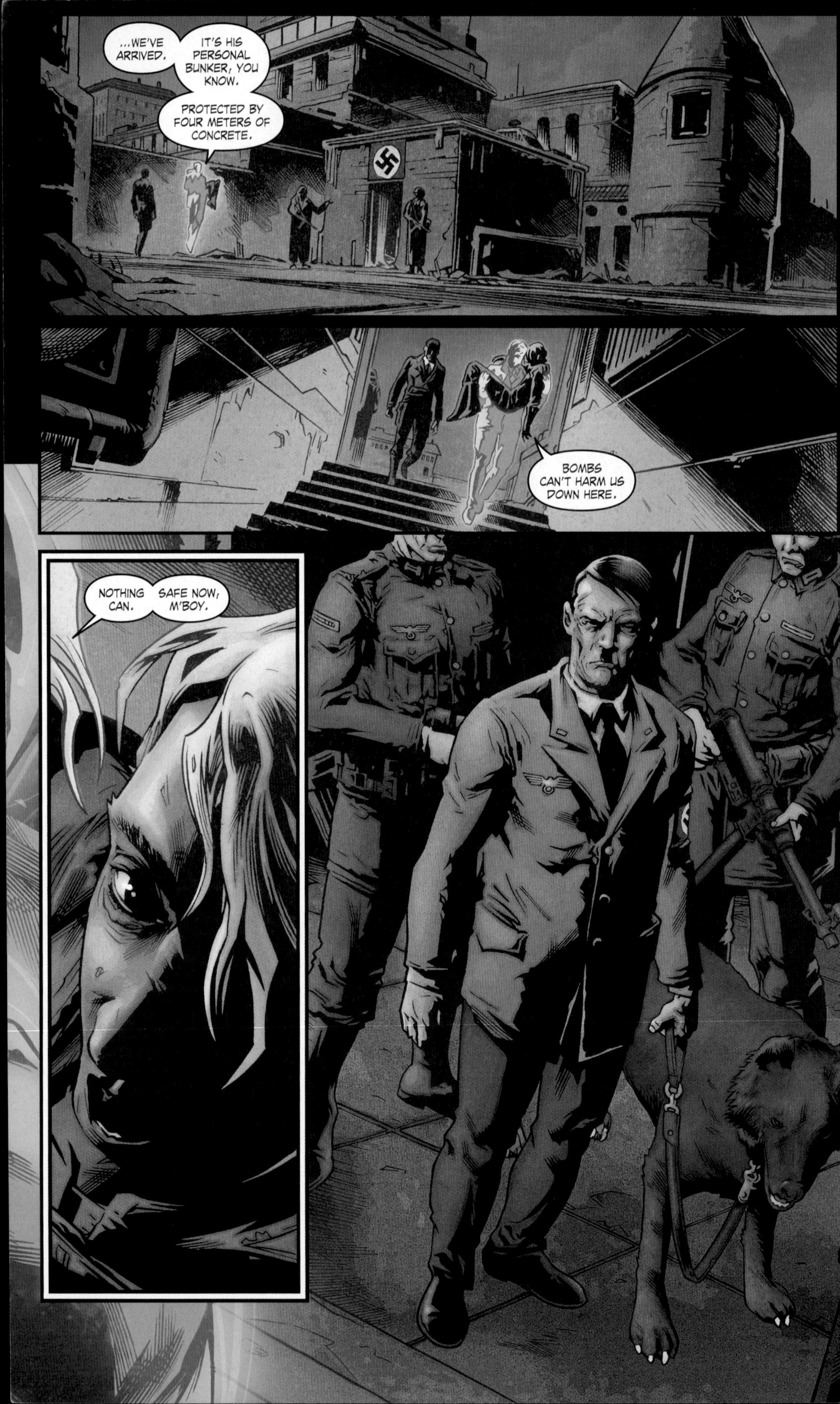
...WE'VE ARRIVED.
IT'S HIS PERSONAL BUNKER, YOU KNOW.
PROTECTED BY FOUR METERS OF CONCRETE.
BOMBS CAN'T HARM US DOWN HERE.
NOTHING CAN.
SAFE NOW, M'BOY.

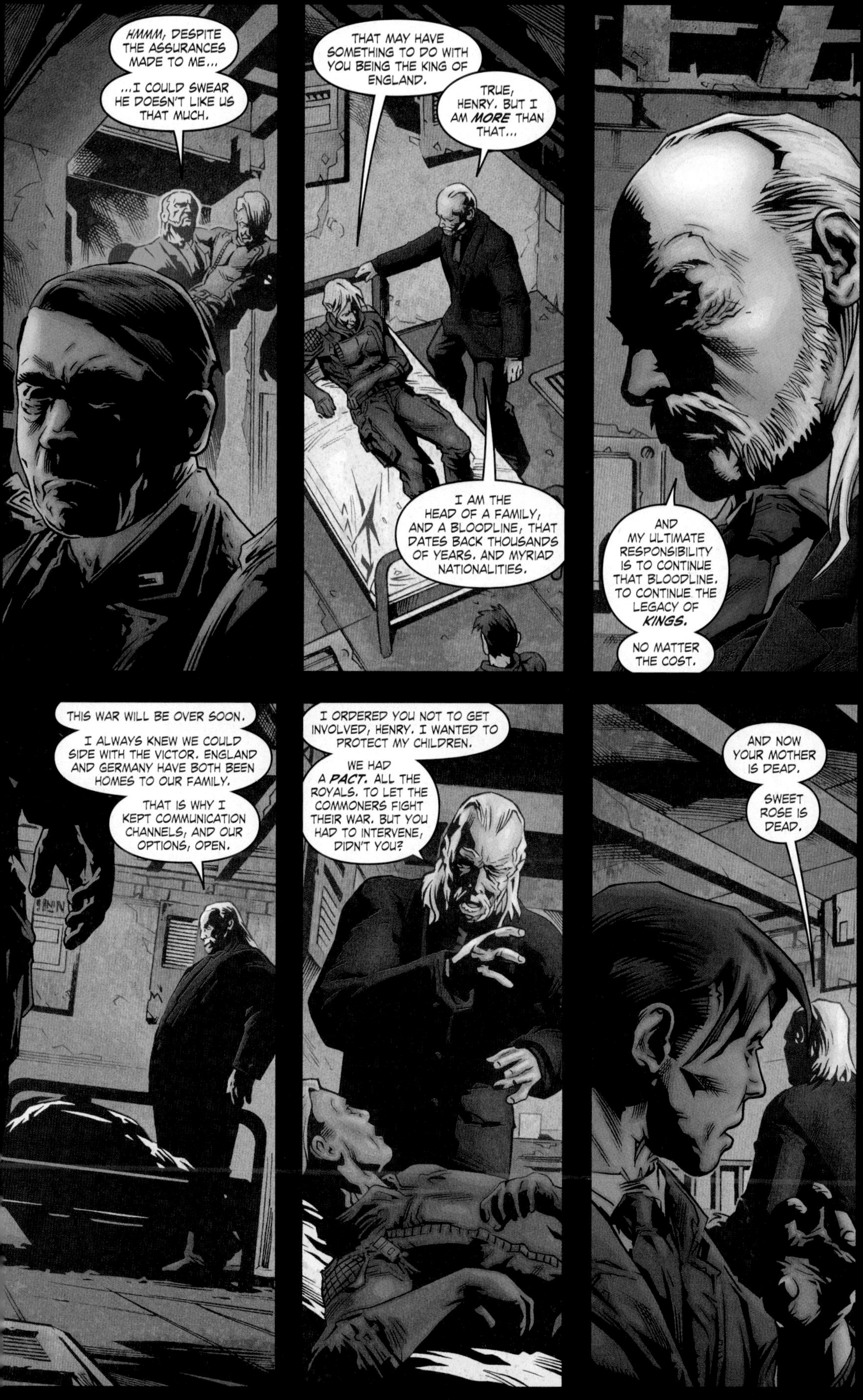
HMMM, DESPITE THE ASSURANCES MADE TO ME...
...I COULD SWEAR HE DOESN'T LIKE US THAT MUCH.
THAT MAY HAVE SOMETHING TO DO WITH YOU BEING THE KING OF ENGLAND.
TRUE, HENRY. BUT I AM MORE THAN THAT...
I AM THE HEAD OF A FAMILY, AND A BLOODLINE, THAT DATES BACK THOUSANDS OF YEARS. AND MYRIAD NATIONALITIES.
AND MY ULTIMATE RESPONSIBILITY IS TO CONTINUE THAT BLOODLINE. TO CONTINUE THE LEGACY OF KINGS.
NO MATTER THE COST.
THIS WAR WILL BE OVER SOON.
I ALWAYS KNEW WE COULD SIDE WITH THE VICTOR. ENGLAND AND GERMANY HAVE BOTH BEEN HOMES TO OUR FAMILY.
THAT IS WHY I KEPT COMMUNICATION CHANNELS, AND OUR OPTIONS, OPEN.
I ORDERED YOU NOT TO GET INVOLVED, HENRY. I WANTED TO PROTECT MY CHILDREN.
WE HAD A PACT. ALL THE ROYALS. TO LET THE COMMONERS FIGHT THEIR WAR. BUT YOU HAD TO INTERVENE, DIDN'T YOU?
AND NOW YOUR MOTHER IS DEAD.
SWEET ROSE IS DEAD.

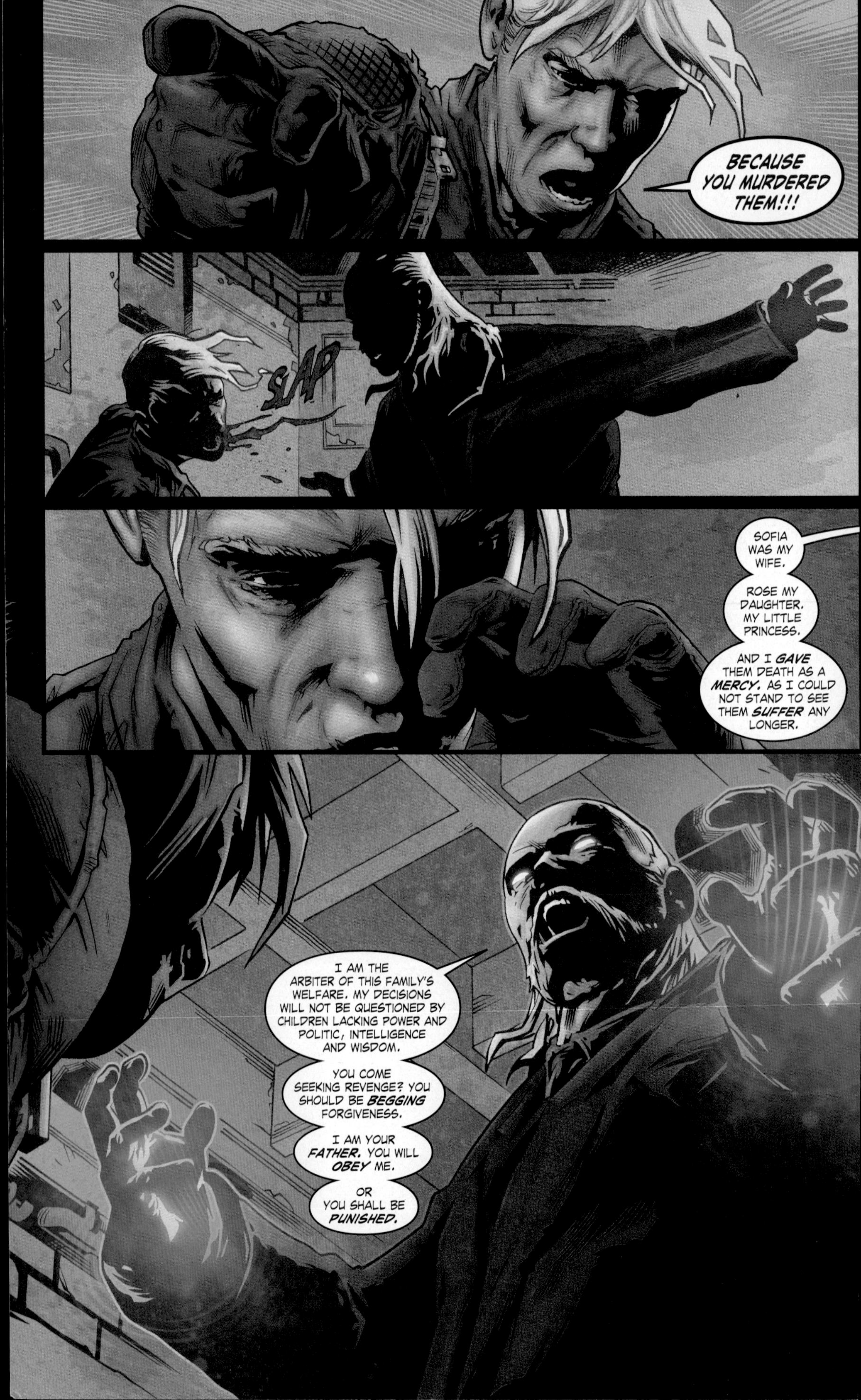
BECAUSE YOU MURDERED THEM!!!
SLAP
SOFIA WAS MY WIFE.
ROSE MY DAUGHTER. MY LITTLE PRINCESS.
AND I GAVE THEM DEATH AS A MERCY, AS I COULD NOT STAND TO SEE THEM SUFFER ANY LONGER.
I AM THE ARBITER OF THIS FAMILY'S WELFARE. MY DECISIONS WILL NOT BE QUESTIONED BY CHILDREN LACKING POWER AND POLITIC, INTELLIGENCE AND WISDOM.
YOU COME SEEKING REVENGE? YOU SHOULD BE BEGGING FORGIVENESS.
I AM YOUR FATHER. YOU WILL OBEY ME.
OR YOU SHALL BE PUNISHED.

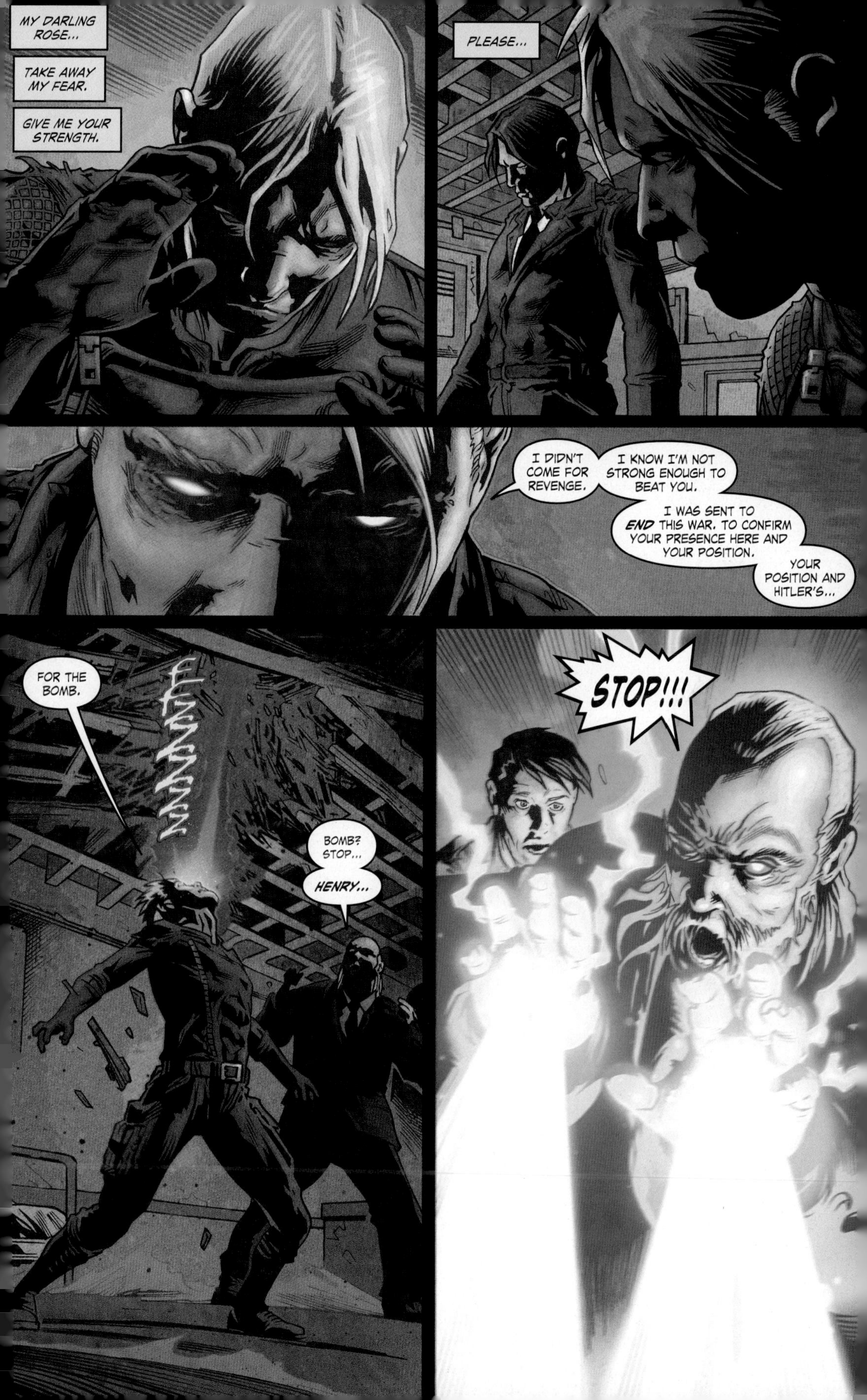
MY DARLING ROSE...
TAKE AWAY MY FEAR.
GIVE ME YOUR STRENGTH.
PLEASE...
I DIDN'T COME FOR REVENGE.
I KNOW I'M NOT STRONG ENOUGH TO BEAT YOU.
I WAS SENT TO END THIS WAR. TO CONFIRM YOUR PRESENCE HERE AND YOUR POSITION.
YOUR POSITION AND HITLER'S...
FOR THE BOMB.
BOMB? STOP...
HENRY...
STOP!!!

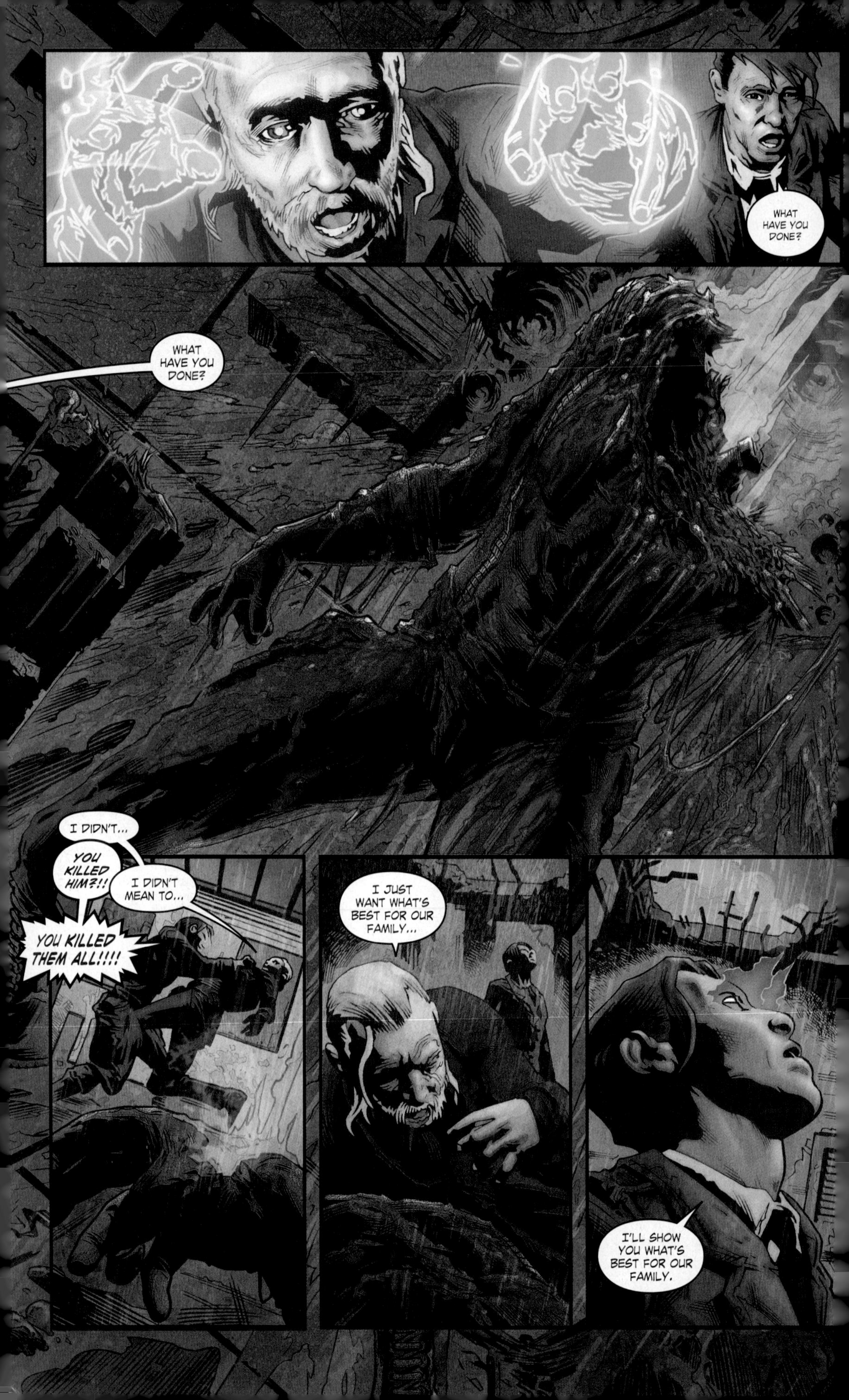
WHAT HAVE YOU DONE?
WHAT HAVE YOU DONE?
I DIDN'T...
YOU KILLED HIM?!!
I DIDN'T MEAN TO...
YOU KILLED THEM ALL!!!!
I JUST WANT WHAT'S BEST FOR OUR FAMILY...
I'LL SHOW YOU WHAT'S BEST FOR OUR FAMILY.

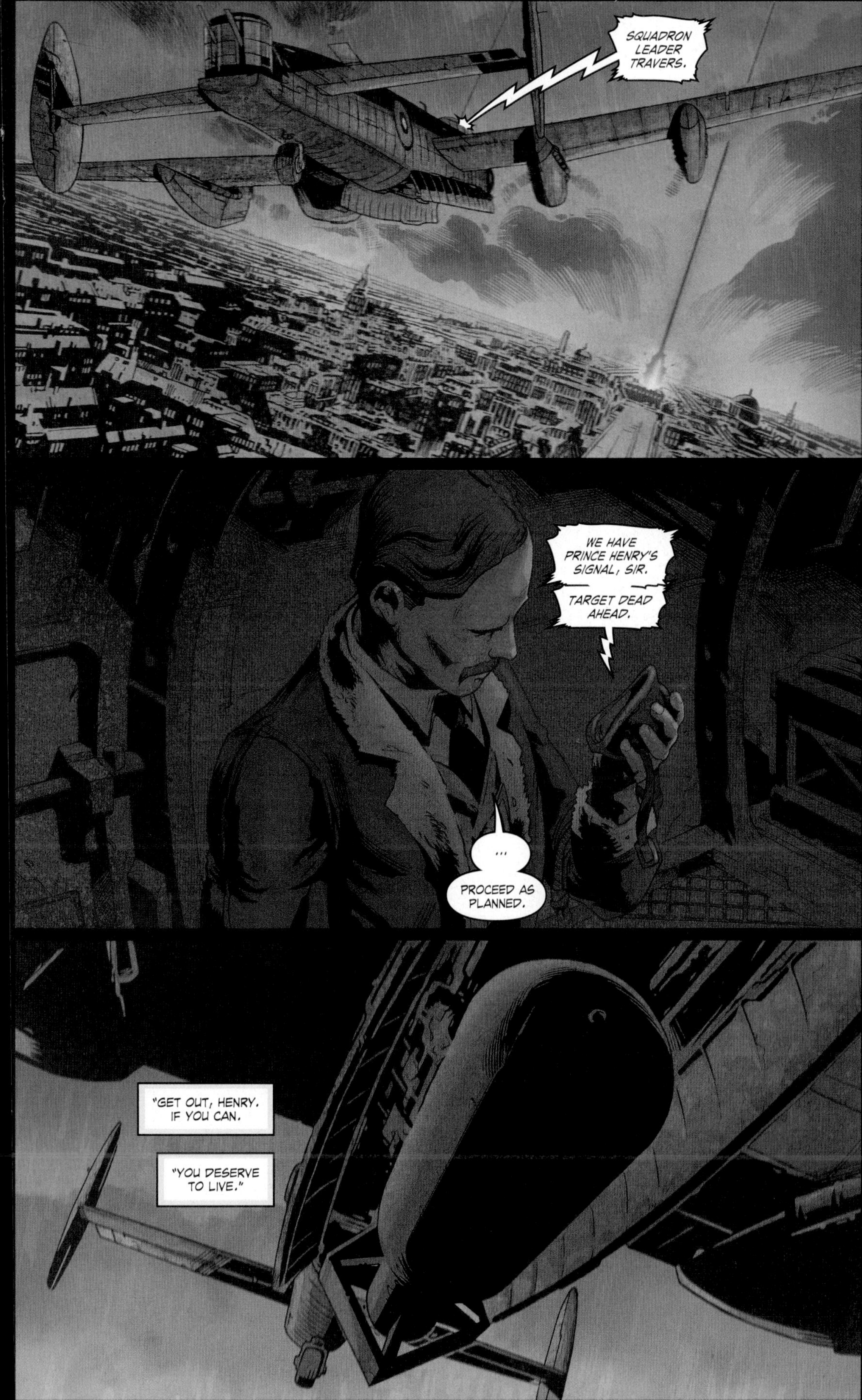
SQUADRON LEADER TRAVERS.
WE HAVE PRINCE HENRY'S SIGNAL, SIR.
TARGET DEAD AHEAD.
...
PROCEED AS PLANNED.
"GET OUT, HENRY. IF YOU CAN.
"YOU DESERVE TO LIVE."

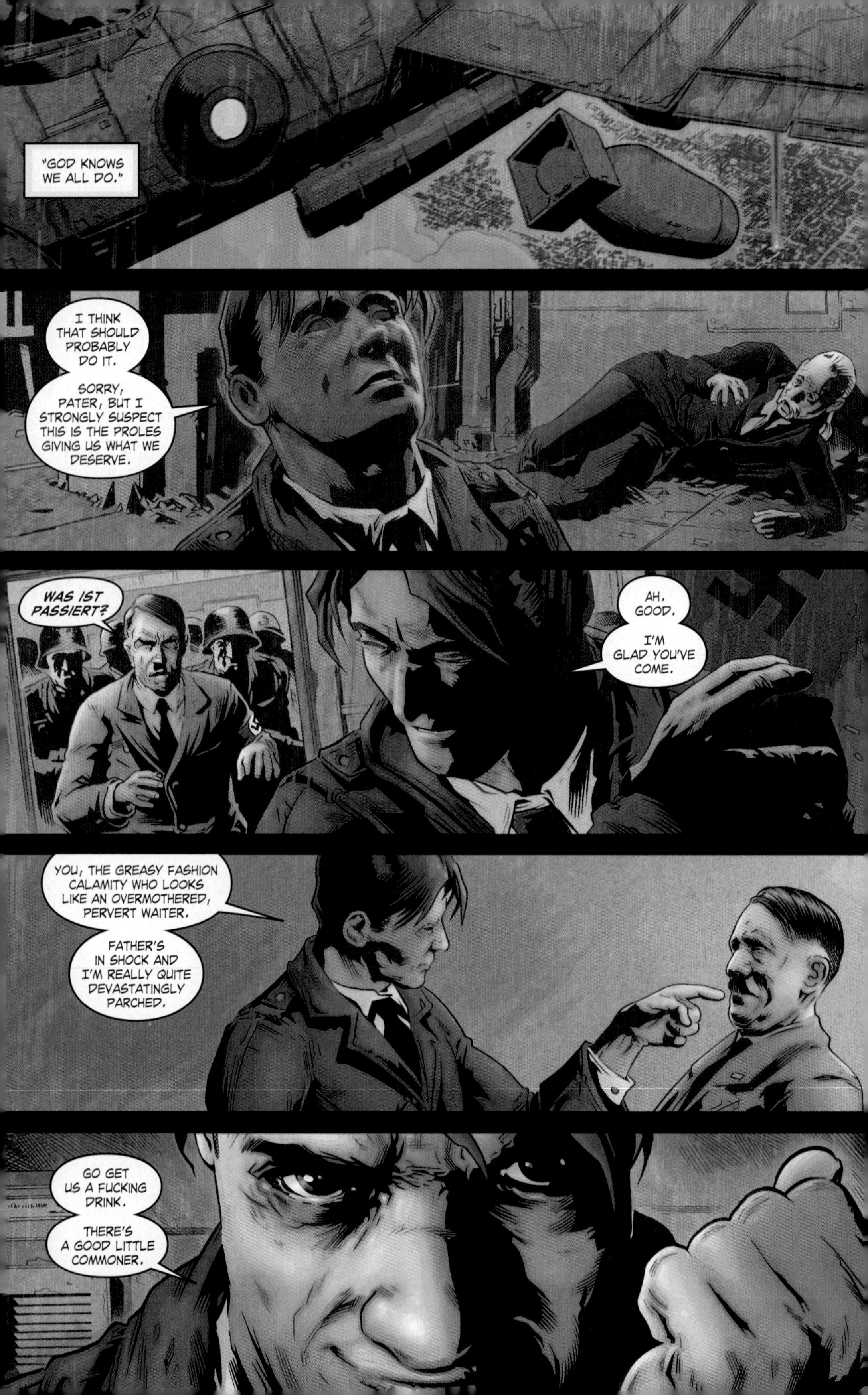
"GOD KNOWS WE ALL DO."
I THINK THAT SHOULD PROBABLY DO IT.
SORRY, PATER, BUT I STRONGLY SUSPECT THIS IS THE PROLES GIVING US WHAT WE DESERVE.
WAS IST PASSIERT?
AH. GOOD.
I'M GLAD YOU'VE COME.
YOU, THE GREASY FASHION CALAMITY WHO LOOKS LIKE AN OVERMOTHERED, PERVERT WAITER.
FATHER'S IN SHOCK AND I'M REALLY QUITE DEVASTATINGLY PARCHED.
GO GET US A FUCKING DRINK.
THERE'S A GOOD LITTLE COMMONER.

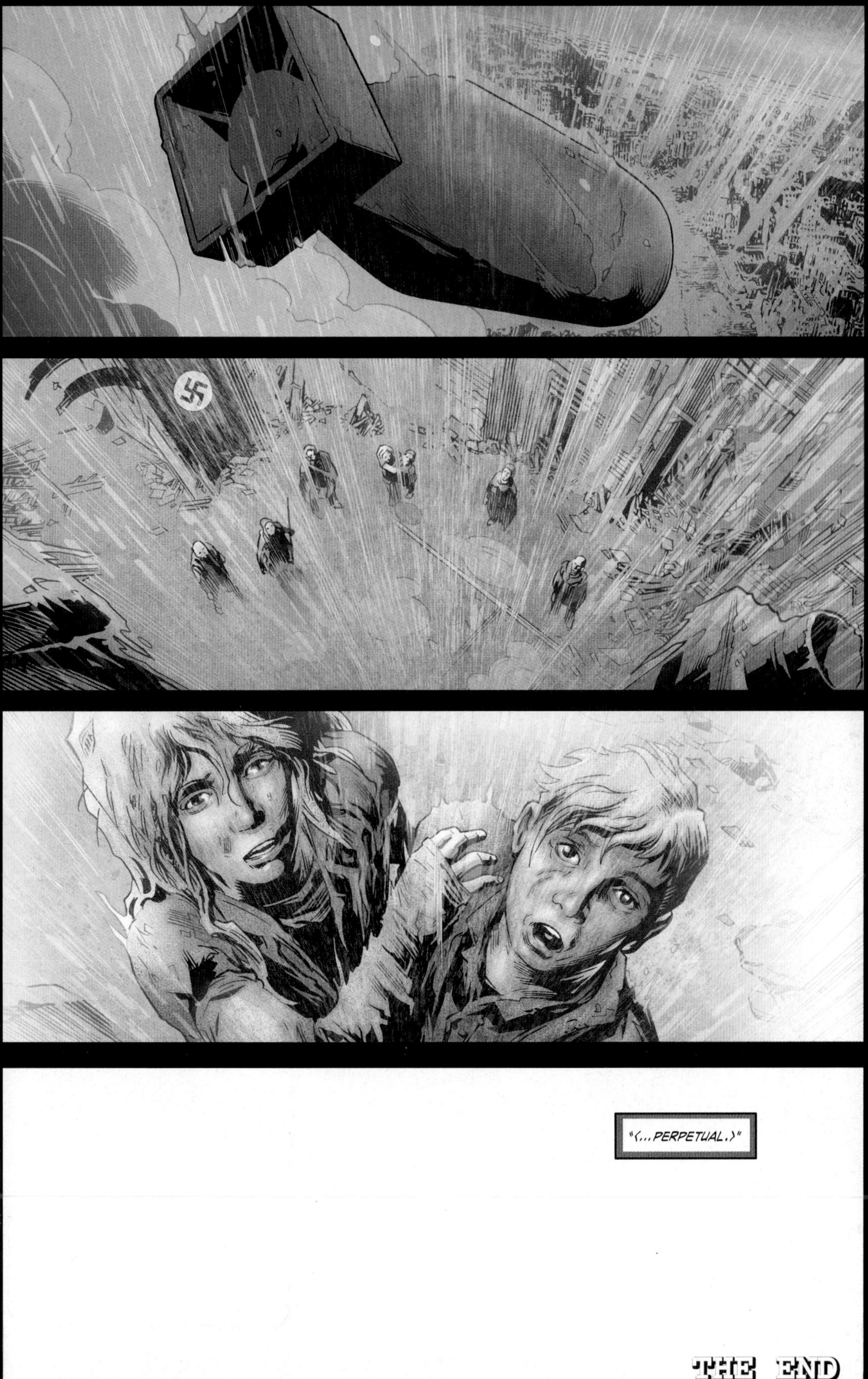
"<...PERPETUAL.>"
THE END

VARIANT COVER ART FOR ISSUE #1 BY BRIAN BOLLAND

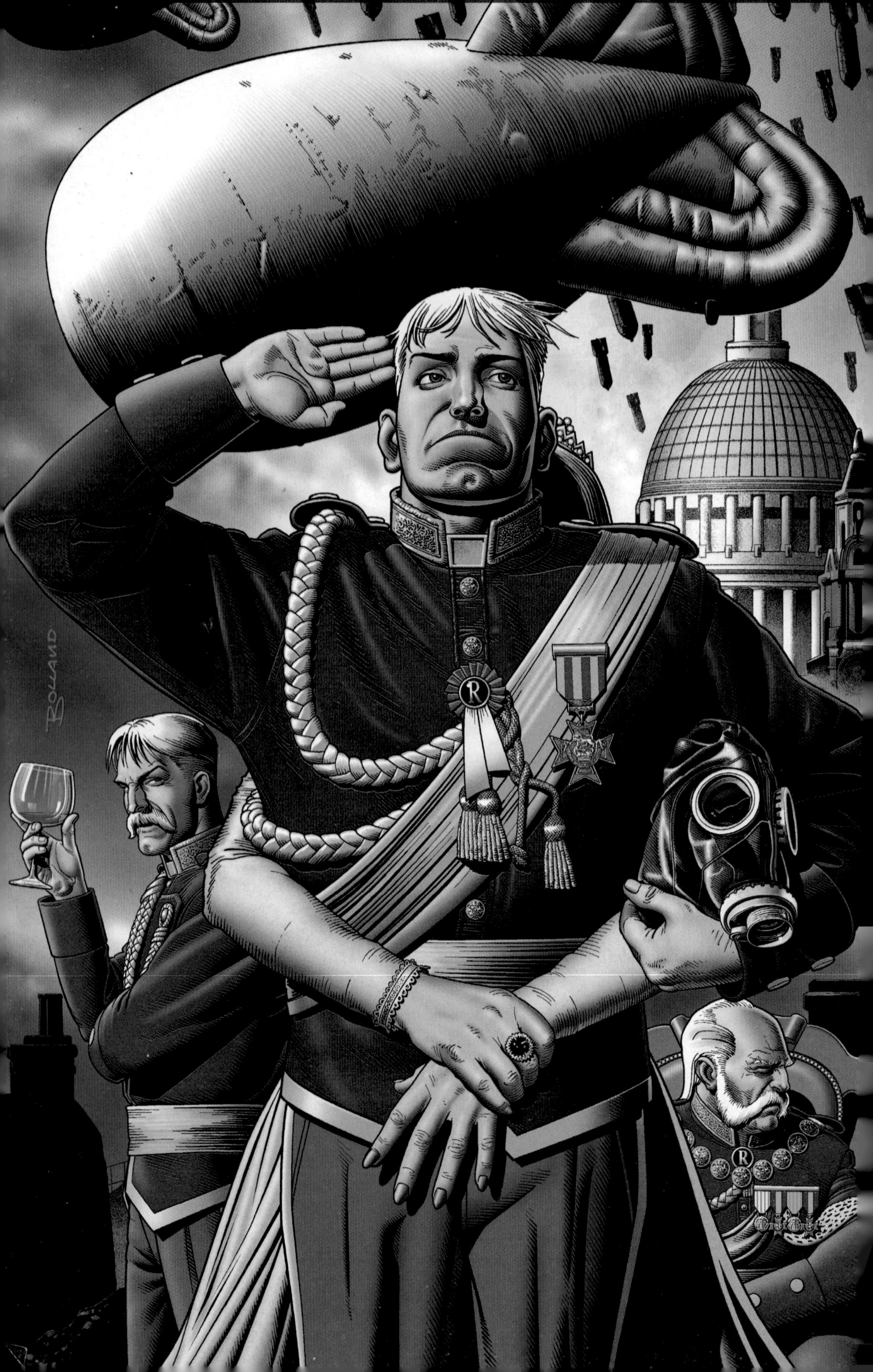
BOLLAND